D0952613

ALSO BY SALLIE BINGHAM

SHORT FICTION

The Touching Hand and Other Stories
The Way It Is Now
Transgressions (published in France as *Libertinage*)
Red Car: Stories
Mending: New and Selected Short Stories

NOVELS

Small Victories
Upstate
Matron of Honor
Straight Man
Cory's Feast
Nick of Time

MEMOIRS

Passion and Prejudice: A Family Memoir
The Blue Box: Three Lives in Letters

PLAYS

Milk of Paradise
Couvade
Paducah
In the Presence
Hopscotch
The Awakening
Treason
A Dangerous Personality

THE
SILVER SWAN

SALLIE BINGHAM

THE
SILVER SWAN

IN
SEARCH
OF
DORIS DUKE

FARRAR, STRAUS AND GIROUX / NEW YORK

Farrar, Straus and Giroux
120 Broadway, New York 10271

Printed in the United States of America
First edition, 2020

Swan art by Thomas Colligan

Library of Congress Cataloging-in-Publication Data
Names: Bingham, Sallie, author.
Title: The Silver Swan : In Search of Doris Duke / Sallie Bingham.
Description: First edition. | New York : Farrar, Straus and Giroux, 2020. |
    Includes index.
Identifiers: LCCN 2017046937 | ISBN 9780374142599 (hardcover)
Subjects: LCSH: Duke, Doris, 1912-1993. | United States—Biography. |
    Celebrities—United States—Biography.
Classification: LCC CT275.D8769 B56 2018 | DDC 920.073 [B]—dc23
LC record available at https://lccn.loc.gov/2017046937

Designed by Abby Kagan

Our books may be purchased in bulk for promotional, educational, or business use.
Please contact your local bookseller or the Macmillan Corporate and Premium Sales
Department at 1-800-221-7945, extension 5442, or by e-mail
at MacmillanSpecialMarkets@macmillan.com.

www.fsgbooks.com
www.twitter.com/fsgbooks • www.facebook.com/fsgbooks

1 3 5 7 9 10 8 6 4 2

Dedicated to
the staff of the David M. Rubenstein Rare Book
& Manuscript Library at Duke University

with special thanks to Melissa Delbridge

and to the memory of Doris Duke

Generosity endures.

The idea of "old money," so dear to the hearts of the Old Rich, is a fiction—a sentimental fiction, not even a legal one.
—Nelson W. Aldrich, Jr., *Old Money: The Mythology of America's Upper Class*

By any definition woman is an outsider. A difficult notion genuinely to digest, as woman occupies one half of the race, constitutes an entire sexual category, cuts across all cultures, classes and conditions, and often occupies positions of honor within those very circumstances in which total rule is exercised, it nevertheless is true.
—Vivian Gornick and Barbara K. Moran, *Women in Sexist Society: Studies in Power and Powerlessness*

"I" must become a "fabulous opera," and not the arena of the known.
—Hélène Cixous, *The Character of "Character"*

Beauty, its creation and enjoyment, is my life's goal.
—Doris Duke

CONTENTS

PREFACE

In the late summer of 1958, I was a shy, nearly silent twenty-one-year-old, awkwardly adjusting to my honeymoon with my young husband, when he took me to a formal luncheon in a grand apartment in Paris; his father moved in that world.

I had no idea what to expect. Raised in privilege, but in Kentucky, I spoke only a little French and, as a beginning writer, had little confidence. Although my mother had worked hard to teach me how to conduct myself at adult occasions, a mixture of reticence and inchoate rebellion had caused me to resist learning her useful lessons, beyond shaking hands and murmuring a few polite inanities.

Yet there I was, sitting at a long dining-room table, with ten or twelve dark-suited French gentlemen on either side. The lunch consisted of four courses, passed by silent waiters in livery. My shyness made me afraid of choking, and I hardly dared touch a drop of the three kinds of wine. Embroidered linen napkins and crystal and silver glinting in the dim Paris sunlight did nothing to make me feel at home. And there was no master of the house sitting at the other end of the table.

Instead, very far from me reigned a distinguished presence: a woman of a certain age, filled with power, authority, and dignity such as I had never encountered. What she wore, or even what she looked like or said, escaped my attention. I was overwhelmed, fascinated, and frightened by her sheer presence. I don't believe we exchanged a single word.

Later, my new husband told me that our hostess was Doris Duke, an heiress and a philanthropist.

Decades later, I visited Duke University in Durham, North Carolina, endowed and named by Doris Duke's father after his family, and a recipient of her generosity. With Jean O'Barr, distinguished professor and founder of Duke's Women's Studies Department, I was setting up the Sallie Bingham Archive for Women's History and Culture, which now, nearly thirty years later, holds an ever-growing collection of the papers of women writers, artists, and feminist activists as well as records of the institutions they founded.

I was staying at the very comfortable, very Southern Washington Duke Inn, named for Doris Duke's grandfather, near the edge of the West Campus of the university. Every day, as I walked to the elevators, I passed a row of impressive black busts on pedestals, commemorating three generations of Dukes: Doris's father, grandfather, uncle, and nephew.

But where was Doris? Her exotic, heart-shaped face, her sly smile and sideways glances had appeared all over the world in news stories and fashion shots, but none of these were framed and hung at the inn. I searched in vain for a bust, a portrait, or even a photograph, both at the inn and on the campus. I found nothing. Eventually, I was led to a small photograph in the corner of a garden center she had endowed.

Whenever I find a trace of a woman whose story has been expunged, I want to know what caused the omission. What characteristics of the vanished woman resulted in her banishment from history? I was mystified. Doris Duke is by far the best-known member of her family; even today, more than two decades after her death, her name usually evokes a look of recognition, whereas her grandfather, father, and uncles, despite their accomplishments, have vanished into virtual obscurity.

Did Doris's absence from the family portrait gallery reflect her well-known reticence; her, at times, distant relationship with the university? Had the rumors that plagued her from childhood obscured her accomplishments? Or had the mere fact of her independence, her choice of an unconventional way of life, been responsible for her excision?

Dubbed "the richest girl in the world" when she inherited, at thirteen, the hydroelectric-and-tobacco fortune of her father, James Buchanan Duke, Doris was pursued nationally and internationally by the tabloids all her life. It was not what she wanted. Was this unwelcome attention the cause of her exclusion?

I set out to discover the answer, probing the recesses of the vast archive Doris Duke left to the Rubenstein Library at Duke. Now, eight years later, I have discovered many more mysteries and exclusions, and, at the center of it all, the paradox of a woman about whom everything seems to be known but who retains a certain mystery, her life a template for that extraordinary phenomenon, the New Woman.

Just two years before Doris Duke's birth, on November 22, 1912, Virginia Woolf daringly claimed, "On or about December 1910 human character changed."[1] As an example, Woolf describes her iconic Mrs. Brown as "capable of appearing in any place; wearing any dress; saying anything and doing heaven knows what. But the things she says and the things she does and her eyes and her nose and her speech and her silence have an overwhelming fascination, for she is, of course, the spirit we live by, life itself."[2] In short, the New Woman—complex, challenging, and, like Doris Duke, a rule unto herself.

THE
SILVER SWAN

PROLOGUE

Wearing her signature two-piece bathing suit, elastic, sturdy, designed for serious swimming, Doris Duke climbs down the steep bluff below Rough Point, her mansion on the coast at Newport, Rhode Island, and plunges into the ocean. For a moment, she disappears beneath the waves, and the gardener, sent by her staff, starts from behind his tree. He is hiding because Doris would be furious if she knew he was waiting there, armed with a coil of rope, in case she needs rescue.

She does not.

She surfaces, swimming strongly toward the calmer water outside of the cove. She breaststrokes out, then turns on her back to float, staying so long in the cold water her fingers shrivel and her lips turn blue, just as when, decades earlier, she swam all morning with her best friend, Alletta Morris,[1] at nearby Bailey's Beach.

Floating, she glimpses her camels, Princess and Baby, lazing on the lawn in front of her house, wearing the pink harnesses she bought for them from Schiaparelli in Paris. Later, she'll twine pink hibiscus from her garden into their manes.

In spite of having shrunk a bit with age from her commanding height of six foot one, Doris is long and lean in the water. In Hawaii, she still occasionally wears her wet suit and surfs off Diamond Head, one of the first nonnative women to brave those waves.

But her time in the water is up. Guests are coming for lunch. She sidestrokes into the cove, clambers out, and climbs up the bluff. The gardener hurriedly retreats before she sees him.

Crossing the lawn, she stops to stroke Baby's furry neck. She has never regretted her purchase of a Boeing 737-300 aircraft to transport the two camels from J. C. Schulz's game farm in Catskill, New York. Along with her dogs, the camels are her greatest comfort.

In her second-floor bedroom, she dresses in one of her gauzy orange caftans, then turns on the radio to check the weather. If an Atlantic storm is brewing, she'll give orders to have the furniture moved out of the ground-floor solarium and straw spread so that Baby and Princess can take shelter there.

Her father, James Buchanan Duke, would have understood. They both loved the horses, the pony, Prince, and the dogs that had lived, during Doris's childhood, at Duke Farms in Somerville, New Jersey. Now, when she visits the farm, she houses her dogs right next to her bedroom on a fenced porch with a door so they can come in to visit her. They sometimes climb up on the bed beside her when she is eating her breakfast off a tray.

Her father would have understood that, too, but he had died years earlier, in 1925, when Doris was a girl of not quite thirteen. He had never had a chance to see his beloved only daughter swimming out to sea at Rough Point or battling the waves off Diamond Head. Battling ocean waves in the Atlantic and the Pacific led Doris to other adventures, not least her involvement in World War II.

 September 1944. In Europe, the war was coming to an end. The Allies had invaded Normandy, and the occupying German army had surrendered Paris. In New York, Doris Duke was fretting that she was missing the experience of her generation. This was the time to go, especially now that her divorce from her first husband, Jimmy Cromwell, was finalized. She had initiated proceedings in 1943 on grounds of extreme cruelty.

Late in September, Doris would receive official permission to go to Cairo. Her U.S. passport, however, did not authorize her to visit other countries except ones she might have to pass through on her way to Egypt.[1] Here begins Doris's struggle with the State Department. Since Egypt was now a backwater in the war, she wanted, instead, to get to a country closer to the fighting in order to write dispatches of consequence for the international news services. But the State Department had other ideas, perhaps in an attempt to disguise Doris's dual role as minor undercover agent for the OSS and war correspondent. She was aware that nothing she could write from or about Egypt would attract the level of attention of dispatches from the war zone.

Her movements in this period are difficult to trace, since she felt empowered to go wherever she wanted, with or without an authorizing passport and visa. She wanted to be able to travel around Europe as freely as she had moved with her parents in the years before the war. Her privilege, at this point in her life, gave her the illusion that she could always go her own way.

Doris's difficulties were compounded by the notoriety of her divorce.[2] She had spent six months in Reno, Nevada, establishing residency in the only state where it was possible to obtain a quick divorce; her decree was issued on December 21, 1943, but then Jimmy had contested it, questioning the legitimacy of her residence in Nevada. The final decree would not be issued until 1948. But Doris would not wait. She was already packing for Cairo.

Into her sunny bedroom, on the second floor of the great white limestone mansion at the corner of Seventy-eighth Street and Fifth Avenue in Manhattan that was built by her father, the porter and his mate hauled two Louis Vuitton steamer trunks. On the right side of each trunk was a capacious cupboard with wooden hangers, covered by a blue silk curtain; on the left, six drawers, each equipped with metal pulls. Her mother's scent, Guerlain's 1912 L'Heure Bleue, wafted out as she opened the top drawer.

Doris selected the various outfits she would need—for England, where Captain Alec Cunningham-Reid might or might not be waiting; for the Continent (as she had learned to call Europe on trips with her parents); and for Egypt.

Into the trunk went bathing suits for the Mediterranean, golf outfits for servicemen's clubs and grand hotels, tennis dresses and rackets for mixed doubles, and proper suits for the work she hoped for as a foreign correspondent. Doris knew what she wanted, if not necessarily how she would achieve it.

In the first trunk, on the hanging side, she arranged size-sixteen prewar Paquin suits (size ten by American standards) and an assortment of evening gowns. She based her choices on her past work: recently she had been running a relief station in New York Harbor for the United Seamen's Service, throwing parties with plenty of food and pretty girls for merchant seamen on leave. A lifetime later, her *New York Times* obituary

(October 3, 1993) reported that she had said of that period, "I couldn't live with myself if I didn't do something real to help with this war. This may sound funny, but I honestly believe I'm happier now than I've ever been . . . I'm doing something worthwhile, earning the right to be friends with a lot of swell, interesting people . . . I've discovered, I guess, that it's fun to work." For her training, Doris had been dispatched in April 1944 for one month to the United Seamen's Service in New Orleans.

On May 29, 1944, J. Reilly Marcus, business manager at the Merchant Marine Relief Center, wrote to his opposite number at the rest center in Oyster Bay, New York, that Doris Duke had arrived in an atmosphere that was colored, inevitably, by expectations the men might have formed from reading news stories about her. Yet Marcus wrote, with seeming surprise, that these expectations were dispelled almost at once by Doris's calm, evenhanded treatment of everyone she met. She accepted all of the men as worthy of whatever help she could provide. Some of the merchant mariners were African Americans, never a problem for Doris, who had loved her father's African American valet and felt an affinity with people of color. She was to be paid a dollar a year, and to serve until the end of the war. A check for her first dollar was enclosed in Marcus's letter.[3]

Her job was not frivolous. Merchant ships carrying essential supplies to England were vulnerable to submarine and air attack; they were lightly armed, if at all, and even in convoys were subject to sinking by the Axis Powers. Rest and recreation for the sailors between these harrowing voyages were essential. Still, Doris had her sights on journalistic work.

It had seemed that Doris's break had come much earlier, in September 1942, when the FBI head, J. Edgar Hoover, wrote to thank her for her intelligence work and raised the possibility of a dual assignment abroad: foreign correspondent and minor operative for the OSS.[4] This explains her posting to Egypt, which was at this point in the war a nest of spies. But red tape and her lack of credentials had kept Doris in the United States for two more years.

Admittedly, she had no training or background as a journalist, and in fact she hardly wrote at all. But that, for Doris, was no impediment. She could always learn. One of the very rare interviews with Doris, conducted by her International News Service boss, Mike Chinigo, on January 30, 1945, was printed in *Stars and Stripes*, a daily publication for United

States forces stationed in Europe. An accompanying photograph of Doris predictably identifies her as the "world's richest girl."

In the interview, she spoke fondly of the service, referring to herself several times as a dangerous woman, like screen stars of the period, such as Hedy Lamarr, whose allure was enhanced by her roguishness. This led Chinigo to conclude that the posting to Cairo was the only possibility for Doris. Her face was not so familiar there that she would have difficulty maintaining dual roles.

Chinigo mentions that in Alexandria, Egypt, Doris had repainted and redecorated the American Seamen's Club and arranged its first dance. Asked if the subject of her fortune ever came up at the club, she said it never had. Chinigo added that she was a tall blonde who seemed friendly and approachable. When he apologized for asking her age, she replied without hesitation that she was thirty-two. After one of the officers attending the interview said that she was three years his junior, she got up, shook his hand, and congratulated him on being even older than she was.

About six months later, on June 23, 1945, Mike Chinigo again interviewed her, this time for an article called "Doris Duke Learning How to Be a Reporter." When Chinigo asked her why she wanted to be a reporter, she replied that she felt compelled to do something worthwhile with her life. She added that her friend the writer Clare Boothe Luce had sparked the idea when she was visiting Doris in Hawaii back in 1941.

Doris told Chinigo that she had been preparing for the job by studying and then rewriting news stories. She said she understood that she might not be taken seriously by editors, since she had no previous experience as a reporter. She knew she would have to establish herself as a responsible professional by proving that she could observe accurately and write persuasively.

She went on to say that during this unorthodox apprenticeship she had begun to appreciate how useful newspaper reporting could be when stories about important events were written responsibly. This work might satisfy her drive to achieve something independent of her family and her fortune, as well as introduce her to a great variety of people. She hoped to write news stories that would appeal to a mass audience, a large swathe of the population she would never have encountered in her post-debutante life in New York.

She had already learned how difficult it was for editors to take their minds off her celebrity and attend to her interest in her work, but she believed she could cut through their fascination with her by presenting herself as a hardworking reporter.

Doris's reporting put to rest one myth—that she could not write—which has been used as an attempt to explain the small number of her letters in her archive. For that there is a more compelling explanation. From an early age, Doris feared the loss of privacy that would result if unfriendly eyes read her correspondence. This apprehension severely curtailed her letter writing. Anyhow, she explained, most of the letters she received answered themselves over time.

After the war, when she began to refuse almost all interviews, Doris was imitating her father's determination to shield himself from scrutiny in an age of gossip columnists and scandal sheets. She would never again feel comfortable enough with an interviewer to talk as frankly as she had with Mike Chinigo.

 Doris's war reporting has been discredited in other accounts as simply a desperate attempt to reunite in England with Captain Alec Cunningham-Reid, the British MP whom she had met in the United States in 1937. Alec did not lack for dash: in 1927, he had been dubbed England's handsomest man when he married the wealthy Honorable Ruth Mary Clarisse Ashley, with whom he had two sons. During their divorce proceedings in 1940, Alec sued his wife for four hundred thousand pounds.[1]

He was known in Britain as the "unconventional MP." The author of a controversial and outspoken book about the Second World War, *Blame the Old Gang!*,[2] he was admired as a World War I flying ace but criticized for blaming the Conservative Party for causing World War II, although he had served as a Conservative Party member in the House of Commons for thirteen years. On July 28, 1943, he came to blows with another Conservative MP, Oliver Locker-Lampson, who accused Alec of fleeing London during the Blitz for the United States and Doris Duke. Both men later apologized to the House, but the incident made all the London papers and was mentioned in Jimmy Cromwell's divorce from Doris as evidence of her adultery.[3]

When Alec heard that Doris was posted to Cairo and not permitted by the State Department to travel to London, he wrote that the news was a "body blow."[4] But in the same undated letter, Alec also wrote that he accepted rumors that she was about to be married again because they were such good friends that marriage was clearly out of the question. Apparently, in lieu of a marriage contract, Doris had offered him "devoted comradeship."[5]

In a letter in which he referred to himself as "Wurtz," Doris's nickname for him, he wrote that he had been living in "a cuckoo dreamland," revealing that he had promised to marry a certain English girl by 1944. By then he expected that Doris would give them her blessing.[6] His fiancée was poor, but charming and sensible, and, according to Alec, apparently accepted quite happily that Doris had been "the greatest thing in his life." If she had not, he continued, he would have walked out on her. He told Doris he felt that his news would come as a relief to her.[7]

Alec and Doris had shared some good times in the early days of their relationship, including an interlude when Doris taught him to crisp bacon by draining it on brown paper. They had especially enjoyed a trip down the Seine. A series of small black-and-white deckle-edged photos show Doris smiling broadly as she sits on deck behind Alec; in another photo, Michael, his eldest son, leans affectionately against his father's shoulder. Snapshots from their 1945 tour of Italy contain familiar views of cathedrals. Doris, in flats, stands shoulder to shoulder with Alec, as though to prove that they are the same height, a recurring issue in all her photos with men.[8]

In an earlier, undated letter to his "Dearest Borgia" (his nickname for Doris), Alec regretted that he hadn't seen her since they rode bicycles together before the war.[9] He remembered saying that Doris was the only person he had ever loved. He claimed to be flabbergasted by Doris's reaction, stating that he would always remember something "whizzing at [him] through the air" after his proposal.

The nickname he used for Doris linked her to the infamous Borgias, the Italian and Spanish family that produced two popes and was accused of many crimes. He was probably alluding specifically to the notorious

Lucrezia Borgia, whose love letters to Pietro Bembo had been much admired by Lord Byron.

At the bottom of his letter, Doris penciled, "Sorry Wurtz. I got you wrong. Let's meet soon. Love and kisses. Borgia." But the war and Alec's next marriage intervened.[10]

Alec compared the loss of their relationship to the blotting out of pages from a copybook. He denied knowing what crime he had committed and surmised that it must have been "a simple misunderstanding."[11] He continued to write her and at one point asked her to pay twenty-seven dollars to a shipyard where Doris had bought a boat she and Alec had christened the *Pious Puffin*.[12] Alec claimed the shipyard was threatening to have a process server visit Doris, and that "interesting particulars" would be revealed to the press, with the possibility of a trial and more publicity. He wanted to visit her to explain the situation.[13]

Doris recognized a threat when she saw one, and cabled Alec, "Your arrival very inconvenient for me at present time. Fail to understand why discussing with me is necessary concerning additional contracts made by you and which are therefore up to you to settle." Alec had overplayed his hand.[14]

In another undated letter, Alec wrote Doris that he "fought back steadily" against insinuations that his trip to the United States to arrange safe conditions for British children to escape the Blitz was a pleasure jaunt to visit Doris. After all, he had returned to London in October 1940, at the height of the German bombardment.[15]

During the Blitz, when he sent his boys to the United States, Doris became their unofficial guardian. She had already spent time with them and their father in Hawaii and California, Switzerland and France, providing not only splendid vacations but also the companionship they craved. But now that Doris was overseas, the boys, twelve and ten years old, were put in the care of a Mrs. Wisner. After an undefined act of disobedience, they were shipped off to the elite Lawrenceville School, near Trenton, New Jersey, which happened to have been Jimmy Cromwell's alma mater.[16]

Between 1932 and 1937, the older boy, Michael, became devoted to Doris, whom he called "Darling Lihi-Lihi," a reference to the nickname Doris had acquired in Hawaii. In fact, Michael wrote to Doris more often than he did to his father in London, causing Alec to complain bitterly of neglect.[17]

On July 6, 1943, Alec wrote a friend that he had tried to arrange for Michael to write to Doris one week and to him the next, acknowledging that the boys owed much to Doris and referring to her as "invaluable and the most wonderful friend imaginable."[18] They also owed a great deal to Marian Paschal, Doris's personal assistant, who oversaw the boys' day-to-day lives when they were not at school.

Alec begged Doris in a cable to tell his sons that he was remarrying; he couldn't face telling them himself.[19] Covering for Doris, Marian Paschal protested in a return cable that it was crucial that Alec discuss his decision with his sons.[20] Alec refused, and it fell to Marian to tell the boys.

Later, Michael wrote to Doris that he and Marian had been floored by his father's marriage to a person they had never met. He continued that they did not know whom or if Alec had actually married, since there were no announcements in the papers and the only information they had was a strange-sounding cable from him.

Alec finally wrote his sons on October 12, 1944, thanking them for their congratulations and attributing his decision to loneliness for Doris, who was "Borgia to me and Lihi-Lihi to you." He blamed time and circumstances for a decision over which he claimed to have no control. Michael and Noel must have been even more bewildered. A year earlier, a Paris newspaper had hinted at Alec's engagement to Doris, but that appears to have been speculation.

In another letter to "Dear Lihi-Lihi," Michael wrote how deeply he missed her. He wished she would become a reporter right away, both because it would please her and because she would be able to travel and see "gloomy me. (I love you, who do you love?)." He closed, "You have heard your problem child speak."

Back in England, after the war, Michael wrote again that he was "homesick" for Doris—so much so that he could "cry all over the place."[21]

In September 1944, when Doris left for Egypt, her mother, Nanaline Holt Duke, a widow since James Buchanan Duke's death in 1925, may have viewed her daughter's adventure with concern. But she may also have admired her energy and drive, qualities that had propelled Nanaline herself to New York from the South many years earlier.

Marian Paschal may have also been worried. Marian, whom Doris called Pansy, supervised the office of Doris's first foundation, Independent Aid, room 250, at 535 Fifth Avenue in midtown Manhattan. Marian called Doris "Holetia" and loved her, she wrote, almost as though Doris was her child, and her eyes had filled with tears when she told her goodbye.[22]

On December 3, 1944, Doris wrote Marian that she had been painting her Cairo office her favorite bright yellow, since "my job seems to be what I make it so I'm continually trying to find things to do." The dances she organized were "a roaring success. In fact, they are beginning to call me Elsa Maxwell," she wrote, referring to the well-known American gossip columnist and professional hostess.[23]

There was not much else for Doris to do. She admitted that idleness was not good for her, although her music had benefited; she had been spending three hours a day on voice and piano. Doris's job at the American Seamen's Club demanded the skills she'd honed during her life as an heiress: charm, tact, and selection of the right evening dresses. But it also demanded a firm hand. The club's chaperoned parties had to welcome the merchant sailors on shore leave, at the same time suppressing their urges.

Doris yearned to get to Europe before the war ended. She wanted to be close to the front with the desperation of a young woman committed to kicking off the chains of her class and its expectations. In March 1945, she finally received security clearance to leave Egypt for Italy.

Her friends in Cairo soon missed her, as letters from her friend Brigadier General Benjamin Franklin Giles, commander of the U.S. Air Force in the Middle East, attest. Giles wrote that he couldn't believe Doris had stayed out of trouble since she left Egypt, but since, according to the old saying, bad news travels fast, he had to assume that she had been behaving, because he had heard nothing to the contrary. He wrote that her friends in Cairo asked about her all the time, and that there hadn't been any parties in her old flat since her departure. He added, "You certainly grow on a guy."[24]

In May 1945, Doris finagled a trip to Vienna through her connection with General George Patton, whom she had known before the war in Hawaii—

smitten with the handsome, swashbuckling general, Doris had bought him two polo ponies.

After his victory at Messina, in which he took western Sicily back from the Germans, Patton's military career seemed to have suffered from the news of his having slapped an enlisted man who was suffering from battle fatigue, calling him a "coward." Scolded by General Eisenhower but not officially reprimanded, he was now stranded on the volcanic Italian island as viceroy of Sicily. Compared by the actress Marlene Dietrich to a tank bigger than a village square, Patton was, like Doris, longing for action. Her adulation must have been balm to his wounded spirits, and he invited her to join him behind the Russian lines.

In an undated letter, Doris wrote Marian in New York: "Have been having fun lately. Went on a junket to Austria with a bunch of correspondents. But the jokers ran off and left me while I was prowling around looking for a story and as a result I scooped them and were they burned up?"[25] As the only American correspondent, she got to cover the meeting between Soviet marshal Fyodor Tolbukhin and General Patton. Tolbukhin, one of the most respected of Russia's generals, had invaded southern Hungary as commander of the Fourth Ukrainian Front in September 1944, driving the Germans out with frightful losses on both sides. After Tolbukhin gave Doris a medal, she joked that perhaps he was bestowing it on her because she hadn't slid under the table from drinking vodka. In her dispatch, she wrote, "Dashing General George S. Patton gripped Marshal Fedor Ivanovitch Telbukhin's hand and said, 'This is the greatest day of my life.'"[26]

Doris went on to describe the Russian soldiers lined up in dress uniform at the meeting, including a "Russian WAC [sic] very smart in full black skirt, khaki jacket and black boots." Afterward, there was a procession and then a celebratory dinner with many champagne toasts—including toasts to Stalin—and a "wild musical theme strikingly reminiscent of primitive savage music."[27]

Before the dinner, she was shown into a room where a burly Russian general was seated at a dressing table while a woman wearing a lot of makeup sprayed eau de cologne on his bald head. Doris wrote that the cologne seemed to be expected, and that she, too, had been sprayed. Her dispatch was never distributed by the International News Service, perhaps because Doris was in Vienna without the requisite visa.[28] But the meeting would have unintended consequences. Since Doris's passport did not authorize her to visit Austria, the State Department abruptly ordered her home. She was instructed to use her temporary passport to return to the United States within thirty days to apply there for a new one.[29]

But according to a 1965 article in *The National Observer* written by Doris's old friend John J. Pullen, Doris stayed with Patton for four more days. Her flouting of official regulations may have been the act of an entitled young woman, or of one who was naive, fearless, or both.

Difficulties attended her return to Italy, but according to Pullen, an airman in an F-38 finally arrived and took her back to Rome, where she intended to continue writing dispatches. Another rumor at the time placed Doris in Linz earlier in May, while Patton was planning the rescue of the Lippizaner stallions; still others linked Doris romantically with the sixty-year-old general.

On May 5, 1945, Patton and Undersecretary of War Robert P. Patterson had seen a Spanish Riding School performance by the famous stallions. The head of the riding school, who knew Patton because they had both competed in the Olympics, asked him to take the horses under his protection, because he was worried that the Russians might slaughter them for meat when they arrived. Through a series of dramatic maneuvers memorialized in Walt Disney's 1963 film *The Miracle of the White Stallions*, Patton had his soldiers ride, herd, and truck the stallions over the German border, possibly saving them from extinction.[30]

In Rome, Doris sorted out her passport issues. When her New York lawyer, Tom Perkins, tried to help her solve these problems, his efforts were rudely rebuffed by a State Department functionary. He wrote to Doris that a Mrs. Shipley insisted that Doris had been in Italy illegally, since her passport had been limited to Egypt. She claimed, he continued, that a scandal had been narrowly avoided.[31] Mrs. Shipley routinely gave women war correspondents a hard time, canceling their passports when they were at home on leave. She believed that writing about the war was men's work.[32] Clearly, Doris did not agree.

Until the fall of 1944, Doris was confined by the expectations of her class and her times: to be a debutante and marry early. A superb athlete, she was too tall at six foot one to fit that framework, too strange in her beauty, with her heart-shaped face, narrow eyes, and ironic mouth. She was always questing for meaning in a life that provided only the rubric of the Social Register (from which she would be excised) and the list of the Best Dressed Women. Attracted to both men and women, comfortable with dark-skinned friends and lovers, kicking off her shoes as often as she could get away with it, Doris was ranging widely. Several men offered possibilities, both professional and personal, after her marriage to Jimmy ended; one of the first was General Patton. He was in the mold set by Doris's father. She would always admire large men who instinctively knew how to command.

 In Egypt, Doris was still working in a minor capacity for the OSS. This was considered a patriotic duty, one that was undertaken by many U.S. citizens.[1] In 1941, responding to a request from President Roosevelt, Colonel William J. Donovan, known as Wild Bill Donovan, designed the OSS on the model of the much-admired British Secret Intelligence Service (MI6).[2]

In 1943, the OSS had set up offices in Istanbul, but by the time Doris arrived in Alexandria, the Istanbul offices had been closed. The reason for this closing was misinformation supplied by the "Dogwood-chain," at that time the largest intelligence-gathering unit the United States possessed. This left a vacuum that Doris may have been expected to some small degree to fill. The OSS relied on the services of attractive young women for the "pillow talk" that sometimes led to useful revelations. As Doris's friend Brigadier General B. F. Giles wrote to her on August 25, 1945, "We do need some Mata Haris here at this time to look after and check upon some of our friendly enemies."[3]

Writing from army headquarters, Giles warned her that she was becoming too identified with the Special Services. He added that there was so much work of this kind to be done that it would never be finished. But he hoped that she would soon be transferred to the front, to do the reporting that was her real goal.[4]

Since she kept no diary and wrote few letters, Doris's three months in Egypt are refracted through letters to her from Giles and from Captain Tex McCrary. This smooth-faced Texan, who headed the photography unit of the OSS, was in love with Doris for years, having met her in California before the war.

Tex had been trying for months to arrange a professional assignment for Doris. In February 1944, he had written to his "Dear Daisy Mae Duke" (a sly reference to the gorgeous and libidinous cartoon character in the comic strip *Li'l Abner*; it was also Doris's OSS sobriquet).[5] Unfortunately, a very attractive deal involving reporting in China had fallen through. (The OSS was active in China from 1943 to 1945, arming, training, and supplying Mao Zedong's Red Army.) Tex still hoped to pull strings in Alexandria with William Randolph Hearst of the Hearst News Corporation. Tex was sure he could arrange some kind of assignment for Doris with Hearst as a reporter. He knew the exciting work would be covering the Allied assault on Italy in the spring.[6]

"I'm afraid you never did have much faith in guys in general," Tex continued. He believed this was because other men didn't act natural around Doris, whereas he did. She was pretty, he wrote, and he liked how hard she tried to learn new skills, such as diving. He had watched her in Santa Barbara before the war, practicing diving over and over in a swimming pool. He also liked her long fingers and the fact that she didn't tolerate formality or people she thought were artificial. He admitted that he would have liked to persuade her to be his lover, adding that he would have enjoyed it thoroughly.[7] He signed off "L'il Abner" [*sic*], Daisy Mae's naïve, hulking, and seldom amorous love interest in the comic strip. This was an unlikely moniker for the seductive Texan.

In his next letter, Tex apologized for not coming to see Doris when he was in Cairo. He explained that he was trying to determine whether or not he and Jinx Falkenburg were in love and, if so, whether they should get married. He was still uncertain and felt that seeing Doris would not have helped him find the right answer.[8]

Later, on June 15, 1945, Tex and Jinx were married. After the war, they would host two radio programs—the first called *Hi, Jinx*—and a television show, in which they would discuss politics and international affairs. They would be on the air nationally seven days a week during the late 1940s and early 1950s.[9]

In Jinx, Tex found the glamour that had excited him in Doris but without the threat of Doris's independence and fortune. Jinx's path was a very different one from Doris's. She was the first Miss Rheingold, and *Life* magazine had referred to her as the leading candidate for America's number-one girl for 1941. Tex and Jinx separated in the 1980s but were never divorced.[10]

Tex may have detonated his chances with Doris long before he decided to marry Jinx, when he wrote a detailed letter asking Doris to subsidize an international news service to compete with Associated Press and United Press. He requested $30,000 to start, with more money to come later.[11] Doris could not have been pleased. She wanted to be a career correspondent herself, not to fund the journalistic careers of others.

Tex feared that Doris might still be married to Jimmy Cromwell or involved in complicated romantic relationships that would make her life as a reporter difficult. Perhaps speaking another language would help with an assignment. When he asked what languages Doris spoke well, she replied that she spoke fluent French from her years with her governess, Mademoiselle Jenny Renaud.

Since he was supplying photographs for the *New York Herald Tribune*, Tex believed he might be able to arrange a job for Doris as a special correspondent for that newspaper through his friendship with the paper's owner, John Hay Whitney. He'd heard that Whitney had offered the job to Averell Harriman's daughter Kathy but didn't think her father would allow her to take it. He added that he knew Doris "couldn't" write—she almost never answered his letters—but that he would find a friend to write her dispatches for three weeks, which was all the time she would need to learn how to do it herself.[12]

Many years later, in 1969, Tex would write to Doris again: "You and I bump into each other and twenty-five years is suddenly twenty-five minutes."[13] Tex's affection, his respect, and his faith in her strength were elements of what Doris was seeking as she tried to work her way into writing about the war. Apparently, Tex never forgot her. In 1969, he would write that he wanted her to remember that he had always admired her resilience. It was not toughness—a quality he personified—but an enduring tenderness that was full of love. Doris expressed her love with her fingers and her eyes, her thighs, and even her "long fin-feet." Their relationship had been short, but for the rest of his life, Tex would be grateful for what Doris had given him. He admitted that he'd never been able to tell her this before because he couldn't bear "to confess his need."[14]

Finally, Doris received a passport dated January 2, 1945, authorizing travel to Italy. But that same day it was stamped "CANCELLED" in four places, despite the original handwritten instructions signed by the consul of the United States of America stating that the bearer was a United States employee traveling on business that would include trips to Egypt and Italy, as well as countries she might pass through along the way.[15]

Ultimately, however, Doris believed she did not really need a passport, since she had already obtained an AGO card (Adjutant General's Office, issued to active and retired military personnel), though it did not specifically list the countries where she was permitted to travel. For that, another permit was needed. It had been granted in a secret order issued by Brigadier General Giles on January 5, 1945. For six months, from January to June 1945, Giles's order authorized what he called temporary duty, connected with the U.S. armed forces' work in that region. After June, however, this order was to be reduced to "RESTRICTED."[16]

Now Tex urged Doris to go to Corsica. The little island held seventeen Allied air bases, used for the attack on Italy. Knowing that she was lonely, Tex hoped Doris would find a "Fortress pilot" worthy of her love. She would also be close to the action.[17] A photograph shows her in a dark suit and kerchief, camera slung over her shoulder, as she shakes hands with a GI.[18]

On January 22, 1945, she wrote for the International News Service an account of what was happening in Trieste, where the Allied and Yugoslav forces were facing each other for a final showdown. The partisans were asking that the United States abide by the Atlantic Charter. Signed in August 1941 by Winston Churchill and Franklin Roosevelt, it stipulated that the will of the people would govern any territorial changes.

Referring to the work she was doing—taking dictation from soldiers, then turning the dictation into scripts for the soldiers to record and send to their families in the United States—Doris admitted that it was very hard, but said she was enjoying it. A photograph shows her operating her recording apparatus while a serviceman prepares to read his script.[19] Then, in November 1945, in belated consequence of her unauthorized trip to Austria, she was again told by the OSS that she had to return to the United States at once for "proper indoctrination."

The entanglement of her reporting and her secret work was now complete and was causing some concern at home. Apparently in response to anxious questions, she replied in a letter to Tom Perkins, dated November 17, 1945, that General Giles had originally referred her to the OSS because he believed it was "more flexible." Wild Bill Donovan, who ran the OSS and knew Doris through their overlapping social circles,[20] obliged, telling her to start packing and be prepared to leave Trieste for Rome.[21]

Then President Roosevelt's right-hand man, Harry Hopkins, made matters difficult by announcing at a military dinner that men who came into contact with Doris were likely to suffer what he called burned fingers.[22] Hopkins, President Roosevelt's closest personal adviser—he and his wife lived at the White House during the war years—would have known of Doris's undercover activities as well as the gossip about her affair with Tex. The combination, he warned, could be dangerous.

Doris's mother was also concerned. Five letters written by Nanaline between 1945 and 1947 show her trying to advise her daughter. In 1945, she wrote to Doris that she understood her need to be "very guarded," because of the publicity caused by her divorce from Jimmy, as well as the inevitable jealousy aroused by her legacy from her father. Nanaline understood that great wealth, especially when it is inherited rather than earned, could cause unfortunate public perceptions. Significantly, Nanaline closed her letter by urging Doris always to trust her, because she loved her deeply and was "disinterested."[23]

Once again, Tex stepped in, arranging for Doris to work in Rome under Mike Chinigo, bureau chief for Hearst's International News Service. She rented a small apartment and rode a bicycle to work. Her salary was a mere twenty-five dollars a week, but this may have been one of the happiest times of her life.

In an undated letter to her assistant, Marian Paschal, Doris wrote that she had finally been accredited to Italy by the Joint Chiefs of Staff. She felt that the delay had been discriminatory.

From Rome, she described for her U.S. readers the lead-up to Italy's first elections since the war and the elections' possible outcome. She admired Randolfo Pacciardi, who was assembling a government to take charge upon King Umberto's exile on June 12, 1946. After interviewing him, Doris wrote in her dispatch that she believed he was the leader of "the real Republicans" in Italy. She also noted his suave appearance, which reminded her of the polish displayed by some American politicians.[24]

In 1945 and 1946, Doris was given assignments like those she would have received working for the society page at a U.S. newspaper—soft news, designed solely for women readers. Meanwhile, Italy, prostrate after the war, provided countless opportunities for serious reporting, but that was not Doris's beat.[25] On the rare occasions when she was able, for instance, to interview someone major, like Donna Rachele Mussolini, the dictator's widow, the result was superficial. Doris's insistence on seeing her subject in the context of the stereotypical Italian housewife prevented her from digging beneath the surface.[26]

Writing about visiting Rome's soup kitchens and talking to fallen notables, Doris mentioned that here soup kitchens served everyone, from out-of-work musicians to employees of the government and even retired officers. She was particularly charmed by one elderly lady who showed up wearing a purple turban. This visitor confessed that she had used up all her savings in just a few months, buying supplies on the black market, and now depended on the soup kitchen, where she could find not only good food but pleasant company.[27]

Doris commented in her dispatch that both the newly impoverished and the newly rich offered fertile ground for communism. Both groups believed that the "leveling" of society would prove to be their salvation, and that this change would come either through the establishment of a democracy or through civil war. But in the end, Doris agreed with the purple-turbaned lady that the scarcity or the abundance of food would ultimately decide the political future of the Italians, as it always had.[28]

These dispatches show that Doris was able to handle the facts of postwar Italy, even if her insights were not particularly profound.

Still, she had broken out of the role her family and her society expected her to fulfill. She would find it impossible to return to her conventional life in New York, although her mother and half brother, Walker Inman, wanted her to return. Walker was burdened by responsibilities at Duke Farms, which he and Marian had managed for the duration of the war. He needed Doris to make decisions about hiring and firing staff, and about management of the gardens and the herd of cattle.

Doris hadn't yet mastered the complicated affairs of Duke Farms, which she had fought to inherit after her father's death. But she was learning. In an undated letter to Marian, sent from Rome, she wrote that she realized she should not have invested in a herd of Angus cattle, which required so much "manicuring." But she didn't want to sell off the herd until later in the year, when they could no longer subsist on grazing. She also felt she might get a better price at that time of year.

She warned Marian, "And don't tell me we are out of the red." Doris knew that the expenses of running the farm were considerable. She also knew that Marian always put the best possible interpretation on their shared projects.[29]

After Germany's unconditional surrender, Nanaline again urged her daughter to come home. Would she stay on to continue to direct the Rome *Daily American*?[1]

Doris had invested heavily in the Rome *Daily American*,[2] surely knowing that the CIA owned 40 percent of the newspaper's stock. This was to provide cover for its operatives and to undermine Italian support for the Communist Party in the upcoming elections. Started by three GIs in the immediate postwar period in reaction to the demise of the army's *Stars and Stripes*, the newspaper was modeled on the *International Herald Tribune*, which took three days to travel from Paris to Rome, too long for news-hungry expats to wait.[3]

The newspaper might have provided a good excuse for Doris to stay in Rome for a few more years. But in May 1947, she moved to Paris, where she lived until October at 118 rue du Bac, on the Left Bank. Carmel Snow gave her a job for this brief period, as a photography assistant at the Paris *Harper's Bazaar*. Snow, the daughter of an Irish immigrant, had worked in her mother's dressmaking shop until she was discovered by the magazine publisher Condé Nast. Managing *Harper's Bazaar* and hiring such figures as Richard Avedon, Diana Vreeland, and Henri Cartier-Bresson, Snow, during her twenty-four years as editor in chief, developed what became the leading fashion magazine of the twentieth century.[4]

Doris would have known and admired the magazine for years, drawn to its breezy style and irreverence. *Harper's Bazaar* was, for instance, the first fashion magazine to run a photograph of a model in a swimsuit running toward the camera on a windy beach. Until then, all fashion shots were static ones of clothes displayed on mannequins.

Snow was quite an autocrat, though. Richard Avedon requested an interview fifteen times before she finally consented to see him. After she hired him, he became the best-known photographer *Harper's Bazaar* ever employed and one of the foremost photographers of the twentieth century.

Snow, who would have appreciated Doris's charm, style, and social connections, quickly took her under her wing.[5] By now, Doris may have planned to stay in France indefinitely. Her exposure to unwelcome publicity had dulled the lure of New York City.

In 1940, the Social Register had dropped Doris. This would have aggrieved her socially conscious mother, but Doris may have laughed it off. Among the other outcasts were the Duke and Duchess of Windsor and Gloria Vanderbilt—all apparently blackballed for bad marriages and worse divorces—but what exactly had Doris done to explain her exclusion? Five years later, Jimmy Cromwell's accusations in the New Jersey divorce court of Doris's unfaithfulness—he suspected, with reason, Alec Cunningham-Reid—reverberated in scandal sheets like *Los Angeles Confidential*. But that was long after the Social Register had dropped her.

In its May 1955 issue, *Confidential*'s cover story attempted to link Doris sexually with her African American chauffeur. A photograph on the magazine's cover showed Doris with her "African Prince," his headshot clearly superimposed on someone else's body.

Confidential, through its network of spies operating under the aegis of Hollywood Research Inc., aimed to expose interracial affairs among Hollywood celebrities. *Newsweek* had called *Confidential* a gossip sheet with conservative political leanings. The magazine was sued by Liberace, Frank Sinatra, and Groucho Marx, as well as Doris—the suits totaling $12 million in damages—and by Hollywood producers fearing damage to their stars' carefully cultivated images.[6] In 1955, the U.S. attorney general would ban *Confidential* from the mails as obscene.

Confidential secretly collaborated with the gossip columnist Walter Winchell, who tirelessly attacked Doris in his column in the New York *Daily Mirror*, "On Broadway"—the first syndicated gossip column. From April 1947 until Doris's death in 1993, *Confidential* carried sixty-three articles, with headlines such as "Doris Duke Daddy's Rich Girl," "Doris Duke's Number 2 Stars in Tale of Death and Gems," and "Doris Duke in Reno Sheds Latin 2nd Hubby."

Doris's *Confidential* suit—for $3 million—went nowhere, but it stirred up a lot of dust. Commiserating with her daughter over her problems with *Confidential*, Nanaline wrote that she hoped the controversy would be less damaging to Doris given that the magazine had lost earlier legal battles. She always tried to support and advise her daughter during difficult times.

Around the time of the *Confidential* brouhaha, Doris was receiving letters from Russell McKinnon, an important collector of French and Italian antique furniture. McKinnon may have acted as an agent for Doris, perhaps buying and selling furniture. An affectionate friend as well as a fellow collector of antiques, McKinnon wrote that he hoped Doris would always stay as beautiful as he had found her on their most recent evening together, when she had been wearing a dark blue satin dress with her hair piled on top of her head: "Yeah! Kisses!"[7]

But a later letter may have ended their friendship. In it, McKinnon mused that he would love to write an article about her for one of the fashion magazines, going into detail about her interests, her views on life, and her charitable giving. The article might even appeal, he thought, to *The Atlantic Monthly*.[8] This article, which he never wrote, would certainly have seemed to Doris a betrayal of their intimacy.

She would not have found it reassuring that McKinnon had first thought of writing it when "those thugs" had visited him in his house on East Eighty-first Street in Manhattan, apparently seeking information to fuel another negative news story about Doris. McKinnon felt sure the men were sent by *Confidential*.[9]

Around the same time, Nanaline had again been begging Doris to tell her when she planned to return to the United States. But Doris was not inclined to explain herself to her mother. On November 26, 1945, Doris scrawled in black pencil, "You asked me about plans but I have had none . . . tentative ones, but who knows what will become of them. I might return in a month but then again I may not."

Now thirty-three, Doris was assuming the role of international celebrity and icon of fashion. Her newfound confidence stemmed from her wartime experiences, and was enhanced by the extraordinary clothes she was ordering from the Paris couturiers, who had shown their courage during the Nazi occupation by refusing to move to Berlin and Vienna as ordered. According to Lucien Lelong, president of the Chambre Syndicale de la Couture Parisienne, fashion was in Paris or it was nowhere.

A worker from the milliner Reboux described the attitude of her fellow workers during the war: "We all wore large hats to raise our spirits. Felt gave out, so we made them out of chiffon. Chiffon was no more. All right, take straw. No more straw? Very well, braided paper. Hats have been a sort of contest between French imagination and German regulation. We wouldn't look shabby and worn out. After all, we were Parisiennes." Around this time, Doris began to wear large felt and straw hats, which became her signature.

Very tall and slim, Doris was perfectly suited to the designs of the resurgent French fashion industry and daring enough to carry them off. She particularly enjoyed wearing Christian Dior's New Look, its billowing skirts symbolizing the relaxation of wartime cloth restrictions. Dior's New Look was named and championed by Snow. The rounded shoulders, nipped-in waists, and full skirts were becoming to Doris, especially when balanced with one of her new broad-brimmed hats. This was the period when Doris, who loved going barefoot, seldom had the chance. Instead, she increased her height with three-inch heels, showing off the long legs that a sneaked photograph in *Confidential* showed when she had stretched at the barre in Martha Graham's New York dance studio.

She might have worn a red velvet jacket from Balenciaga for late-evening nightclubbing, during which she heard the black musicians who had fled New York for the warmer welcome offered in France. To the fashionable nightclub Le Bœuf sur le Toit she might have worn the short Dior black-lace-over-silk-chiffon evening dress. For embassy receptions, she would have worn beautifully tailored suits. All these clothes worked for the receptions, dinner parties, and dances where Doris was meeting the international set, who were once again moving from Paris to Nice for the spring racing meets, to Monte Carlo for the casinos, and to the Riviera for the life that F. Scott Fitzgerald wrote about in *Tender Is the Night*.

At *Harper's Bazaar*, Doris's wealth was certainly part of her identity. Snow must earlier have asked her protégée for a contribution to the coffers of the magazine. In the spring of 1945, Doris ordered her lawyers to send off the substantial sum of four hundred thousand francs. In the same letter, she asked that all recent issues of *Harper's Bazaar* be sent to her, explaining their absence from the Paris office as a case of the shoemaker's children having no shoes.[10]

That same spring, Doris met the Dominican diplomat Porfirio "Rubi" Rubirosa when she interviewed his wife, Danielle, for a story in *Harper's Bazaar*. Rubi later wrote in his unfinished memoir that upon meeting Doris he found her happy, elegant, and enchanting. Before long, he divorced Danielle, who said he was a man who could never be satisfied with just one woman. Doris and Rubi were soon seen at night spots around Paris.

Rubi was a self-styled playboy who would bring sex and fun to Doris's life. But he also embodied a risk far greater than that posed by Jimmy Cromwell or any of her other suitors, which was surely part of his allure: El Tiguerón, as he was called back in the Dominican Republic, was the biggest tiger in the Paris jungle, and he would not be tamed. His evident virility may have meant, for Doris, a chance to become pregnant. If so, she would be disappointed. Although his sexual prowess was supposed to have inspired Paris waiters to nickname their giant pepper grinders "Rubirosas,"[11] he was in fact sterile.

Doris was enchanted by Rubi's joie de vivre. When a journalist asked him about his work, Rubi explained that it was impossible for him to do a conventional job. As he explained, being an international playboy was a full-time occupation. Expertise in at least one sport—for Rubi, it was polo—great skill as a dancer, knowledge of several languages, the right social connections, an extensive bespoke wardrobe, a sense of humor, and, above all, plenty of free time to entertain and be entertained, these were essential. And Rubi possessed it all, as well as exotic good looks and a sophistication that made him feel at home anywhere in the world.

Claude Terrail, a close friend and owner of one of Rubi's favorite Paris restaurants, La Tour d'Argent, recalled of Rubi, "He was a gentleman, and a gentleman who has a lot of success with girls keeps his big mouth shut."[12] Doris, haunted all her life by intrusions of the press, could count on his discretion.

Mildred Ricart, a friend from the Dominican Republic whose husband had been in the foreign service with Rubi, remembered that he never let an unlit cigarette touch a woman's lips. And any woman he was talking to had his full attention. She added that a lot of men are good in bed, "but you can't go out to dinner with them."[13] This savoir faire was essential for a man navigating Doris's world. Yet Taki Theodoracopulos, raconteur and bon vivant, remembered that when Rubi was drunk, he would take out a guitar and sing, "I'm just a gigolo."

The waspish Truman Capote, according to a 2002 article in *Vanity Fair*, referred to Rubi as "a kinky-hair octoroon," a phrase with less-than-subtle racial overtones.

Born on January 22, 1909, in San Francisco de Macorís, Dominican Republic, Porfirio came from an educated family whose members were often drawn to public service. After attending school in Paris, where his father was counselor to the Dominican embassy, he spent most of his life in and out of diplomatic roles. An ambitious athlete, he trained as a boxer and skied at Saint-Moritz. Doris must have found his athleticism and the discipline it required—a discipline inevitably undermined by his determined carousing—attractive. She, too, was an athlete who took her physical ability, as well as the diet and rest it demanded, seriously.

Rubi had joined the army at seventeen, just as General Trujillo seized power. Impressed by his prowess in a polo game, the dictator asked, according to Rubi's memoir, what he was planning to do with his life, to which Rubi replied that he was training to be a lawyer. Trujillo told him that he should instead be measured for a uniform as presidential guard, which appealed to Rubi because it would attract women. One such woman was the dictator's seventeen-year-old daughter, Flor de Oro. Elegant, sophisticated Flor invited Rubi to a party in the presidential palace, where they danced every dance, which was unheard of in polite society and a death wish for a man attracted to Trujillo's daughter. Flor forced her father to agree to their marriage by going on a hunger strike.

Trujillo named Rubi to a legation at the Dominican embassy in Berlin in July 1936, as Germany was preparing for the Summer Olympics in Munich. There, Jesse Owens, the African American track star, would win innumerable medals, and would then travel freely throughout Germany, staying in hotels whose counterparts in the United States would have barred him on grounds of race. Later, Owens said that whereas Hitler had praised him, President Roosevelt had ignored him. Apparently, the president had not even sent a congratulatory telegram.

The darkening political situation in Berlin as Hitler gained power was of little interest to Rubi. He played polo, went to nightclubs, drove fast cars, and danced at the popular five o'clock tea parties at the Eden Hotel—teas that often involved flirtations with other women. Flor, who was trying and failing to become pregnant, soon became jealous. After their divorce in 1938, the two remained on friendly terms. Even more surprising, Rubi retained Trujillo's friendship and political patronage as well as the dictator's financial support.

Trujillo's actions in the Dominican Republic probably did not cause Rubi to lose any sleep. In 1929, a treaty had been signed delineating the boundary between the Dominican Republic and its neighbor, Haiti, on the island of Hispaniola. In 1937, angry that the border was being disregarded, Trujillo ordered the slaughter of thousands of Haitians still living on what he considered Dominican soil. Trujillo ruled the island through violence and intimidation.

In 1938, on his return to Paris from Berlin, Rubi raced sports cars at Le Mans, frequented the race track at Longchamps, and became involved with Gaby Montbreuse, a cabaret singer with the stage name of "La Môme Moineau" (the bratty sparrow). Also in 1938, Rubi was hired by the sparrow's wealthy husband to spirit her jewels out of Franco's Spain. Driving to Spain from Paris with an accomplice, Rubi managed to rescue only half the jewels. The accomplice disappeared, as did the other half of the jewels, which were appraised at $160,000—$2.8 million in today's dollars.

Rubi was often engaged in Trujillo's activities. In 1935, he had been involved in the unsolved murder of Sergio Bencosme, sidekick of Dr. Angel Morales, leader of the opposition against Trujillo, who had fled to New York after the dictator came to power. At Trujillo's request, Rubi became bagman to Morales's murderers, carrying $7,000 in a suitcase to the Dominican consulate in New York for the payoff before departing in haste.

In 1939, Trujillo appointed Rubi chargé d'affaires in Paris, where he is said to have personally sold visas to Jews fleeing the Nazi occupation. He was briefly arrested by the Gestapo. Upon his release, he began an affair with the French actress Danielle Darrieux. When Gestapo officers saw the pair dining at L'Aiglon in Paris, they were repelled by the sight of a dark-skinned man with a blond woman. Rubi was interned in Germany for a year.

In 1942, Rubi and Danielle married, divorcing in 1947. At the time of their marriage, he was thirty-three and she was twenty-four. In the summer of 1944, as Paris was being liberated, Rubi was shot in the back three times while driving his wife out of the city. Seriously wounded, he spent months recovering in a Paris hospital. Later, Rubi reflected that his would-be assassins were young men who, as part of the Franc-Tireurs et Partisans, a splinter group of the Communist Front National, had been looking for Germans still lurking in Paris. When Rubi failed to stop and show them his papers, the young men assumed that he was a fleeing German and fired.

Once he recovered, Rubi was appointed chargé d'affaires to the Dominican embassy in Rome, where he met Doris. After a fast courtship, Doris married Rubi on September 1, 1947, startling everyone in her circle. Her divorce from Jimmy would not be granted for several more months, until January 16, 1948, meaning that her marriage to Rubi was not legal.

In March 1947, Doris had flown back to New York to receive a few days of training at the midtown office of *Harper's Bazaar.* One of her lawyers, Stuart L. Hawkins, accepted a paycheck for her from the magazine covering the weeks from March 27 through April 15—the only paycheck Doris ever received for her work there. Her salary was fifty dollars a month.

Meanwhile, her lawyers were eager to meet with her. In late 1945, Tom Perkins had written her a strong letter advising a visit home so they could sit down and draw up a plan for her finances. He also wanted her to execute a new will and to clarify which responsibilities she wanted her lawyers to assume.

To underscore what she expected those responsibilities to be, Doris gave Perkins her power of attorney in March 1947 so that he could settle questions about her gift-tax payments with the IRS. Problems continued to arise, perhaps because of Doris's use of tax-free funds, dispensed through her charity Independent Aid, to help her friends. Perkins also needed her power of attorney to reach a final divorce settlement, for an undisclosed amount, with Jimmy, who wanted $7 million.

Her half brother, Walker, always intimately involved in all of Doris's financial affairs, telegraphed her on November 14, 1947, about the successful result of his March negotiations with Jimmy. He told her he could settle at the cost of about $650,000, netting Jimmy $350,000, the balance to go to his attorney and gift taxes.[14] (Jimmy's "gift" would be worth more than $4 million in today's currency.) Without a prenuptial agreement, Jimmy had been free to ask for anything he wanted.

Walker's cable suggested that he could possibly negotiate a better deal, but that he needed to know exactly how much Doris wanted to offer to Jimmy. He asked for a fast response, signing off, "Love, Walker Inman."

Perkins sent off another cable two days later, asking Doris to authorize him to resolve the matter of the settlement.[15] Apparently, the amount that Walker had offered was not enough, in Jimmy's eyes. Doris, Walker, and Tom Perkins must all have known by the spring of 1947 that there was only one way to get Jimmy to agree to divorce: ever more substantial amounts of money.

Did guilt enter into Doris's calculations? It's impossible to know, although the fact that she continued to give Jimmy money for years after their divorce seems to indicate a bad conscience. As well, she may have gone on giving Jimmy money to maintain a connection to her early life that she couldn't bear to lose.

Doris also gave Jimmy many promissory notes over the years. One, drawn up as late as December 14, 1967, was in the amount of $325,000 "for the purchase of equipment and working capital to be used by Waterloo Building Products, Inc. and for working capital for Kardar Canadian Oils Limited, at an interest rate of 6% per annum." But on October 17, 1968, Jimmy replied to a letter from Doris's advisers at 30 Rockefeller Plaza, communicating that Miss Duke "does not wish to make any additional investment in the Kardar enterprises."[16]

Annoyed that she was withdrawing support just as Kardar was beginning to emerge from the red, and despite what Jimmy called his remarkably successful business career, he assumed that Doris had been offended
by something he had said or done between dinner on August 20 and a
telephone conversation on August 25. This meant, he asserted, that her
withdrawal of financial support was based on personal pique rather than
on sound business practices. Since then she had refused to see him. He
was now requesting a meeting to repeat his demands, saying that he could
give the information only to Doris herself, rather than send it through a
third party. Apparently, the meeting never took place.

In June 1947, Rubi had flown back to the Dominican Republic to
consult with Trujillo, who must have been delighted by the news of his
former son-in-law's conquest. As canny as he was ruthless, the dictator
would have immediately grasped the possibilities inherent in Rubi's controlling the Duke millions, and especially the Duke Power Company,
with its grid covering the Southeastern states.

Doris did not inform her family or friends at home of her 1947 wedding
before it took place, either to avoid controversy or because there was
simply no time before the ceremony at the Dominican embassy in Paris.
A more wicked interpretation is that Rubi conspired to marry Doris at
the embassy so that the Napoleonic Code, still in effect in the Dominican Republic, would grant him the Duke fortune. In accordance with
the Napoleonic Code, Doris did promise during the ceremony to obey
her husband. But if Rubi's motive was control of her fortune—and there
is no proof of that one way or the other—he was, according to news stories, thwarted by the appearance, minutes before the wedding, of two
briefcase-toting French lawyers, who obtained his signature on a prenuptial agreement. This agreement overrode the financial regulations of the
Napoleonic Code. Additionally, Rubi had signed a note weeks before, re-
nouncing his potential claim on Doris's estate, in return for cash and gifts
in the event of a divorce.[17]

Rubi smoked during the brief ceremony, grinding his cigarette out
just in time to put a gold ring encrusted with rubies on Doris's finger. In
exchange, she gave him a plain gold band. Rubi would prove to be the only
man in Doris's life, other than her father, to give her expensive jewelry.
Perhaps he even paid for it out of his own funds.

On October 10, Doris wrote to Nanaline: "The wedding was certainly a mess through no fault of either of us. We were just the unfortunate victims of the consul who is either half-witted or publicity-crazy. And, I rather think he is both." There were apparently more reporters in attendance than guests. "But, there's no use crying over spilt milk and anyway we're both very happy." The two were looking forward to going to Argentina, where Trujillo had appointed Rubi Dominican ambassador, and where they would escape the cold.

"Actually, the only part of the [news] stories that upset Ruba [*sic*]," she told her mother, "was when they said he was three inches shorter than me. He's not. But it may have looked that way as I had on very high heels and masses of false hair piled on top of my head—trying to be sheeek [*sic*]."[18] Since Rubi was five foot nine and Doris hovered around six feet, the reporters were in fact correct.

Doris explained to Nanaline that she hadn't written earlier because she had expected to see her in New York, "but a reporter called me up and told me that Cromwell was up to his old tricks again"—trying to prove her Nevada residency invalid—"and so I decided I had better stay put." She continued, "Actually I'm very disappointed to have missed that trip to New York. Not only would I have loved seeing you and the farm," but she needed to visit her doctor for an unexplained internal problem. However, she couldn't allow Jimmy to "pull more fast ones . . . More lousy publicity would not be good for my boy in his career."[19] Her suggestion of a medical issue echoes the complaints of Rubi's first wife, who said that when her honeymoon was over, her "insides" hurt a lot.

For her second wedding, Doris wore an emerald-green taffeta cocktail dress, its V-neck stopped by an enormous artificial rose. A dark green velvet beret was perched on the side of her upswept hair, lending her a rakish air, reinforced by her mysterious smile and slit eyes. Although a news story described her as "glittering with diamonds," in a wedding photograph she wears a simple one-strand necklace.

Now, with her piled-up hair and high heels, she was claiming the power inherent in her height as well as in her personality. In this same wedding picture, she smiles at Rubi, who looks slight and somewhat childlike beside her. Her expression is charged with the sexuality that was their strongest link.

That same sexuality would harm Doris's legacy in ways she could never have anticipated, given the apparent freedom of the immediate post-war period, when sexual restrictions, even for women, seemed to have eased. But the double standard still ruled. Potent female desire invited scurrilous innuendo—especially in Doris's case, because of her attraction to dark-skinned men.

On September 2, Walker Inman fired off a cable addressed to Mr. and Mrs. Porfirio Rubirosa at 118 rue du Bac. The cable was full of bluster intended to conceal hurt feelings at not being invited to the wedding. "You blank youngster," Walker's cable begins. He was furious that he had missed the chance provided by Doris's wedding to flirt with the "gay demoiselles" of Paris. Still, he sent his best wishes to his sister and Rubi.

After her wedding, Doris sent Walker a brief undated cable: "Great got hitched to Porfirio Rubirosa stop (no) worry he is nice you will like him love Doris."[20] Realizing that Walker needed to be soothed, she wrote in a subsequent letter, "I don't wonder that you were slightly confozed [sic] by my last cable." Then she told him that her "ever-loving ambassa-dor has recently gone nuts on the subject of aviation. He cut his teeth on a Navion [a 1940s single-engine, unpressurized four-seat aircraft] but of course is rapidly outgrowing it."[21] Doris told her half brother that if he found another plane like the one he owned on the market, equipped with a good pilot, he should let her know.

Three weeks before the wedding, Perkins wrote Doris to advise her of the way marriage would change her legal status. After congratulating her, and wishing her happiness, he went on to say that he had understood from her mother that Doris had signed a prenuptial agreement, one, he believed, that was drawn up by an American lawyer in Paris. He also worried that she would lose her U.S. citizenship if she lived for five years outside the country.

Therefore, he advised, she should keep Nevada as her residency no matter where she and Rubi decided to live. He also suggested that, if the Paris lawyer had drawn up a new will, he should send a copy to Perkins. If, however, Doris had not executed a new will, she should add a codicil to her current will immediately, to define Rubi's rights as possible inheritor. Perkins would have been concerned about the potential threat of the Napoleonic Code, should it be deemed to apply to Doris, creating the possibility that Rubi would inherit her entire estate. Further, Doris's power of attorney, which her lawyers held, would be superseded by the laws of the Dominican Republic. Those laws treated marital property as held by both husband and wife, but with the husband alone having the power to make all decisions. Doris had always depended on her lawyers to protect her, although, in the case of the note Rubi had signed before the wedding, she had exercised her own judgment without seeking Tom's counsel.

On November 27, 1947, Doris flew to New York. She was telling reporters that she had come to visit her mother, but someone from the Duke Business Office claimed that the real reason was to prevent the State Department from killing her passport. Washington might even "use its influence" to prevent Argentina from accepting Rubi as ambassador, because if he was accepted, Doris would be snubbed there, thereby damaging U.S. prestige.[22] Of course, in the Argentina of flamboyant First Lady Eva Perón, a glamorous ambassador's wife dressed in couture fashions was unlikely to be snubbed by anyone.

In the end, Doris was able to obtain her passport, and Rubi his ambassadorship. But the scrutiny continued. Notified of the marriage, the FBI head, J. Edgar Hoover, ordered his office to open a file on Rubi; it would bulge over the years. Hoover himself penciled on it, "What do we have on him?"[23]

5 During their honeymoon on the Riviera, Rubi gave interviews wearing an "atomic bathing suit" that, according to a news story, showed off his "athletic physique." Meanwhile, Doris was trying to reform him, replacing all-night frolicking with an early-to-bed, early-to-rise regime.

Initially, Rubi complied, but it was not in his nature to sacrifice having a good time, which involved plenty of liquor and pretty women. Yet his affection for his new wife is clear in a tender note he penciled that described looking in on Doris and finding her sleeping peacefully. Unwilling to disturb her, he left his message on the nightstand, explaining that he was going out to look for "some old antique jewelry" as a present for her, and hoping that they might be able to go sailing together the next day.[1]

The couple's subsequent stay in Buenos Aires was brief. In July 1948, in a column called "The Smart Set" published in the *New York Journal-American*, Cholly Knickerbocker claimed that they had left Buenos Aires because of a "delicate situation." According to Knickerbocker, an unnamed woman in Buenos Aires "had become violently infatuated" with the ambassador and was stalking him. This caused Doris and Rubi to flee to Paris. Though the woman followed them on the next plane, she was made to feel very unwelcome. It may have been the only time in Rubi's career when a wife managed to scotch one of his flirtations.

Still, his behavior in Argentina, gaudier than it had been in Paris, had offended Doris. Before they had hurried off, Rubi had formed a relationship of some kind with Eva Perón, wife of president Juan Perón.[2] Having visited every corner of the country to promote her husband's candidacy, Evita, as she was known, was idolized because of her support of trade unions and women's suffrage. She formed the Female Peronist Party while also running the Ministries of Labor and Health. Doris knew that she had encountered a formidable adversary.

The traditional narrative of the ending of relationships pictures the woman as disconsolate and abandoned, as is often the case. However, with Doris, a different narrative prevailed. She was always the one who left first. She divorced Rubi amicably in October 1948, in Paris, just thirteen months after their wedding. Fortunately, Doris's wealth, now estimated at $200 million, was protected by the note Rubi had signed. To obtain the divorce quickly, Doris flew to Nevada and cited Rubi's "extreme mental cruelty" as grounds.[3] Such language was necessary, at the time, to obtain a divorce.

Yet divorce did not end their friendship. Two years later, when Rubi was in Santiago playing polo, he cabled Doris that he believed she had listened to unspecified "untruthful reports" about him. In spite of their fraught past, he urged her to visit him.[4]

Rubi expected Doris to continue to support his endeavors. In 1951, when he was organizing the fishing industry in Santo Domingo, he would write his "Baby Darling" to ask for a loan of $100,000 for this project. He ended by saying he loved her. Doris may have wondered to what degree his financial need inspired his love. In 1952, he would cable that he loved her completely and wanted to "reestablish love." In 1954, he suggested that if they became lovers again she would have his undivided attention. Dozens of affectionate cables followed, some of them requesting that Doris draw up a new power of attorney. This intertwining of love and money was, to say the least, problematic. During their brief marriage, their relationship had drawn equally on their individual sources of power:

Rubi's virility and Doris's fortune. Yet their continuing friendship argues that affection had always been a part of the mix.[5]

That it continued is proved by a cable from Rubi and his third wife, the Woolworth heiress Barbara Hutton, whom Rubi married in New York in 1953. Thanking Doris for her "sweet cable" of congratulations, the newlyweds assured her that her good wishes made their happiness "complete," and ended by promising devoted love and hoping to see her soon.[6] The two were married for a total of seventy-three days.

Hutton and Doris were often linked in news stories, since they were both glamorous blond heiresses. But the two women were never close. Doris may have found it hard to understand why Barbara wasted so much of her inherited fortune on her seven husbands. She would also have found Barbara's media nickname, "Poor Little Rich Girl," unappetizing. This moniker was never applied to Doris.

Rubi would go on to have an affair with actress Zsa Zsa Gabor, whom he had begun to see during the run-up to his marriage with Hutton. True to the attitudes of her times, Zsa Zsa excused the black eye he gave her during an argument, telling reporters that men assault their wives only when they love them deeply.[7]

Later, Rubi would be linked romantically with Ava Gardner, Rita Hayworth, and Soraya, the ex-wife of the shah of Iran, whom the shah divorced in 1958. Nevertheless, in 1956 Rubi married a French model and actress, Odile Bérard, whom he met at a polo match in Deauville. He was thirty-one years her senior.

Trujillo continued to support his former son-in-law, appointing him ambassador to Cuba in early 1958. The following year, Fidel Castro came to power. When a bomb exploded in the embassy's inner courtyard, Rubi and Odile decamped. Then Trujillo appointed him ambassador to Belgium. When Rubi failed to report for duty, Trujillo dismissed him, but soon thereafter appointed him inspector of all embassies and legations. Clearly, Trujillo's loyalty to Rubi ran deep. Both men embodied a notion of unabashed masculine power: Rubi with women, and Trujillo with a nation.

In August 1961, Rubi and Odile visited President and Mrs. Kennedy in Hyannis Port and sailed on the president's yacht. Short on money after Trujillo's assassination on May 30, 1961, in the Dominican Republic, Rubi imagined marrying the president's sister, Patricia Kennedy Lawford, who at the time was still married, or the Mellon heiress Peggy Hitchcock. But the opportunity did not arise. He died when he crashed his Ferrari into a tree near the Bois de Boulogne on July 5, 1965.[8] The accident happened after an all-night session at a Paris nightclub to celebrate his winning the polo Coupe de France.

Rubi's death further enhanced the romantic legend that drew Doris, and many other women, to men society deemed unsuitable. Rubi was a handsome, seductive risk taker whose recklessness was more exciting than the bland conventionality of suitable men who recognize reasonable limits. Doris, who took risks herself with her reputation and her relationships, found much to attract her in men who took even greater risks— some of them, as in Rubi's case, fatal.

In 1947, while she was enjoying the early days of her marriage to Rubi, Doris struggled, at long distance, to save her investment in the Rome *Daily American*. The newspaper was bedeviled by mismanagement. Doris gave its parent company, the American Publishing Company, $132,000 between 1946 and 1952.

Aided by Tom Perkins, who at one point was vice president of the newspaper's corporation, Doris hired and fired various executives who were also board members and stockholders, trying to "to clear up the terrible mess Jack left." Apparently, Jack Begon, the original publisher and president, had "milked the corporation to obtain funds to buy control," according to a letter from Perkins to Doris on October 26, 1951.

In New York in 1951, Perkins was trying to persuade two essential but disillusioned Rome *Daily American* executives, Louis Cortese and James Wick, to drop their lawsuit against Begon and remain in their positions. Ignoring Perkins's advice, Doris wrote to Cortese, whom she wished to replace with her old friend Mike Chinigo—"a natural for the job"—that "Jack left the paper saddled with so many burdens that unless radical

steps are taken it can never pull itself out." Even the State Department
had canceled its subscriptions, though Clare Boothe Luce, U.S. ambassador to Italy, promised to resubscribe if the company was reorganized.

On November 5, 1951, Jack Begon tendered his resignation, as requested by Perkins, insisting, "I have at all times acted in good faith and
for the best interests of the company," spending, he claimed, $30,000 of
his own money to supplement what he viewed as an inadequate salary. Yet
he ended his letter by apologizing for having let Doris down.

A flurry of directors' resignations immediately followed Begon's departure, causing the newspaper's meager profits to decline so precipi-
tously that, later in November, Perkins wrote Doris that the company
had only about $3,000 in cash and owed between $85,000 and $90,000,
most in the form of a loan from the Banca d'Italia, which Begon had
arranged. Meanwhile, Doris gave Chinigo, newly installed in his role as
president, her power of attorney. Perkins urged Chinigo to hire more staff,
including a man named Jesse James, son-in-law of Perkins's friend
Admiral Flanagan.

In July 1953, Chinigo received a reprimand from Perkins for allegedly
exceeding the limits of Doris's power of attorney by initiating a lawsuit
against Cortese. Chinigo complained in a cable that he regretted his involvement in the whole messy business.

Perkins dispatched the advertising executive Ray Vir Den to Rome to
get to the bottom of the situation. On November 13, 1953, Vir Den wrote
Perkins that the Rome *Daily American* was riddled with problems. Four
pages of detailed analysis followed, leading Vir Den to conclude that the
newspaper was now entirely composed of wire-service stories and that all
the staff needed to know was how to use scissors and paste.

Chinigo responded to a letter from Doris announcing her withdrawal
from the American Publishing Company, saying that he was amazed, cha-
grined, and insulted. Having read Chinigo's reply over many times, Doris
responded, "It seems to me you have completely lost sight of the main
point in our agreement—namely, the welfare of the RDA." She went on to
say that Chinigo seemed to think that she, "in some sort of a Xmas spirit,
made you a present of some notes or machinery or whatnot. A strange idea
to say the least." In a draft she may never have sent, she accused Chinigo "of
welching on agreements and double-crossing at random, and never getting

to the main point." (This clause is faintly crossed out.) She stated that he seemed to have forgotten that "the aim of those notes in the first place was simply to help along a struggling American paper (which wasn't too bad at the time)" in an attempt "to sell America to a country torn apart by un-American political factions. Since then the paper has disintegrated."[1]

The rest of this letter is lost, but its tone, crossed-out phrases, and rewrites convey Doris's anger. Yet she later appointed Chinigo as a consultant to her foundation. He remained a friend as well as a financial drain for many years.[2]

On February 28, 1954, Chinigo wrote to Doris to ask for $10,000 as payment for a year and a half's work on the Rome *Daily American*, as well as $1,000 for a Monsignor Pietro Barbieri, who, according to Chinigo, had been fighting communism single-handedly and wanted money to help Alexandria's orphans. He received both checks, made out to him personally.

But on at least one occasion, Chinigo seemed to menace Doris by acting as conduit for untoward revelations. On March 10, 1955, he wrote her that her former maid in Rome, Paola Riva, wanted help and knew that Piero Piccioni used to come to visit Doris and play the piano in her apartment.[3] Piccioni was a well-known musician and composer, so the veiled threat seems fairly toothless. Later, Chinigo returned to the United States to marry Marajen Stevick, who had inherited her father's Illinois newspaper, the Champaign *News-Gazette*.

In a 1954 news story in the *Chicago American*, Chinigo revealed information about his connections with the Italian Mafia (he said he'd been warned that the story would endanger his life), including his meeting with Don Calogero Vizzini, reportedly the chief of the Mafia, in Sicily. Chinigo had tried to "establish a link between his cooperation with American troops and Lucky Luciano, the American gangster," in an attempt to support the American invasion.

On August 13, 1974, Chinigo was wounded at midnight on a street in Rome, apparently by his companion, a man named Giarizzo. He lingered for two months. The case was never solved. *The New York Times* called the death a suicide. The Rome police report stated that Chinigo had reached into his companion's pocket, grabbed a .38 pistol, and shot himself in the left temple with his right hand, surviving for two weeks in the hospital before finally dying as the result of an operation for a bone splinter in his brain.

Chinigo was of Yugoslav ancestry. Born in Italy in 1908, he had moved with his family to the United States in 1914, attended Yale, and become a member of Skull and Bones, an elite secret society and breeding ground for undercover operatives. During the war, he worked for the OSS, with the code name Sorel. He was awarded a Silver Star for valor by the U.S. government after he landed as a war correspondent with the first wave of U.S. soldiers in Sicily on July 3, 1943. He returned from that foray with two truckloads of Italian POWs. Described in Bayard Stockton's *Flawed Patriot* as trailing "a heavy miasma of bad taste, double dealing, petty crime," Chinigo was helpful to the spymaster James Angleton in his undercover campaign in Yugoslavia, thanks to Chinigo's knowledge of an obscure local dialect.[4]

Doris tended to be entranced by men she viewed as heroes, and she admired Chinigo's war record. Also, since she saw herself as notorious, especially after the scandalous news stories of the 1940s and 1950s, she often felt a kinship with men who lived on the shadow side. In Chinigo, she saw a man with one foot in each realm.

The failure of the Rome *Daily American* was not surprising in view of Doris's physical distance (after she left Rome) and her lack of newspaper experience. By relying so heavily on Perkins, whose good intentions could not compensate for his own distance from Rome and his own lack of journalistic experience, Doris showed that she preferred to trust an old retainer rather than an expert who might be tempted to betray her.

Doris's departure for Paris did not end her connection with Jack Begon. She wrote on May 15, 1947, to Stuart Hawkins, another of her New York lawyers: "Jack Begon, of the *Rome American*, is arriving shortly in New York, and is sure to call on you. He's an awfully nice guy and I'm sure you'll like him. Incidentally, I owe him $1,145.00."[5] Begon was another of the ambiguous men who appeared regularly in Doris's life during this period.

A former undercover agent, Begon was a correspondent for the Rome *Daily American*, as well as for the American Broadcasting Company

(ABC), when he apparently faked his own kidnapping, disappearing from Rome for a month. Upon his return, he told police that he'd been captured by the Mafia and transported back to the United States. The police were unconvinced. At the same time, he would be accused of embezzling funds from ABC, but the Roman court cleared him of criminal charges on both counts for lack of evidence.[6]

Given this scandal, Doris may have tried to distance herself from the Rome *Daily American* when she moved to Paris, but she remained involved until 1953. On August 15, 1951, she explained her position as investor to the former editor William B. deMeza: "I supported the paper because I felt that you and Jack and Lou could do a good job running it—and now you have left and sold your interest to Jack and Lou is suing Jack."[7] Feeling that she lacked sufficient information to make a decision about what was happening, Doris asked deMeza for his opinion.[8]

Doris's request reveals some aspects of her business savvy—or lack of it. She didn't realize that although deMeza's financial involvement with the newspaper had ended, he could still retain a grudge against the other editors.

For this brief period in Rome and Paris, Doris's work seemed to free her from some of the complexities of her inheritance. She may have viewed herself, and perhaps even been viewed, as just another American girl journalist. Still, she would not be able to leave her history behind for long. One of the great forces of that history was the influence of her father.

No one would ever call James Buchanan Duke—Buck Duke—graceful. At six foot two, weighing in later life more than two hundred pounds, with his curious pigeon-toed walk, the result of a foot injury, and his North Carolina tobacco-field accent, he seemed, at best, a curiosity. In 1890, a New York newspaper dubbed him "The Tarheel Nobody Knows," which was exactly the way he wanted it.

Even his foot injury was mysterious. At the height of his success, he responded to a lady who asked, at a New York dinner party, what his feet looked like by taking off his shoe and sock and displaying a foot she pronounced "beautiful."[1]

Perhaps he was being playful. This quality often surfaced when he wrote to his brother Ben. In the tone of intimacy that characterized their close and loving partnership, Buck described an incident that occurred early in his career, when he was peddling the family's loose-leaf tobacco.

About a visit with their uncle John Taylor Duke in Milan, Tennessee, Buck wrote: "On my arrival there at Uncle John's I found Miss Mattie Patton, the liveliest girl I think God ever put breath in . . . I romped and

played with the girls so much I declare I was so tired at night I could not
sleep . . . It first started by Lyda and Mattie putting some water on me &
got me started I then you know wanted to get the best of them so it went
from droppers to dripperfull [sic] and finally ended in Bucketfulls on top
of one another until we were wet from head to foot. Old Uncle John (about
half stued [sic] most of the time) would urge us on & I thought he would
split his old sides laughing. Cousin Lockie gave us plenty of wine & I got
a gallon besides so we kept the crowd jolly all the time."[2]

Buck had been one of many poor urchins in the post–Civil War South
when he worked in the North Carolina tobacco fields of his father, Washington Duke. He went largely unacknowledged as an entrepreneur in his
youth, while he was creating one of the great fortunes of the early twentieth century. Even once the work of making his fortune was done, Buck
Duke remained hidden except to his business associates and his family.
He did not give interviews and permitted few photographs, developing a
passion for secrecy that Doris would imitate.

A singular power drove him through childhood hardships: first, the
death of his mother, Artelia, from typhoid in 1858, when Buck was not
even two years old, followed ten days later by the death of Sidney, a child
from his father's first marriage, to Mary Clinton, who had died in 1847.
Then there was his family's upheaval caused by his father's being drafted
in 1863 into the Confederate Navy. Washington Duke—or Wash, as he was
called—was drafted by the Confederacy even though he was a staunch Republican, as all his offspring would be, an admirer of Presidents Lincoln
and Buchanan. But slaves were included in the list of his household be-
longings, auctioned before Wash left for the war; the "eight or ten likely
NEGROES"[3] certainly made the meager pickings more attractive.

Forced to "brake [sic] up" his household in Durham, which consisted
of his and Artelia's three children—Mary, Benjamin, and James (Buck)—
Wash sent the children to live with their grandparents in Alamance County,
North Carolina. Brodie, an adult son from Wash's first marriage, was not
sent to the front, because he weighed only ninety-six pounds. Instead, he
worked as a guard at the Confederate Prison in Salisbury, North Carolina.

Wash served in the Confederate Navy obscurely but unharmed. After
Appomattox, he walked more than a hundred miles home and went to
work to restore his three-hundred-acre farm in Durham, which had been

despoiled by outliers from Sherman's rampage. His four children labored beside him.[4] Buck's first duty was to help rebuild the farm. Already, the teenager possessed extraordinary energy and focus.

Twenty years later, that energy would propel him to New York, the big city that was next on his list of places to conquer. From his humble two-room rental in Harlem and the Bowery taverns and greasy spoons where he took his meals, Buck would ascend in two decades to a classically proportioned limestone mansion on the corner of Fifth Avenue and Seventy-eighth Street, soon adding a vast farm in Somerville, New Jersey; a summer "cottage" on Bellevue Avenue in Newport, Rhode Island; and a pretty and adept Southern wife, Nanaline, as mistress of all of these grand properties. Though Buck Duke's success mirrors that of the creators of other early-twentieth-century fortunes in oil, steel, and rails, no one rose faster.

It all began with the tobacco plant, a suitable symbol for Buck himself. Towering at full growth to over nine feet, with a thick stalk covered with hairs and leaves emitting a potent insect-attracting ooze, tobacco depleted the soil and demanded the most scrupulous and unrelenting care. Buck, his brother Ben, his half brother Brodie, and their father had tended it as women tend sickly children, debugging, pruning, working ceaselessly toward the perfect big leaf that was called Bright for its light caramel color and its mild aroma.

In the rough frame house in Durham that Wash built for his family, his daughter, Mary, sewed small cotton pouches for the tobacco, stamping each one with the sentiment that sprang from Wash's Whig convictions: "Pro Bono Publico."[5] It takes some mental maneuvering to fathom the name, which the Dukes soon dropped: How could tobacco, suspected as early as the late nineteenth century of causing lung problems, be deemed to contribute to the public good? Perhaps Buck Duke thought, as many have before and since, that because people all over the world have always smoked, his "pure" tobacco (he would later deny its purity) was their best and most wholesome choice. Decades later, he would ask an amused Newport audience where else a poor man could procure such pleasure for ten cents.

The Dukes cured their tobacco in their open-slatted barn, using the new long-flue curing process. Legend holds that a slave set to watch the curing process overnight once fell asleep and let the leaf scorch to the newly desired golden color. Whatever precipitated the discovery, the Dukes found that this type of curing changed the chemistry of the tobacco leaf, making it acidic rather than alkaline, and therefore much easier to inhale. Smoke from Virginia and Kentucky dark-leaf tobacco was usually held in the smoker's mouth, whereas milder smoke from North Carolina Bright Leaf was drawn straight into the lungs. With this inhalable smoke, nicotine addiction was born.

Buck planned on further improving the processing of tobacco; he wrote Ben that he intended to dry the leaves and then dip them in rum to improve their flavor.[6] After the cured tobacco leaves were dried, the sons and their father flayed and sifted them, added the rum or molasses, and packed the final product into Mary's little bags, to peddle it across the state in a battered cart drawn by a pair of mules Buck later claimed were blind. They bartered or sold their tobacco to small-town customers, many of them friends or acquaintances who were glad to help fellow strivers in the hard days of Reconstruction.

Buck, as strong as an ox and utterly confident, soon took the lead in the family, becoming at nineteen his father's partner. He later said there was nothing more exciting than creating that business. It was sheer fun to begin what would become in a few decades an empire: to imagine, to plan, to maneuver; to advance, to retreat, to flirt, or to threaten, always hedged by a loyal cadre of men—first of all his father and his brothers—always operating in fraternal secrecy. By 1914, Buck's British-American Tobacco Company owned 95 percent of all the tobacco grown, processed, and machined into cigarettes in the United States and Britain.

From the early days, Buck realized that his biggest market lay in China. Asking for an atlas, he laid his finger on the country that even then numbered 450 million people. Today, its more than one billion inhabitants lead the world in rates of tobacco consumption.

Buck succeeded rapidly. In 1874, when Wash had acquired a small warehouse in Charlotte, the firm of W. Duke & Sons was valued at $90,800. By 1889, its value had risen to $600,000, partly thanks to the money and labor saved by buying tobacco from neighboring farmers rather than raising it themselves. Over time, the Dukes would come to control the price of tobacco sold at auction.[7]

On April 23, 2012, the Kentucky-born writer Wendell Berry remembered in his Jefferson Lecture for the National Endowment for the Humanities that his father had been ruined at the 1907 tobacco auction by the (then) American Tobacco Company, which, Berry said, was a monopoly that squashed competitors by controlling, and lowering, the prices paid to them at auction. Berry railed against Buck Duke, who, he said, had followed "a capitalistic logic" to ruin tobacco farmers, including Berry's father.

Berry described visiting the Duke campus and viewing, with horror, the statue of the founder, standing in front of its cathedral-like chapel with its majestic tower and soaring stained-glass windows.

Buck's statue—he is holding a cigar in his left hand—is inscribed on one side of the base "INDUSTRIALIST" and on the other side "PHILANTHROPIST," which Berry felt showed that he was "terrifyingly ignorant, even terrifyingly innocent" of the unavoidable contradiction between the fortune he had made through the manufacture and sale of cigarettes and any possible public good his philanthropy might finance.[8] A similar ignorance, or innocence, would haunt Buck's daughter.

Buck Duke differed from the other robber barons of his period, as his friend Bernard Baruch, the financier, remembered. Asked to compare Duke with his peers in the financial world, Baruch said he lacked the "verve and dash" of Henry Clay Frick. Buck was a man "with every hair in place," but he used rough language and didn't speak grammatically. According to Baruch, Duke was "one of the first very great merchants . . . Duke was a very solid kind of fellow. He never showed much emotion, around where I was. He was very devoted to Doris." Baruch remembered Doris running to greet her father "with her pigtail streaming out behind her back."

Baruch described "trading at the curb" in the early days, saying that Buck gave him orders for tobacco and left the negotiating to him. After Buck bought the Liggett & Myers tobacco company, "a very fine concern" for which he paid $12 million, he gave Baruch $150,000 for his share. "He said I was the only Democrat he knew that ever had any sense," Baruch recalled.[9]

In the early years, the Dukes produced only smoking tobacco for pipes and chews. In 1881, they began to produce hand-rolled paper-covered cigarettes, packing them in small, stiff pasteboard boxes to prevent breakage. Wash ordered fifty thousand boxes at first, but within a year needed to buy them in lots of a million. Buck would make the boxes more attractive to buyers by adding colored lithographs of vaudeville stars and famous athletes.

His little lithographs, with their sharp white borders and colorful backgrounds, are now collectors' items. In the May 6, 2013, issue of *The New Yorker*, Reeves Wiedeman wrote in "The Talk of the Town" that one of the American Tobacco Company's 1909 cards had sold recently for $2.1 million at a public auction. The card, Wiedeman explained, was particularly valuable to collectors because it carried an image of Honus Wagner, shortstop for the Pittsburgh Pirates. Because Honus opposed smoking and fought the use of his image on the card, few were printed.

The buyer, Jonathan Gallen, described by Wiedeman as supporting his collecting of sports memorabilia by running a hedge fund, told the reporter that owning the Honus card "means you're the man," a sentiment Buck Duke might have guessed would help to sell cigarettes as well as baseball cards.[10]

Two inventions were needed to fuel the growth of the Dukes' tobacco company.

The first was Joshua Pusey's creation of matchbooks with a striking surface in the 1890s; he sold his invention to the Diamond Match Company, which continues to produce matches today. These matches replaced the older friction matches, which sometimes spewed balls of fire, scorching carpets and dresses.

The other invention was the cigarette-rolling machine. In 1880, James Albert Bonsack read of a contest with a prize of $75,000 for such a machine, sponsored by tobacconists Allen & Ginter. Bonsack left school to work on his invention, a giant mechanical spider with multilevel belts and moving cogs that frequently broke down.[11] Bonsack's first customer, the North Carolina firm of W. T. Blackwell, grew frustrated with the machine's many failures. Through a secret deal, Buck Duke acquired the patent and hired the expert engineering help required to make his first four machines fully operational. This marked the decline of marketing hand-rolled cigarettes.[12]

Until then, cigarettes—called "short smokes," and used during the Crimean War and the Civil War because of their cheapness and

portability—trailed chew and pipe tobacco in sales. Hand-rolling cigarettes, begun in the famous Seville warehouse that was the setting for
Bizet's *Carmen*, could not produce anywhere near the number per day
that Buck desired, even in the hands of expert rollers, who were paid two
dollars an hour. He knew he needed a cigarette-rolling machine to replace
all those hands, many of them the smaller hands of underpaid women
workers.

With the shadow of the then far larger and more successful W. T.
Blackwell Tobacco Company of Durham hovering over him, the thirty-
year-old entrepreneur took the risk that would propel his future, buying
the patent to the Bonsack machine. It must have given him particular
pleasure to prove that he could make it work.

Blackwell had been ahead of him, building a new factory in Durham
in 1874—the same year Wash Duke moved his enterprise to Charlotte—
and installing the latest machinery. Blackwell also pioneered the use of
advertising to sell tobacco, spending enormous amounts of money to
place ads for Bull Durham pipe tobacco in magazines and newspapers,
and offering buyers premiums from razors to mantel clocks with the purchase of every pack.

The Blackwell factory dominated the entire city of Durham. At noon,
a steam whistle on the factory proclaimed the hour with a tremendous
roar, and the fierce bull, symbol of Blackwell tobacco, was plastered on
signboards all over the country and in Europe. It was a potent symbol for
male consumers; women would not smoke in public until the 1920s.

Buck eagerly rose to the challenge Blackwell offered. But he admitted that his company could not "compete with the Bull" in pipe-tobacco
sales. "I am going into the cigarette business," he declared.[13]

Brodie, the eldest, and the only surviving offspring of Wash's first
marriage, soon went his own way, starting a small tobacco business in
Durham in 1869 in a frame house on Main Street. He lived on the second
floor and manufactured tobacco on the ground floor, calling it "Semper
Idem" (Always the Same), in reference to the consistent flavor. Sharing the
house and workshop with his father, Brodie also created the first cigarette
brand to find widespread favor, Dukes of Durham. But his alcoholism
produced a rift in the family, widened by his four marriages—especially
the final one, to twenty-nine-year-old Wylanta Rochelle. Brodie was more

than thirty years her senior. None of the Dukes came to his funeral when he died in 1919.[14]

By the early 1880s, the Dukes' Pin Head, Cross Cut, and Dukes of Durham cigarettes were selling well, propelled by an advertising campaign that first featured a French actress, performing in Atlanta, who was persuaded to pose for a lithograph holding a package of Duke cigarettes in her hand over a caption that read "Atlanta's favorite." In spite of his earlier objections to such images of scantily clad women, Wash was said to be smitten.

As a result of the success of his advertising campaign, Buck began to focus on New York, where he introduced his extra-mild Cameo brand, which was soon "catching on very nicely."

In Durham, the Duke salesman Edward Featherston Small boasted that the Duke cigarette business was booming, with orders ranging from 200 million to 400 million daily, while Bull Durham was selling only about 250 million. Profits rose from $25 million in 1890 to $350 million in 1910.[15]

The Dukes were also getting "some strong medicine" prepared for their competition, Buck announced. This turned out to be the Cross Cut Polo Club, a roller-skating team in Durham, at a time when roller-skating was becoming a fad. Men in the audience were given a free five-cent pack of Cross Cut cigarettes, and women were offered small lithographs, even after Buck warned that these expensive inducements must be used judiciously.

Slashing prices to undercut competition, W. Duke, Sons & Company took advantage of the 1883 cut in federal taxes on tobacco to announce that they would use the new policy to lower their prices rather than increase their profits.

In 1890, Buck was ready to announce, privately, the consolidation of the business. He was combining five companies into the American Tobacco Company, which soon controlled 95 percent of the national market. After he acquired the majority of the British tobacco companies, he changed the name to the British-American Tobacco Company.[16] The creation of the British-American Tobacco Company was a triumph of consolidation that came at great public cost to tobacco farmers in the region.

The auctions were frequented by speculators who saw a way to profit enormously as middlemen between the growers and the buyers. They pounced upon the farmers as soon as they arrived, outsmarting them by purchasing their tobacco and selling it for more money to the highest bidder—which would be James B. Duke.

By 1890, the growers were fighting back, joining the Farmers' Alliance, created in 1887, to force lower selling charges at the auction houses and to organize against "the schemes and plans used by large manufacturers to monopolize the trade." The growers planned to start their own auction houses and to begin manufacturing cigarettes themselves. In 1888, some months before Buck incorporated his American Tobacco Company, the alliance scored a few successes. But when the American Tobacco Company was incorporated, planning to fight the speculators in leaf tobacco who had caused the growers so many problems, they were confronted with a dilemma. Should they fight this new trust, with its threat of becoming a monopoly, or join it to fight speculation?

In Kentucky, the growers' efforts against the big tobacco firms took the form of "Night Riders," growers who rode around the countryside issuing threats to prevent farmers from selling their tobacco to ATC. However, the alliance failed to enforce any action that could have injured ATC, such as withholding their crops; indeed, tobacco production in the region increased.[17]

The growers were stuck. If they withheld their tobacco, they lost their income; if they sold it at ruinously low prices, they could not cover the cost of planting next year's crop. Though their problems predated the formation of Buck's company, its growth and development exacerbated matters.[18]

The politics of white supremacy also figured here. From 1897 to 1901, agitation against "Negroes" voting and holding state offices began to threaten the Republican Party, which was dependent on the black vote. The Dukes, as Republicans, were seen as allies of African Americans: Wash's philanthropic efforts on behalf of the first African American hospital in North Carolina were seen as particularly incendiary.

After state legislatures following Reconstruction succeeded in wresting rights away from blacks, agitation against ATC began to decrease. By 1890, North Carolina African Americans were fully disenfranchised, and the efforts of the Night Riders and the Farmers' Alliance had failed.

Buck was now powerful enough to insist that he would buy no tobacco except through the auction houses he controlled. Consolidation proceeded at a furious rate. One of Duke's most important purchases was of the R. J. Reynolds Tobacco Company, which was closely allied with the Raleigh *News & Observer.* The newspaper had run many editorials blasting the American Tobacco Company. After Buck's purchase of R. J. Reynolds, the *Observer* fell silent.[19]

Bitter struggles and long negotiations led to ATC's purchase, within just a few years, of all its major competitors. Owners were forced to realize that they could not win against the monopoly; stockholders expected their firms to accept the highest price offered. Although the criticism never stopped—an editorial in the *Southern Planter* expressed dread that the pampered daughters of the old aristocracy would now find themselves laboring in the Dukes' tobacco factories[20]—it lacked teeth, and even *The News & Observer* began to suggest that the small leaf-growers had participated in their own ruin by growing too much tobacco.

Meanwhile, cigarette sales boomed. While chewing, pipe, and roll-your-own tobacco, as well as cigars, dominated the market from 1880 to 1905, cigarette smoking began to increase in 1905 and achieved almost total dominance by 1950 before undergoing a slow, ragged decline. Sales began to decline only after the first widely disseminated studies linking tobacco and lung disease presaged the Surgeon General's report in 1964.[21] By 1980, the decline was well under way. That year, annual cigarette production was seven hundred billion, with a per-capita purchase of twenty-five hundred cigarettes annually by smokers over eighteen.

Buck did not live to see these changes, although he would have applauded the tobacco companies' wily response to criticism: the introduction of filtered cigarettes, deemed to be less harmful to health. Like the later companies, Buck knew that profits must be put back into the business.

In 1889, his company spent $80,000 of its $4 million in net sales on advertising. Buck targeted young men. His stern resistance to his wife's occasional cigarette, and the fact that his daughter, Doris, never smoked, may indicate that he knew of the health problems associated with smoking. Yet Buck, a lifelong smoker, consumed twenty-five to thirty specially manufactured cigars a day.

In the early days, when he was his own best salesman, he knew how to court jobbers, undersell his more successful competitors, offer "premiums" to tobacconists who refused to carry other brands, and extend his markets to Europe and China. On these sturdy steps, he built his empire. He was an engine of desire.

Intuitively, Buck seemed to know from early on that even with the booming success of his tobacco monopoly, he needed to diversify. In 1892, he began what would become a major investment in textiles with the purchase of Erwin Mills in Durham. In 1905, he plunged into hydro-electric power, creating what would become the vast Duke Power Company, which dominated the creation and distribution of electricity in the Southeast and eventually began the transition to nuclear power.[22]

In the midst of his success, Buck repeatedly confronted human frailty. His mother died young; Brodie suffered from alcoholism; Buck's sister, Mary, died prematurely; and his brother, Ben, suffered from depression.

Buck would write to Ben in 1919 that he sympathized with his brother's troubles. To bolster Ben's self-esteem, Buck had put him in charge of nearly all the family's charitable endeavors.[23]

Washington Duke's philanthropy was entwined with his involvement in the Methodist Church, which inspired his sons with a profound sense of duty, both to their families and to the community. Wash was profoundly influenced by the Methodist doctrine of the stewardship of wealth. John Wesley had said in 1739 that the world was his to lead. His church advocated helping ordinary people, especially the poor. Doris certainly inherited the family tradition of philanthropy, but without its Christian trappings.

Washington Duke devoted a significant portion of his new fortune to philanthropy, especially after selling his interest in W. Duke, Sons & Company in 1880 for $23,000 to Richard Harvey Wright, who became the firm's principal salesman. By 1882, the Old Gentleman, as Wash was known, was moving decisively into philanthropy, long before federal tax exemptions for charitable contributions became both spur and reward for givers.

In 1901, Wash helped found Lincoln Hospital, the first hospital for African Americans in Durham. Both Buck and Ben also contributed.

After a fire destroyed the hospital in 1922, Buck gave money sufficient to rebuild it.[24]

For all three Duke men, who were deeply committed to North Carolina, the state's lack of institutions of advanced education was a major concern. In 1892, Wash persuaded little Trinity College to move to Durham, out-bidding Raleigh as a site with a gift of $85,000. In 1896, he donated another $100,000 with the stipulation that the college would open its doors to women, "placing them on an equal footing with men." Four female day students were already enrolled, but it was the construction of the Mary Duke Building, a dormitory for women, that made full-time residency possible. At first, when too few women had enrolled to fill the rooms, the president of the college took the radical step of making the dorm coed. One Durham woman said that if her girl was living there she would take her out at once.

Washington Duke was part of a national trend in the late nineteenth century of advancing women's education. He followed the first female students closely. One young woman remembered that Mr. Duke was amused by their accomplishments.

Dismayed by the high cost of supporting the university, Wash at one point expressed regret that he had ever donated a dollar. But in 1898 and 1900, he made two more gifts of $100,000 each, so it is hard to know how seriously to take his stated ambivalence.[25]

Though well off by the 1880s, Wash could not rival the fortunes of someone like George W. Vanderbilt, who erected his enormous estate, Biltmore, in western North Carolina between 1889 and 1895, at the cost of several million dollars. In any event, Wash was never interested in conspicuous consumption; that would begin with Buck after his move to New York City in 1894.

Nor was Ben Duke interested in the excesses of the Gilded Age. When he built his frame house in Durham in the late 1880s, Ben paid the builder $8,000. The house had all the modern conveniences—a furnace, running water, and electricity—but it was not grand.

Wash and Ben chose for their rare vacations Buffalo Lithia Springs or other old Virginia resorts, rather than East Coast retreats such as Newport. Carteret Lodge, the fishing camp in eastern North Carolina they co-owned with business associates, was a modest affair. When Ben bought a farm outside of Durham, he planned at the same time to build a house for his pastor, decreeing that his house and the new parsonage should cost no more than $20,000 each.[26]

According to a close friend, Ben "gave generously . . . and did a great deal more . . . charitable work than Mr. J. B. did." Ben sometimes gave away so much money his family worried that he would be ruined.[27]

 When Doris returned to New York from Paris in 1947, she went to see her mother in the mansion on Fifth Avenue. Their relationship was cordial, although Doris was living in a world very different from the one Nanaline had known as a girl in Macon, Georgia.

Baptized Nannie Lane Holt when she was born in 1872, Nanaline came from a distinguished Georgia family that, like many others, fell on hard times after the Civil War. Her father, Judge T. G. Holt, had been a captain in the Confederate cavalry; the white-columned Holt mansion was said to be the finest in downtown Macon. But in 1885, when Nannie was about thirteen, the mansion was sold and the family moved into a boardinghouse.

A series of disasters followed. When Nannie was fifteen, her father drowned at sea and her older brother died, leaving the widowed Florine Russell Holt with two daughters to raise—her namesake, Florine, and Nannie. Mrs. Holt was forced to sew party dresses for well-off neighbors to earn a living.

Given the late-Edwardian propensity for saving face, Nannie probably never had anyone to comfort her or even to tolerate open expressions of grief. Stiff-lipped Calvinism and ironclad manners would have created a world of silence around the growing girl, which may explain her strangely absent gaze in later portraits, where, beautifully dressed and decked in pearls, she seems perched like a bird about to take flight.

Nannie had a pretty face to recommend her as well as an unusually complete education for a young woman of the period, especially under the circumstances—first at the Branham School in Macon, and then at nearby Wesleyan Female College.

Founded in 1836 as Georgia Female College, Wesleyan was one of a small group of colleges—which included Mount Holyoke, Wellesley, and Vassar—that granted women college degrees based on four years of courses in philosophy, history, ancient and modern languages, math, and natural science. The courses were designed to be equal intellectually to those offered at men's colleges. These colleges reflected the period's progressive ideals: they took stands against slavery, overindulgence in alcohol, and the problems of substandard prisons.

The college graduated the first woman in Georgia to secure a medical degree and the first women from that state to argue a case before the Supreme Court. Its Alpha Delta Pi sorority was called the "mother of the sorority system" in the school's literature. This blending of higher education and social graces, resting on the creation of strong bonds between women, would have appealed to Nannie and her mother. Nannie's graduation from Wesleyan in the class of 1886 would have been a source of pride and hope for them both.

Curiously, Nannie's education in the 1880s was more complete than Doris's would be three decades later, perhaps because Nannie's expectations for her daughter seemed to be largely social: debut, marriage, big houses, and travel, none of which demanded advanced education. In addition, the progressivism that had swept the country in the early and mid-nineteenth century had ebbed, because of the disappearance of the first wave of suffragists—Elizabeth Cady Stanton had died in 1902—and a general mood of conservatism in the country.

Nannie's education in the liberal arts did not equip her to take a job, which would have been unimaginable in any event; the only professions open to women at the time were as governesses, teachers, or nurses. But her mother was in no position to continue to support her grown daughter, which may have contributed to Nannie's decision to marry, in 1890, a wealthy Atlanta cotton broker, William Henry Inman.

With William, Nannie gave birth to two children, but by 1900, only one of them, five-year-old Walker Patterson Inman, had survived. The death of the older child was never discussed. The boy, whose name was not recorded, died before he was two.

Nannie's husband, William Henry Inman, died quite young, in 1902, at age thirty-eight, apparently of complications from diabetes. Nannie was left widowed, like her mother, with young Walker to raise on her own. Determined to escape Macon, Nannie began to call herself the more sophisticated "Nanaline," and with her mother traveled to New York in 1907, to shop and to meet eligible men.

At a dinner party in Newport soon after their arrival in New York, Nanaline and her mother were introduced to the recently divorced North Carolina tobacco magnate James Buchanan Duke. Nanaline and Buck were married on July 23, 1907, after a courtship of only a few months.[1] The union of a rich parvenu and a member of the impoverished Southern gentility was too familiar to arouse comment. Other American girls would marry minor European royalty in a similar exchange of dollars for pedigree. In fact, these young women would be called "Dollar Princesses."

Upon the marriage of Buck and Nanaline, newspaper society columnists speculated that her genteel heritage would provide Buck with an entrée to society while his money would keep his wife steeped in luxury. Like all oversimplifications, this explanation for the marriage of two complex individuals contains at least a grain of truth.

In 1893, his tobacco business booming, Buck had bought a 2,500-acre estate in Somerville, New Jersey, and christened it Duke Farms. It was designed to imitate the grand estates he had seen on his trips to Europe. Buck always felt at ease amid the rolling fields and tranquil woods of his property.

In the spring of 1909, as a present for his wife, Buck bought the Cook

House and its entire block at Seventy-eighth Street and Fifth Avenue in Manhattan, on the border of Frederick Law Olmsted's Central Park. Two years later, he had the house rebuilt as an enormous limestone mansion, establishing his presence in the city. This stretch of Fifth Avenue would come to be known as Millionaires' Row.

The Cook House, built in 1880 for $500,000 by the railroad and banking magnate Henry C. Cook, created by Cook's fiat a restriction that exists to this day: height mandates ensure that only private houses may be built on what became known as Cook's Block, between Seventy-eighth and Seventy-ninth Streets on Fifth Avenue. As a result, it is one of the few blocks on Fifth Avenue that preserves its pre–World War I appearance and character.

Cook's faux-French château was torn down and replaced for Buck Duke by the prominent Philadelphia architect Horace Trumbauer. The house was modeled on the Hôtel Labottière, built in Bordeaux in 1773 and ascribed to Étienne Laclotte. Trumbauer's design for Buck is chaste in its classic simplicity, well suited to the size of its lot. Philip Johnson called it the most successful of all the Greek Revival houses in New York City.

The massive white two-story façade is faced with marble-like limestone panels. It seems at first glance both to seek and to repel attention. Pilasters guard the six long, regularly spaced windows on the ground floor. The stone balustrade along the sidewalk prevents the curious from approaching the house too closely.[2]

Buck's choice of location was prescient. Gilded Age society had been defined by the four hundred people who could fit comfortably in Alice Vanderbilt's ballroom in her huge mansion at 1 West Fifty-seventh Street. In 1925, the then eighty-eight-year-old Alice built a new, smaller house on the corner of Fifth Avenue and Sixty-seventh Street, signaling the removal of society farther uptown. Buck Duke's house, eleven blocks higher up on Fifth Avenue, was an important part of the northward migration. By then, the wrecking ball would have taken down most of the enormous houses built on lower Fifth. As Clarice Stasz writes about the Vanderbilts, "The wrecking ball, the disbursement of treasures to museums, the contracts of sale—all mirrored a disintegration occurring on a more private level."³ Indeed, that disintegration opened a social void for Buck and Nanaline to fill.

On November 22, 1912, Doris was born in the house on Seventy-eighth Street. Her father immediately cabled his friend Lady Paget at 55 Belgravia Square in London, "Fine girl just arrived. Mother and child progressing satisfactorily."⁴ This was the same Lady Paget who in 1893 had engineered Consuelo Vanderbilt's marriage to the Duke of Marlborough. That Buck Duke knew Lady Paget well enough to communicate news of Doris's birth—perhaps through an earlier introduction from the remarkable Alva Smith Vanderbilt Belmont, a childhood friend of Minnie Stevens, later Lady Paget—shows that his entrée and Nanaline's in London and New York society may already have been accomplished.

The life that victory created would absorb Nanaline's time and energy throughout Doris's childhood. No one would have expected her to lay her social activities aside because she had a child, especially a daughter.

According to the received wisdom of 1912, and of her class, Nanaline seldom held Doris when she was a baby. One of the pediatric authorities of the time, Dr. John B. Watson, believed that cuddling was detrimental to infant development. Nanaline may also have doubted her maternal competence after the death of her first child, prompting her to turn her baby daughter over to a series of uniformed nurses. Doris's care would have been, at best, efficient.

However, habits of child rearing in Macon also exerted some influence. Old New York noticed that newcomers from the South—like Nanaline, and Alva Smith's family—tended to allow their offspring more physical freedom, especially in places like Newport, where the Smiths went during the summer. There, Alva as a child, long before her marriage to William Kissam Vanderbilt, rode horseback all day, and, by her own account, beat up little boys. Doris would enjoy some of the same experiences.

During her first year, Doris was blessed with the robustness that would be one of her strengths almost to the end of her life. Her uncle Ben, responding to a letter from a Texas cousin, wrote from New York on December 3, 1913, that Doris "is now a few days over one year of age, and

she is well, good-looking, and a great comfort to her mother and father."
Ben was replying in Buck's stead, as he often did, to a letter asking for
money. He enclosed a $1,000 check to the Texas cousin with a note, "He
[Buck] says to tell you not to save this money, but to spend it for your
comfort and pleasure."

Two years later, Doris's health caused both parents some concern, but
a telegram of July 13, 1915, from her mother in Newport to her father
at his office at 200 Fifth Avenue in New York is reassuring. "Babys [sic]
temperature normal continues to improve daily and strong appetite."

Buck's response to his wife, who was then staying at Inchiquin House
in Newport before their mansion Rough Point was ready to be occupied,
expressed his relief that "Doris is improving so nicely." It is signed, "Best
love."[5]

Three weeks later, Buck cabled his baby daughter in Newport: "Have
been to Somerville" (Duke Farms). "Prince Shep Rose all want to see
you."[6] A photo taken a few years later shows Prince pulling Doris in her
pony cart, a top-hatted groom holding the reins. Most of her childhood
was spent in New York City, in the Seventy-eighth Street mansion, with
weekend visits to Somerville and six-week summer vacations in Newport.

What would her childhood have been? As a baby, she received strictly
monitored feeding at fixed intervals, bottle rather than breast—breast-
feeding was considered a mark of poverty and ignorance, as well as injuri-
ous to a woman's figure. Typically, forced toilet training began as early as
two months, and an emphasis on neatness, cleanliness, and manners left
little room for exploring or playing. Doris's nurse would have taken Doris
for daily visits to Central Park, wearing the elaborate dresses and high-
buttoned shoes of the time, which would not have allowed Doris much
freedom of movement. Companionship with other children would have
been limited to those of her class, especially since she and her mother
shuttled from New York to New Jersey to Rhode Island and back. Doris
sometimes played with her older half brother, Walker, who would become
an adult friend.

The august presence and massive scale of the Seventy-eighth Street
house certainly influenced the atmosphere of Doris's childhood. It's easy
to imagine her skipping down the broad front steps with their bas-relief
of acanthus leaves—that is, if her nurse allowed her such freedom. There

are nine of these steps, which Doris would have learned to negotiate, first with the one-step-at-a-time of toddlerhood, her hand firmly grasped, and later more lightly and freely, especially after she began to learn to tap-dance, but always within the framework of the great front doors with their ironwork tracery, surmounted by a small grim marble head—Athena?—and a row of ironwork goddesses. These immense, well-attended doors would have been too heavy for even a very sturdy child like Doris to open. A footman would have opened and closed them, controlling Doris's access to the outside world.

The second floor, where Doris had her bedroom, was flooded with light. On the Fifth Avenue side, the greenery of Central Park partly ob-scured lawns running down to the boat basin, where small sailboats were launched. Stone garlands over the windows and low iron railings empha-sized privacy, but the great mass of trees across Fifth Avenue beckoned toward a civilized degree of freedom in a grand public space.

Small bedrooms housed the maids and the cook on the third floor. The footmen and butler lived in the basement. A pretty little mirrored elevator ran from the basement to the third floor. On the third floor, each servant had a private bedroom with a closet. Two large bathrooms were shared.

Had Doris explored the servants' bedrooms, which would have been strictly forbidden, she would have sensed the atmosphere of servitude: immigrant girls like the 140 who died during the Triangle Shirtwaist fire of 1911. As children, many of these girls would have lived in the window-less tenements of Jacob Riis's Lower East Side. Many such immigrants were from Ireland.

However, a remark made by their butler Edward Hansen indicates that Nanaline, like many women she knew, preferred not to hire Irish servants. Interviewing Edward for the job, she asked him only where he was from. When he replied that he was born in Norway, she said, "All right," and promptly offered him the job. The names of some of the other servants further suggest Nanaline's preference for Northern Europeans: Mrs. Hulda Goudie, cook; Germaine Moulanne, companion to Mrs. Duke; Olga Olofsson, maid; Adeline Norholm, laundress; Greta Johnson, maid. Edward was first apprenticed to the senior butler, who said that life at the Dukes' house on Seventy-eighth Street was much like life in other grand houses in the neighborhood.[7]

In the center of the ground floor, a sweeping staircase led to the upper stories. On the ground floor were the dining room and the paneled library—the top shelves filled with what Edward called "false books."[8] A gilded music room and drawing room opened off the main hall. Buck and Nanaline hired the distinguished French firm of Alavoine and Carlhian to decorate the house, probably at the suggestion of Joseph Duveen, the well-known British art dealer who sold Titians, Botticellis, and Vermeers to newly minted American millionaires such as J. P. Morgan, John D. Rockefeller, and Andrew Mellon.[9]

Many original design details remain even now, long after Doris and her mother gave the house to the New York Institute of Fine Arts, including the pale blue-gray paint, a favorite family color that also appeared at Duke Farms. The layout of the bedrooms on the second floor still tells much about the daily life Doris knew as a child and an adolescent. Her parents shared a bedroom—rather unusual for this period—on the northeast corner of the house, furnished with twin beds. Next door was the governess Jenny Renaud's bedroom, which had a raised ceiling to accommodate Doris's books, according to Edward. Doris's love of reading contrasted with her father's attitude toward books. According to Norman Atwater Cocke, Buck's longtime friend and employee and one of the original trustees of the Duke Endowment, Buck read only one book in his lifetime, *The Swiss Family Robinson*, with its tale of heroic endurance and family solidarity.

As Cocke remembered, Buck would scan the headlines of the daily paper before tossing it aside. Even the market results didn't seem to interest him. But in Gilded Age New York, Buck's lack of education surprised no one. Many of the newly minted millionaires had no formal education. J. P. Morgan was the exception, educated in Connecticut, Massachusetts, and Switzerland, but Andrew Carnegie had only a few years of schooling, Henry Frick did not graduate from college, John D. Rockefeller graduated from high school but went no further, and Cornelius Vanderbilt dropped out of school at age eleven. Certainly, Cocke remembered, lack of education never seemed to bother his boss. Even music was of little interest to Buck, except when Doris was playing the harp.[10]

According to Edward, the household ran smoothly, with little strife. The butler remembered only once hearing Buck in a temper. He was so angry that the elevator was not available all the time that he forbade the staff to use it, but after a year he relented, feeling that they had learned their lesson. Nanaline was often irritated when the elevator was occupied by her maids, but, being younger and slimmer than Buck, she would sometimes climb the stairs. Doris as a girl probably flew up and down the stairs rather than wait for the overcrowded lift.

Doris's bedroom adjoined her sitting room. Next came her bathroom, with a door to her mother's double-height dressing room. Nanaline's sitting room was on the west side of the house, next to Buck's official bedroom, where he seldom slept because of his sensitivity to the traffic noise on Fifth Avenue.

A dumbwaiter connected the basement kitchen to the butler's pantry next to the dining room on the first floor, then continued on to the second floor for those times after Buck's death when Nanaline was served on a tray in bed.

Doris did not eat with her parents, which was typical of the times. Instead, she took her meals with Jenny in her sitting room. Edward remembered that Doris and Jenny were always speaking French. Since neither parent knew French, it was their private language.

Nanaline ran her household with a certain hauteur, insisting that the servants wait to be addressed before speaking to her. Other details of life in the big house, as remembered by Edward, contributed to a sense of rectitude, order, and security that both nourished and constrained Doris as she grew up.

The staff would have ministered to virtually all of Doris's needs. Her clothes would have been laid out in the morning by Jenny, and as Doris grew up, her evening dresses would be laid out as well, and then her nightgown and robe. She did not yet have the extensive wardrobe that filled Nanaline's dressing room. It contained roughly two dozen closets, some specially designed for her shoes (sixty pairs, satin, dyed to match her evening gowns, showing off her tiny feet), a vault for her jewelry, and an upper tier of closets for her fur coats.

Later, Doris would come to love clothes and jewelry; both she and her mother developed an eye for fashion and the taste for luxury that was expected for their class. But for Doris as a child, a certain simplicity of attire prevailed. The only remaining elements of her childhood wardrobe are two small barrettes, gold with seed pearls, to hold back her long, light brown hair.

In early childhood, Doris could always depend on her father's affection. In 1923, when Doris was eleven, Buck wrote to his daughter, who was in Paris with her mother: "You certainly are the dearest daughter that any daddy ever had. Your affection and devotion to me are the brightest spot in my life."[11] In a studio portrait taken some years earlier, Doris sits with supreme confidence on her father's knee.

Buck continued, to Doris, "Sending Crocker"—the chauffeur—"and your Packard on the Aquitania to London for you and your mother." He expected to meet them later in Paris and hoped they would have finished their shopping so that he and Doris could explore the city together. "I want to do everything I can to give you the best time you ever had in your life . . . I love you more than I can tell and I want you to develop into the grandest lady in the world and have no doubt that you will do so."[12]

But there were undercurrents in Doris's childhood. When she was sixteen, a fire broke out in the corner of her bedroom. The only record of the fire, the cause of which has never been ascertained, is a bill submitted to Nanaline by Mr. Verpilleux of the decorating firm Carlhian on September 29, 1929. Mr. Verpilleux had inspected Doris's room; the carpet was burned "right in the center" and the flames had scorched the chandelier. The ceiling was blackened and would have to be repainted, and the carpet replaced. The bill came to $3,960, the majority of it for the Axminster carpet.

Few details are known about Doris's childhood, but it is likely that she was raised in accordance with the principles current at the time. Mothers at the beginning of the twentieth century and for decades afterward subscribed to the advice offered in Dr. Luther Emmett Holt's popular *The Care and Feeding of Children*, first published in 1894, and republished regularly until 1943.[13] Holt's book gave detailed instruction about feeding and airing, and the causes and treatment of crying, which Holt thought was useful as exercise but, if indulged, would become a bad habit.

Holt also advised mothers not to play with their children. The aim was to produce what Daniel Beekman later called a mechanical baby, divorced from human contact.[14]

The Mothercraft Manual, another popular handbook of the period, first published in 1916 and still in print today, warned that a child should never touch its genitals.[15] Doris's lifelong search for freedom, physical and social, may well have been rooted in the social constraints of her childhood. Throughout her life, she would always seek to escape confinement.

Yet the house on Seventy-eighth Street was full of light and air. Like Doris's bedroom and sitting room, all the rooms on the second floor were high-ceilinged and bright. They were decorated with gilt-framed mirrors, chandeliers, brocade curtains, and silk shades, which maids lowered at night. Doris's room would have looked as formal as a guest room, with most of her toys hidden from sight.

In 1920, Doris and her mother could not have failed to notice the great parades of the suffrage movement. A referendum on women voting, which had failed in New York State in 1915, led to vigorous support for the 1920 constitutional amendment, bringing throngs of women dressed in white, along with swarms of hecklers. The Nineteenth Amendment was finally passed in 1920, when Doris turned eight—old enough to be aware of the commotion. Not only did thousands march, but nearly a million people watched from the sidewalks. The movement was so widespread, and generated so much publicity, that it would have been almost impossible to ignore. Suffrage souvenirs were even sold at Macy's in Herald Square.

Nanaline may have been the one to decide that her daughter needed at least a few years of formal education. When Doris was eight, her mother enrolled her in the distinguished Brearley School for Girls, at Park Avenue and Sixty-first Street. Two years later, in 1922, while Doris was still at Brearley, Nanaline hired Mademoiselle Jenny Renaud as governess and companion. Jenny remained with Doris until 1935. The long-standing companionship she provided, the affection, understanding, and sheer fun, proved essential to Doris's development. With Jenny, Doris would venture out into the world.[16]

Jenny probably took Doris to the Metropolitan Museum of Art on Fifth Avenue, just north of the Duke house. This would have provided the girl with an important introduction to visual art. That certainly could not have happened at home. Unlike the great collectors of the period—J. Pierpont

Morgan, Charles Lang Freer, the Henry O. Havemeyers, and Albert C. Barnes—Buck Duke showed little interest in decorating his houses with art that might have expressed his, or Nanaline's, personal taste. Instead, the Seventy-eighth Street house was hung with conventional if highly priced portraits of eighteenth-century gentlemen and ladies, often purchased through M. Knoedler, such as Thomas Miller Hiddell by Gainsborough, and four portraits of ladies by John Hoppner.

If Doris had studied the portrait of Mr. Hiddell sitting at a table next to a window with a view, she probably would have felt little connection with the subject or his pose. The pensive pastel ladies in the Hoppner portraits, who always seem to be waiting for something to happen, could not have excited her, either. But when Jenny began taking her to museums, new worlds opened up to Doris.

In 1891, Edward C. Moore had given the Metropolitan Museum an astonishing bequest of four hundred objects of Islamic art. Moore's collection, which he amassed to help him in his work as artistic director of the silver department at Tiffany and Company, included ceramics, glass, metalware, embroidery, and wood. The artifacts reflected the growing American fascination with Orientalism, spurred by increasing travel to Syria, Iran, India, and Egypt, as well as Jordan and Lebanon. One of Doris's schoolgirl drawings, made in colored pencil, predicts to an astonishing degree her later fascination with Islamic tiles.[17]

Doris drew six meticulously detailed designs: a star in a square, a stylized flower in a circle, a five-pointed figure, a delicate arabesque in a circle, and two more squares with smaller squares inside, all in brilliant colors. These designs are unlike anything she would have seen at home or in books of reproductions of European art. Abstract, brilliant, floating in space, her designs can easily be interpreted as tiles. Doris's imagination would have been stirred by what she saw at the Metropolitan Museum and in the houses of family friends with great collections like the Havemeyers.

Jenny's influence on Doris's education ended in 1935, when she retired. Later, after Jenny returned to France, she was partly supported by a trust fund Doris established with 885 shares of common stock in her father's Duke Power Company. Unfortunately, Doris's intention to provide for Jenny was not fulfilled. In a pitiful 1955 letter to her trustee in New York, Jenny lamented, "I am myself most disappointed to have so many unexpected charges." That year, she had received only $1,400 of the trust's annual income of $2,000 and the French government had heavily taxed even "money not received." Apologizing for writing, Jenny explained, "I am in bed ill since months." She died soon after.[18]

 Oriental tiles were far from the world of Doris's grand-
father Washington Duke, who seldom left North Caro-
lina, except for a trip to Europe to try to restore the
health of his daughter, Mary. But other interests of her
grandfather's may have influenced Doris. Involved, to a degree, with the
black community in Durham, Wash supported a cotton mill briefly run
by African Americans, as well as a black hospital. According to Dr. Wilburt C. Davison, head of Duke Medical School, the hospital, supported
especially by Buck's brother Ben, was established in gratitude to the
slaves who cared for their white owners during the Civil War.

But there was a disturbing side to this story. According to Davison,
Ben's barber, a man named Merrick, told Ben while shaving him about
the Royal Knights of King David, a member-owned burial society that
covered the cost of burial for poor African Americans. Merrick complained that he and his fellow white trustees could provide themselves
with a lot of money—the society had many members—if "we could just
get these [African American] stockholders out."

Ben Duke told Merrick that would be easy. Just hold a meeting and

tell them you were going to have to levy an assessment, then offer to buy
their stock and spare them the tax. This familiar Jim Crow ploy worked
like a charm. Merrick announced the following week, "Mr. Duke, we got
it all." The white trustees made off with the money the African American
stockholders had invested to cover their funeral expenses.[1]

Such maneuverings did not tarnish the family's reputation—the ethos of
the Gilded Age came close to endorsing such behavior—nor did the scan-
dals that occurred at the end of Washington's life. Having called Buck
and Ben to his bedside in 1904, Wash apparently extracted a deathbed
promise from his forty-seven-year-old son, Buck, that he would marry his
companion, Mrs. Lillian McCredy, a divorced woman of charm and sub-
stance. Accordingly, Buck married her in New Jersey at her aunt's house,
as quietly as possible, on November 29, 1904.

Wash never learned of the marital misadventure of Brodie, his eldest
son. After two weeks of merrymaking in a New York hotel, Brodie married his third wife, Alice Webb, on December 19, 1904. For unknown
reasons, Ben rushed to have Brodie committed to what would have been
called a lunatic asylum in that era, a strategy sometimes used to control
unruly family members.

According to Mrs. John Williams, Brodie was considered by the family
to be a failure, but he was also intelligent and a charmer. Mrs. Williams,
the remarried widow of Buck Duke's nephew Buchanan Lyon, remembered: "Uncle Buck didn't want to leave him and his crowd in on this
endowment. I told him it wasn't right. 'He is your brother, your father's
son, and you can't do that.'"[2]

Washington Duke died on May 8, 1905, at the age of eighty-four. A
newspaper account of Wash's funeral described Brodie sitting crestfallen
on the steps of the church and referred to him as the son Washington
loved.[3] Wash left parts of his fortune—never as large as his sons'—to
the Methodist Church (for the relief of "worn-out preachers") as well as
$250,000 to Trinity College, which Buck would later transform into Duke
University.[4]

Meanwhile, Buck, traveling in Europe with Lillian, may not have
known that another contender for her affections, one Frank T. Huntoon,

described in a newspaper account as an elderly bon vivant, was placing personal advertisements in the newspapers, recalling memories too sweet to be forgotten. He called Buck the "Octopus."[5]

The very year Buck and Lillian married, while Buck was back in Europe on cigarette business, Lillian and Frank were seen at the racetrack and at various New York restaurants. On his return, Buck had Lillian tailed not only by private detectives but also by two executives of the British-American Tobacco Company.

In 1906, with a great deal of press attending the process, Buck obtained his divorce. Lillian had testified that he beat her and called her "vile names." Since Buck had already given her $250,000, there was said to be no further financial settlement, and with the divorce speedily granted on the grounds of separation, Lillian McCredy might have disappeared into obscurity along with her paramour. However, although married to Buck less than two years, Lillian continued to call herself Mrs. Duke for the rest of her life.[6]

Marital problems did not hinder Buck's rise. By 1894, when he came to New York, he had consolidated virtually all of his smaller competitors into the American Tobacco Company, withholding twenty cents of every sale dollar for advertising and promotion. His Dukes of Durham billboards were plastered everywhere, and his salesmen gave out free folding chairs and other inducements to tobacconists who would grant his brand favored treatment. As a result, American Tobacco was netting a colossal 33 percent yearly in profits on its tangible assets.

In 1902, after consolidating with British Tobacco, Buck's company attracted the zeal of President Theodore Roosevelt's trust-busting efforts, as did Standard Oil and the railways. Taken to court for obstructing trade in 1911, Buck explained matter-of-factly that a lot of smokers just preferred his brands.

The government was not persuaded and ordered Duke to devise a plan for breaking up his monopoly. His strategy was to spread his business among three large subsidiaries, the largest of which retained the American Tobacco Company name. Smaller percentages of the business were allotted to Liggett & Myers and Lorillard; United Cigar Stores,

British-American Tobacco, and R. J. Reynolds spun off to continue business on their own.[7] This seems rather like giving the fox access to the
henhouse. Buck Duke could hardly have been expected to be objective in
breaking up his own monopoly. But then President Roosevelt, although
credited with being trust-buster-in-chief, "declined to break up Standard Oil and permitted J. P. Morgan to establish monopoly control of
the steel industry."[8]

Whether disillusioned with the tobacco business or simply realizing
that the glory days of building a fortune were over, Buck then turned
his efforts to creating what would become the Duke Power Company;
initially, it had provided hydroelectric power for the mills in North and
South Carolina, beginning with Durham's cotton mills, but then it expanded through the Carolinas, Indiana, and Kentucky. In the last two
decades of his life, Buck became fascinated by the building of his power
plants and visited Charlotte frequently to supervise construction.

Nanaline's girlhood friend Mrs. Edward Carrington Marshall remembered Nanaline's telling her that when Buck had completed his first steam
plant, he said it would help prevent droughts in North Carolina. Perhaps
in his later years, Buck Duke found some reassurance in the thought that
his steam plants would reduce hardship in the Carolinas. His investment
might be seen as a counterbalance to his cigarette industry, especially as
the harmful effects of smoking became better known.[9]

How much did Buck Duke know about the damaging effects of cigarettes, and when did he know it? Just as Nanaline in New York in the
early 1900s could not have avoided knowing about the fight for suffrage,
Buck could not have missed reading the reports that began to be published on the threat of smoking.

The revelation began with a May 1906 article in *Harper's Weekly*, stating that "the toxic qualities of tobacco [are] freed by combustion."[10] This
seemed to blame health effects on the burning rather than on the inert
toxicity of tobacco. Soon after, boys were warned in magazine and newspaper articles that the increased mildness of Duke's Bright Leaf tobacco
was offset by early-onset smoking and the practice of inhaling. Then a
professor at the New York School of Clinical Medicine argued that the

cumulative effect of smoking cigarettes was more damaging than that of smoking a pipe or a cigar. As early as 1912, *Harper's Weekly* warned readers that smoking was a sure way to an early death.[11]

Buck might have argued that no one really knew which element in tobacco caused addiction, although if he was honest, he would have admitted that the additives, such as rum, licorice, and molasses, certainly increased the appeal. As he turned his attention to the more or less benevolent issues of hydroelectricity, Buck Duke left most of the criticism of tobacco use behind.

At sixty-eight, overweight, physically inactive, and himself a regular smoker of cigars, Buck had rapidly failing health. He must have had a sense of foreboding. In 1924, with his financial advisers—and nearly-twelve-year-old Doris often at his side—Buck drew up the terms of his will and of the Duke University Endowment.

Edward Hansen, the longtime butler at Seventy-eighth Street, was one of the last people to see Buck Duke alive. In an interview, he stated that a nurse had rung for help, and when Hansen went into the bedroom, his employer was in bed, his breathing labored, and he was hooked up to an oxygen tank. "I am in bad shape, Edward," he said. The butler tried to reassure him, but both men knew the end was near. Buck was dying of pneumonia, untreatable before the advent of penicillin in 1928.

That Saturday night, Hansen said, was the only night he didn't see Nanaline sitting beside her husband's bed in her fur coat with the windows thrown open, as was the custom in sickrooms of the period. Buck died at 6:00 p.m. on October 10, 1925.

The next morning, as Hansen related, the body was taken downstairs and laid out in an open casket. Hansen remembered that some of Nanaline's friends said they preferred to remember Buck as he was and went directly into the ballroom for the service.[12]

The Reverend Raymond L. Forman, pastor of the Dukes' church, St. Paul's Methodist Episcopal at West End Avenue and Eighty-sixth Street, read excerpts from John Greenleaf Whittier's poem "Immortal Love," the Twenty-third Psalm, and the fourteenth chapter of Saint Luke. For Buck, who rose from poverty to great wealth but never earned widespread respect among his peers, these verses from Saint Luke had particular relevance: At a wedding, Jesus had advised his disciples, "Sit not down in the highest place, lest perhaps one who is more honorable than thou be invited . . . But . . . go sit down in the lowest place . . . that when he that invited thee cometh, he may say to thee, Go up higher. Then shall thou have glory."

Twelve honorary pallbearers attended the burial, in North Carolina. In Buck's will, they had been named trustees of the Duke University Endowment.

Doris may have been at her father's burial, in Maplewood Cemetery, Durham, or she may have been left at home, as was often the habit at that period, when such events were considered too disturbing for children.

Along with sixty relatives and friends, the pallbearers rode a special train to Durham, where Buck Duke's body lay in state in the main hall of Duke University. During the funeral, all work on the campus stopped. Ben, the older brother Buck loved, was too sick to attend.[13]

A memorial chapel was added to the plans for the soaring Gothic chapel on the university campus, built in 1930. It was designed, like the rest of the university, by the Philadelphia firm of Horace Trumbauer (the same firm that designed Duke Farms and the Seventy-eighth Street house). The "brains" of the project, however, according to Trumbauer, were supplied by a long-unrecognized African American architect, Julian Abele.

At twenty-seven, Abele, the University of Pennsylvania architecture department's first African American graduate, became Trumbauer's chief designer. Later, Abele designed Harvard's Widener Library and Philadelphia's Free Library and Museum of Art, as well as four hundred other buildings. But when he visited Durham, he was not allowed to stay at local hotels.

In 1929 Buck Duke's body was buried in the crypt under the Duke University Chapel, memorialized in one of the three white Carrara marble sarcophagi there. Enveloped in the gloom of a side chapel, they commemorate Washington Duke and two of his sons, Benjamin and James "Buck" Buchanan.

Dressed in formal twentieth-century suits, Washington, Ben, and Buck are laid on their backs like medieval knights, but lacking shield, sword, and buckler. Covered with marble sheets from which the toes of their laced-up shoes protrude, these male forms strike an ironic note—not knights, not saints, yet presented as secular saints who earned their three tons of marble through the grandeur of their ambition and the size of their fortunes.

Buck's obituaries in East Coast newspapers reflected the discretion typical of the period. The *Washington Post* obituary summed up his life: he had loved business more than anything else. *The New York Times* issued a long, admiring obituary, describing the life and the accomplishments of a man it called a great figure in American industry and an important philanthropist. The obituary cited Buck Duke's last words as ensuring the future of his many investments because they were all in great shape.[14]

His largest gift, $40 million, went to the Duke University Endowment. He also created through his will the Doris Duke Charitable Trust, to hold one-third of his residuary estate of $100 million for his wife and daughter. Doris's trust would dispense income to her at regular intervals: when she turned twenty-one, thirty, and thirty-five. It was almost entirely made up of shares in Duke Power. Nanaline was appointed as Doris's guardian and was to receive income from the trust for the duration of her life.[15]

Buck explained in his will that he was not leaving large amounts of money outright to his wife because of his generosity to her during his lifetime. One hopes Nanaline had the foresight to save some of her allowance. In any event, she had her clothes, furs, and jewelry as well as a life tenancy in the house on Seventy-eighth Street, at Rough Point, and at Duke Farms—the last of which she would seldom visit.

Buck left the servants at his three houses the equivalent of two years' pay. Two million dollars went to various relatives, and handsome gifts were bequeathed to an array of business colleagues. Another provision of his will directed that both Rough Point and Duke Farms be sold at auction, with the proceeds going to the trust's shareholders.

But one year after Buck's death, thirteen-year-old Doris challenged this provision, which her father probably intended to free her of responsibility for the demanding properties. Doris, who loved both places, went to court with her lawyers—a legal nicety, since her mother had graciously complied with her wishes. For the price of one dollar, Rough Point and Duke Farms became the property of a thirteen-year-old girl.[16]

But the past is never entirely and safely the past. Ten days after Buck's death, news stories surfaced about the economic and health problems of his long-divorced first wife, Lillian McCredy. For years, she had survived in her small West Side studio apartment by giving voice lessons, but only one student remained with her. Her attorney, Miss Lucille Pugh, reported that on visiting her she found Lillian morose, destitute, and on the verge of death.[17] Six months earlier, she had gone to court to have her divorce from Buck Duke set aside on the grounds that she refused to recognize the jurisdiction of the New Jersey court. Her application had been denied.[18]

A friend wrote a letter of condolence to Benjamin Duke on October 11, 1925—the day of Buck's death—to acknowledge that the loss of his father would be very difficult for Ben, given how close the two had been. Fuller wrote that Buck had been truly a great man, certainly the finest man North Carolina had ever called its own. Buck might have smiled at the narrowness of the definition.

After the funeral, Nanaline and Doris spent the prescribed year of mourning traveling in Europe. A snapshot shows mother and daughter seated side by side on the base of a statue at St. Mark's Square in Venice, contentedly feeding the pigeons.[19]

 It seems, from early photographs and firsthand accounts, that Buck included Doris from a young age in some of his business conferences, passing on the values of his philanthropy. He had been an exceptionally devoted father at a time when many professional men did not spend much time with their children.

He was certainly a more spontaneous and indulgent parent than Nanaline. Mary Reamy Thomas Few, wife of the president of Trinity College, remembered Buck's telling her husband that Nanaline had taken Doris to FAO Schwarz, New York's premier toy store, which was founded in 1862. There, Doris saw a wonderful French talking doll the size of a two-year-old child. It had an exquisite handmade wardrobe. Doris asked her mother to buy the doll, but Nanaline told her that $300 was simply too much.

Having warned Doris not to mention the doll to her father, Nanaline secretly paid a deposit and had the doll put on layaway, suggesting to Doris that if she saved her allowance of twenty-five cents a week, she might eventually have enough money to buy the doll. Years later, when Nana-line told Doris that she now had enough money to pay for the doll, Doris replied that she was too old for it.[1]

Naturally, Doris was heartbroken when her father died. Mrs. Few tried to comfort her, reminding her that she still had her mother, but Doris replied, "Oh, Mrs. Few, there's nobody to love me now." Mrs. Few explained that of course Doris's mother loved her, but that she was less demonstrative than her father had been, adding that Nanaline sometimes didn't see Doris for several days. This was not unusual for a woman of that period. As an adult, Doris would deal with some of the same issues, and the tension between personal relationships and social responsibilities.

When Doris was eleven or twelve, Mrs. Few remembered, she said that she wanted to be a chemist and that she had a little laboratory in the basement of the Seventy-eighth Street house, but Nanaline complained about the fumes and had the chemicals removed. "So she had nothing left," Mrs. Few concluded. Nanaline also closely supervised Doris's diet, worrying constantly that Doris would get fat.[2]

John Fox, an acquaintance of Nanaline's from the early days in Charlotte, remembered that he had once seen Doris waiting in the car while her mother was busy in a nearby building. Fox was carrying a paper bag and Doris called to him, asking what was in the bag—a bored child waiting for her mother and hoping for some distraction. When Fox told her that his bag was full of candy and offered it, she took some and started to eat it. While she was eating, Nanaline came out of the build-ing and was furious to see that Doris was eating candy, which would never have been allowed at home. Fox remembered that Nanaline "just turned on me and said I should be ashamed of myself," before jump-ing in the car and rushing away. Doris certainly would have received a reprimand.[3]

Mrs. Few believed this story showed that Doris never had a chance to grow up as other girls did. She remembered Doris confiding that she was desperate to go to college, an attempt to remedy her lack of even a high school education, but that her mother thought the idea was "foolish" and wouldn't allow her even to apply. Nanaline told Mrs. Few that Doris, with her inheritance, would be able to do anything she wanted—including traveling all over the world. She couldn't understand why her daughter

kept harping on going to college. Mrs. Few tried to suggest that an education might be a good idea, but Nanaline insisted that it was irrelevant for
a girl who would never need to teach school.[4]

Swallowing her disappointment, Doris then told Mrs. Few that she
wanted to come down to Duke University incognito and see how college
girls lived. Perhaps she even imagined that by changing her name she
could, for a month, seem to be one of them. She planned to get some "college clothes" so she would fit in.

The visit was arranged, and Doris arrived in an old car, after leaving
her good car back in Williamsburg. The housemother had explained to
the girls that this newcomer to the dorm had not had their opportunities
and should be treated with kindness. The girls invited her to their parties, making sure she had a date.

Doris later confided to Mrs. Few that that month had been the happiest time of her life. She even had her toenails painted, which would never
have been allowed at home. This is not surprising, given that, during this
period, things like nail polish—and pierced ears—were seen as being dis-
tinctly beneath her class.

Doris almost revealed her identity when the girls were collecting money
to pay for a party and she chipped in five dollars rather than the expected
fifty cents, but, Mrs. Few remembered, they believed she couldn't afford
it and gave it right back to her. During her month at Duke, no one recognized her, and she left as she had arrived, incognito.[5]

Then everything changed.

As soon as Doris turned twenty-one and came into the first installment
of her inheritance, her mother told Mrs. Few, she became assertive overnight. She didn't waste time claiming her independence, just announced
to her mother at breakfast on her birthday that she was leaving for Florida that afternoon—with Jimmy Cromwell. A patina of respectability was
supplied by visiting his mother in West Palm Beach, but they would still
be unchaperoned overnight, alone together on the train, which would
have horrified Nanaline. Doris forestalled any discussion by telling her
mother that she didn't care in the least that her mother disapproved of
Jimmy, advising her, "Don't say anything about it."

From that time on, Mrs. Few believed, Doris was not only her own mistress, but also, in Nanaline's words, "her own master." Her display of authority made the word "mistress," with its unsavory connotation, seem both inappropriate and inadequate. Doris was, for the first time in her life, displaying mastery. But she had absorbed her mother's attitude toward money; only after her marriage did she begin to spend freely on herself. Now, when a journalist asked her what she intended to do with her inheritance, she replied that she was going to buy an accordion she had longed for and some costume jewelry at Saks Fifth Avenue—modest wishes, in line with the self-restraint she'd learned when her allowance was twenty-five cents a week.

Years later, when Doris served on the board of the Duke Endowment, she replied sharply when another board member stated, "Mr. Duke would have done it another way." Doris said, "I dislike very much when people say that my father would have done so and so, because I know that he would have kept pace with the times, and what he would have done in 1924 is not what he would have done in 1944."

She never embraced the evangelical philosophy of her father's Methodist church, which sought to convert nonbelievers by giving aid to the poor and proselytizing. In the sophisticated world in which Doris traveled, in Manhattan, Paris, and beyond, this homely sentiment would have seemed threadbare, stitched to a simpler past. Instead, in accord with her times and her experience, Doris would come to believe that possibilities for transformation abide in the creation of beauty through art.

Yet her loyalty to her father's wishes overrode all other considerations when she was sure that she was being told the truth. In 1936, E. R. Bucher, a Duke Power employee in Charlotte, heard that now Judge Tom Perkins (Doris's longtime adviser and lawyer) had told "Miss Doris" that her father had promised Charlotte's First Methodist Church $100,000. In line with her respect for her father's wishes—when she knew what they were—Doris had asked only if the judge was sure her father had given his word that the donation would be forthcoming. She might have wondered why he hadn't included it in his will, as a bequest, but the judge's reassurance was all she needed. She asked for her checkbook and wrote out a check for $200,000 on the spot.

Buck Duke, Bucher remembered, had been a man of simple tastes. On the same day in Charlotte when they had discussed the gift to the Methodist church, the two men had had lunch together at a local tearoom, the kind of unpretentious place Buck preferred, because he could count on the menu's offering simple fare. The men ordered salad, soup, and dessert, Bucher remembered. This was far plainer than the food Buck was served at home. He had always preferred buttermilk, cornbread, and turnip greens, staples of his North Carolina childhood, to the more elaborate food he encountered in New York in later life.

At lunch, the two friends discussed Doris, of whom Buck was obviously very fond. Bucher recalled that anytime she wanted to talk to her father, the family chauffeur was instructed to drive her to Buck's office. Often important business matters were being discussed, but even so, Buck would stop and hurry to receive his daughter.[6]

Bennette Eugene Geer, president of Furman University, in Greenville, South Carolina, also remembered Buck's fondness for Doris, but he drew a different conclusion: he thought Doris had been "a great disappointment." But this seems an unlikely conclusion, since she was only twelve when her father died. Also, Buck's comment years earlier that he believed she would become "a great lady" demonstrates his faith in his daughter's potential.

Asked what Doris's father had wanted her to be, Geer replied that Buck hoped she would be charitable and marry a Southerner, displaying loyalty not only to her father's tradition of giving but to the region where he had made his fortune. Perhaps, Geer speculated, Buck had bought his house in Charlotte hoping that Doris would meet Southern boys.[7]

Doris did have one chance to meet the sort of boy her father wanted her to marry. According to a 1963 interview with A. Carl Lee, one of the original engineers of Duke Power, Buck once loaned his car to a Duke business associate, Mr. George Allen, so Allen's nephew Burwell could date Doris. Family friends wanted a chauffeur to drive, as would have been customary, but Doris insisted on sitting beside the boy while he drove on her first outing independent of chaperones.

Geer enjoyed a special friendship with Buck Duke. Once, when they were traveling together by train, Geer asked Buck if he might help Furman

University. Shortly after the conversation, Buck set up a $40 million endow-
ment, of which Furman was to receive 5 percent.[8]

Doris would follow this pattern in her early giving, rewarding friends
for their friendship with funds for their projects without taking much
interest in the actual projects. Later, she would develop a mature appreciation of the projects themselves.

Few knew the little family in the grand house on Seventy-eighth Street as well as Edward Hansen. Beginning in 1924, Hansen was in charge of fourteen to sixteen household servants. They worked only on alternate days, giving them an unprecedented amount of free time, an example of Buck's kindness to his servants.

In contrast, the Elms, built on Bellevue Avenue in Newport in 1901 for the Pennsylvania coal magnate Edward Berwind, was staffed by fourteen live-in servants who worked sixteen hours a day during the season. The ladies' maids worked even longer hours, because they were often expected to help their mistresses take off their ball gowns at 2:00 or 3:00 a.m., then to have breakfast ready to be served at 8:00. The duties of the laundresses were even more onerous. They were required to wash, dry, and iron all the sheets and towels every day.

Hansen recalled that at the Seventy-eighth Street house the staff was paid $110 a month, which he said was excellent pay during this period. Buck was never a skinflint, either with his servants or in support of causes he believed in, such as Duke University, Davidson College, and

Furman University; not-for-profit hospitals and children's homes in the
Carolinas; and rural United Methodist churches, their pastors, and their
families. Never interested in spending lavishly on himself, he provided
amply for Nanaline, so that she always had beautiful clothes as well as
a dazzling collection of jewelry. But he did not indulge their daughter.
The harp he bought for her is the only gift that Doris remembered. Nanaline's control of Doris's pocket money when she was growing up—the
twenty-five-cents-a-week allowance, for example—probably reflected both
parents' fear that Doris would grow up to be a spendthrift and attract
fortune hunters.

Mrs. E. C. Marshall, Nanaline's girlhood friend, who often came to
the Dukes' dinner parties, recalled Buck as a genial man with a good
sense of humor. He especially enjoyed sitting with a group of ladies whom
Nanaline was entertaining, because he loved to hear them gossip and
would encourage them to "knock each other" verbally. He liked to talk to
people generally, and would ask for surprisingly utilitarian details about
home construction and garden maintenance. From his childhood on his
father's tobacco farm in North Carolina, he had learned respect for the
importance of practical details, which may have surprised his New York
acquaintances.

The routine on Seventy-eighth Street was well established: meals were
served at fixed hours, parties and trips were planned well in advance,
and vases of fresh flowers came in from Duke Farms three times a week.
Nanaline disliked the farm, especially in the hot, humid New Jersey summers, but she, Buck, and little Doris often spent weekends there until
they left for Newport in July.

In New York, Nanaline entertained regularly, sometimes inviting as
many as thirty-eight guests to a formal dinner, during which servants
dressed in livery would stand behind the chairs. She entertained Living-
stons and Vanderbilts, Countess Kotecbuc and Lady Wendell, with open
fires in all the ground-floor rooms and tables set up for bridge after dinner.
Buck usually retired early.

His daily routine seldom varied. Leaving for his downtown office
at 8:00 a.m. and returning at 5:00 p.m., Buck would ask, as soon as he
walked in the door, whether his wife and "the baby" were home. Often
they were out—Nanaline visiting friends, and Doris out and about, some-

times at the movies, with her governess, Jenny Renaud. They saw the popular movies of the period—*The Kid*, with Charlie Chaplin; *When Knighthood Was in Flower*, with Marion Davies; *Little Lord Fauntleroy*, with Mary Pickford; and many others, all listed in Doris's notebook in her firm black-penciled script. When she was twenty-one, Doris used capital letters and large black stars to express her enthusiasm for Rudolph Valentino in *Blood and Sand* and *The Sheik*.[1]

According to Hansen, Doris enjoyed having her half brother, Walker, sixteen years her senior, in the house, although he clearly had a drinking problem. Hansen recalled Walker's asking for a glass of whiskey, diluted with water, to be delivered to his room every twenty to thirty minutes. He often crept in late, riding the elevator to the top floor, and tiptoeing down to his room on the second floor so as not to be heard.

Eventually, as Hansen remembered, Buck threw Walker out, albeit with a tear in his eye, probably concerned about Walker's influence on Doris. Nanaline's reaction to the exile of her son was not recorded.

As Doris emerged from the sadness of losing her father, Nanaline recognized her daughter's growing passion for dance. She enrolled Doris in tap lessons. Doris also loved jazz in the 1920s and 1930s, at a time when it was suspect because of its origins in African American culture. Ballroom dancing and classical piano would have been more appropriate, but Nanaline recognized her daughter's passions, and she honored them.

The girl loved to move. Edward Hansen remembered her practicing dance steps all over the house.[2] She also loved popular music. In 1926, Doris printed her list of favorite songs, titled "New Jazz, Summer, 1926," including "Bye Bye Blackbird," "Valencia," "I'd Climb the Highest Mountain," "The Black Bottom Stomp," and "Sweet Child."

Her 1924–25 report card from Class 111 at the Brearley School records A's and B's in English, history, French, science, drawing, and writing. Her teachers added that she was a diligent student.

Her science paper for that year, "The Expansion of Metals," includes a neat sketch of "The Apparatus," a tin-woodman-like figure attached to a Bunsen burner. Her experiment proved that heat expands metal. Another experiment involved taking two geranium leaves, one exposed to sunlight and one not, and boiling them first in hot water and then in alcohol, before finally adding iodine to determine the presence of starch.

Her report for 1925–26 shows a slight decline from the previous school year: a steady march of B's with a few C's and a rare A, following her father's death in October 1925. Later, teachers remarked upon her improvement.

In 1926–27, the following school year, she was earning A's in all her subjects, a remarkable change that her teachers acknowledged. In gym, however, she was still making C's, which was surprising, given her love of physical activity. But the sports the girls' school offered, with squads of bloomer-clad students lined up for drills, may not have appealed to her.

From 1912 until early 1929, Brearley occupied a red-brick building at 60 East Sixty-first Street, purchased for the school by parents and alumnae. The school offered a conventional curriculum that included exercises in public speaking, spelling bees, and diagramming sentences. The headmaster until 1926, George Northrop, brought representatives from the arts, music, and politics to speak at assemblies. Classes were offered for a half day only, and the students usually went home for lunch.

In 1926, a series of headmasters was replaced by the first full-time headmistress, Anne Dunn, who served for just two years. In 1929, the school moved to 610 East Eighty-third Street. As Brearley graduates became interested in going to college, full-day classes were offered. Nearly all the graduates who went on to college attended Vassar or Bryn Mawr.

Doris's academic success at Brearley is particularly remarkable since she was also engaged, to some degree, in managing her two large and demanding properties, Duke Farms and Rough Point. Her skills in organizing and delegating were developed quite early, making it possible for her eventually to own and manage as many as five properties at once. Besides, managing her estates may have been a good deal more interesting than the curriculum offered at a typical girls' school of the period. For example, classical history was presented as a procession of Roman emperors, with the dates of their battles to be memorized. The only female figure Doris drew for a history homework assignment was Livia, the first empress of Rome.

Doris found it disappointing that Brearley did not offer the serious study of music for which she yearned as a budding pianist. Perhaps this is the reason she left in 1928, when she was in the ninth grade, although she is listed as a member of the class of 1931, and continued to contribute to the school's annual fund for the next fifty years.[3]

Doris's love of music may have been one of the reasons Nanaline moved her to the Fermata School for Girls in Aiken, South Carolina. Fermata was a short-lived finishing school for the daughters of East Coast families who wintered in Aiken, enjoying its strong equestrian community.

Unfortunately, Doris hated the school and pleaded to be allowed to return to New York. Nanaline relented and gave her permission for her to leave Fermata after one semester, according to Hansen, when Doris was in the tenth grade. This was the end of Doris's formal education.

Doris made at least one close friend at Fermata, who later visited her in New York: Dorothy Mahana, whose family lived nearby, at 960 Fifth Avenue. Dorothy was lamed in a riding accident the adults blamed on the groom, although Dorothy insisted it was her own fault. Hansen recalled her as one of Doris's closest chums.

Back in New York, Doris focused on French—she had a female tutor four days a week, in addition to Jenny. She also had jazz piano, voice, and dance lessons at home or in New York studios. Hansen remembered that Doris had had six different piano teachers. As she explained to her mother, each of the six had a different way of teaching the piano, which she would eventually blend together.[4]

At this point, other than her study of jazz, Buck's daughter showed no sign of straying from the path laid out for her: limited formal education, debut, then early marriage to a man who shared her background. Edward Hansen remembered that, at nineteen or twenty, Doris, like most sheltered daughters of privilege, was deferential to her mother, almost never disagreed with her, and asked her opinion before making any decision.[5] The formal relationship between mother and daughter prevented the conflict that might have allowed them to establish a closer relationship. But at nineteen and twenty, Doris was also just biding her time until she would become of age, at twenty-one.

Doris's introduction to society came swiftly. Her debut ball at Rough Point, on August 23, 1930, was described in one newspaper as "brilliant" and "the most elaborate of the entire season." The event was held on the last night of the Newport Casino's invitational grass-court tennis tournament, which assured a good assembly of guests from the summer colony. Six hundred attended the ball.[6]

The gardens at Rough Point, at the end of Ocean Avenue, were lighted, and a large tent was set up on the ocean side for the guests' dinner. The tent was lined with smilax—that staple flora of Southern weddings—and decorated with hanging baskets of gladioli. Two orchestras took turns playing in the ballroom, which was screened with palms and more baskets of gladioli. These may have seemed simple, almost pastoral decorations compared with the silver trinkets, crystal epergnes filled with fruit and flowers, and gold candelabras at other Newport festivities of the time. The event, however, occurred in the first year of the Great Depression, and although the Depression did not substantially affect the fortunes of the Duke family—tobacco use only increased with the stress of the times—it may have cast a cloud over the kind of extravagant social functions that had long been expected of Newport and New York society.

Doris's debut was, for Nanaline, imperative. She knew from her own past as an impoverished daughter of the South the importance of these milestones of acceptance. Her daughter's debut provided further proof that the Dukes were "in."

Their way may have been smoothed by the earlier absorption of the family of the tobacconist Pierre Lorillard into Gilded Age society. Pierre IV bought the first tracts of land in Tuxedo Park, New York, which became, with his grandson's development, a well-known retreat for New York's upper class. The family's neo-Gothic house in Newport was a familiar landmark, and no one seemed to remember that their fortune was founded on an eighteenth-century snuff-grinding factory in lower Manhattan. Perhaps the final sign of Lorillard's status was the use of the word "millionaire" in his obituary—for the first time, according to Cleveland Amory.[7]

Doris's Newport debut was the second in a series of celebratory occasions. Earlier, on May 20, 1930, she had been presented at court in London. Twenty-five of the three hundred girls who had applied were accepted to curtsy before the king and queen. Nanaline would have needed to call on all her social contacts to ensure Doris's acceptance.

For her presentation, Doris would have worn the required full-length white kid gloves, three ostrich feathers in a headdress trailing a veil (this arrangement was said to be the despair of hairdressers), and a long white satin gown with a beaded court train hanging from her shoulders. She would have learned to back out of the room at Buckingham Palace after she was presented to the king and queen, a maneuver that required practice and agility if one was to avoid stumbling over one's train.

Arrangements began years in advance, with the submission of the request to the lord chamberlain. Candidates were chosen according to social status, with a few other considerations thrown in; money was surely one of them. Finally, the selected young women received a gilded invitation from the lord chamberlain commanding them on the part of the king and queen to come to court.

For Doris's earlier debut-year event, on August 6, 1930, Mrs. Rufus L. Patterson in Southampton, Long Island, gave her a luncheon.[8] Rufus Patterson, whose invention of a cigarette-rolling machine in 1930 was predated by Duke's Bonsack Cigarette Machine, was one of the competitors Buck Duke bought out to protect his patent and secure his monopoly. That Rufus Patterson and his wife were now well established socially, and friendly enough with the Dukes, underlines the importance of this party as a link to Doris's past as well as her future. She may have made her debut in Newport and her presentation at the Court of St James's primarily to humor her mother. Mrs. Patterson's party, however, was a tribute to her father.

The jazz scene in New York supplied a potent contrast to the refined and controlled life of a debutante on the Upper East Side of Manhattan and in Newport. At first it had centered on the Cotton Club, on Lenox Avenue at 142nd Street in Harlem, with its Savoy Ballroom ("The World's Finest," according to its commemorative plaque). The club covered a whole city block and featured two bands, so the music never stopped. Much attended by the white audience from downtown, its maple-and-mahogany dance floor wore out and had to be replaced every three years. It was called the "Home of Happy Feet."

Even though African Americans were discouraged from attending as audience members, black performers danced, played, and sang against the backdrop of a Southern plantation house, white columns and all. The floor shows, in the Florenz Ziegfeld tradition, featured scantily clad, primarily light-skinned dancers. George "Shorty" Snowden created the Lindy Hop at the Savoy, named after Charles Lindbergh, and the amateur dancers who thronged the floor learned its complicated steps as well as those of the new swing dances. This all changed after the Harlem race riots of 1935, when the area began to be seen as unsafe for whites, and the Cotton Club closed its doors in Harlem, reopening on West Forty-eighth Street in 1935, where it operated for four more years.

Duke Ellington's orchestra played the Cotton Club until 1931, when Cab Calloway and his Missourians took over and made the club's reputation. These were the musicians Doris heard in the years after her debut. Their music shaped her taste in jazz and fueled the passion that would run like a bright thread through her entire life.

As Ralph Ellison remembered, during the 1920s the jazz clubs in New York were as rich in flavor as a well-spiced stew. They would also have been hazy with cigarette smoke. During this period, cigarette consumption in the United States doubled, supported by the now booming economy and the acceptance of smoking for women.

Once she arrived in her chauffeured limousine, Doris would have entered the nightclub on the arm of a young man-about-town. More and more frequently, that young man would be James H. R. "Jimmy" Cromwell. For five years—or longer, since Doris's future husband would claim he began to "worship" her when she was sixteen—Jenny, along with Nanaline, had tried to protect Doris from Jimmy's strenuous attentions. Perhaps because of his first marriage, to Delphine Dodge, the automotive heiress, whose fortune he had partly dissipated through unwise real-estate investments in Florida, both Jenny and Nanaline were suspicious of Jimmy's intentions. Doris, too, would fend Jimmy off for six years.

The courtship proceeded apace, however, especially after Jenny retired in 1935. For Doris, losing Jenny was a serious blow, no matter how appropriate in terms of what was expected for a debutante: a personal maid, perhaps, but certainly no longer a governess. With Jenny no longer immediately available although still living in New York, Doris lost her first female mentor.

Her other beau, Harry Crocker, was an actor, producer, journalist, and well-known presence on the Hollywood scene who was invited on extensive trips with William Randolph Hearst and Marion Davies. He met Doris in Phoenix in the winter of 1934, writing her that March that he remembered how they had enjoyed long conversations when they were in Phoenix, sitting on the sand. He thought she had an original turn of mind and found her opinions radical yet "completely sound."

Later in 1934, Harry wrote to ask Doris to marry him, insisting this proposal was serious and begging her for a letter in response. For her birthday, he wrote jokingly that he was considering buying her a harness for the seven dwarfs, given that she seldom wore jewelry. Harry and Doris shared a sense of humor and fantasy. Apparently, she responded with a postcard, because he reminded her in his next letter that postcards were inappropriate for their correspondence, since Doris cherished secrets and postcards were not private.

At Christmas, Harry was invited to visit Hearst Castle, which sits on a hilltop high above the Pacific Ocean in California. Harry found "W.R.," as he called him, an amusing eccentric. Between name-dropping and accounts of endless barhopping, Harry reported that Walter Winchell had gossiped in his notorious column about Harry and Doris's impending marriage.[9]

Marian Paschal, Doris's assistant, wrote from California that Harry seemed to think Doris would be returning. They had had lunch together and were close enough friends that Harry didn't hesitate to regale Marian with all his "woes and longings" about Doris. Marian admitted that she had been very interested in hearing what he had to say, reminding "Holetia"—Doris's now familiar nickname, which was never explained— that Harry was "simply daft" about her. Relishing private revelations about Doris's relationships with other people, Marian wisely suppressed whatever jealousy she might have felt in order to keep channels of communication open.

Harry remarked that Doris didn't read much—which other friends also noticed—reflecting her lifelong self-consciousness about her lack of education. Besides, she was always more engaged in the life of her body. Harry called her Skippy, reflecting her physical exuberance.

Doris never answered Harry's proposal. After all, he was a Hollywood habitué, without fortune or family to recommend him. Instead, after painful bouts of indecision, Doris stumbled toward her first marriage. Perhaps recognizing that any marriage, especially one to the likes of the ambitious Jimmy Cromwell, might compromise her goals for her fortune, she took her first tentative steps toward sequestering some of her inheritance for philanthropy.

12 Like Doris Duke, James H. R. Cromwell, younger son of Lucretia Bishop Cromwell—later Eva Cromwell Stotesbury—was born to great expectations. His father, Oliver Eaton Cromwell, was defined by his membership in New York clubs and his passion for sailing. He was chairman of the New York Yacht Club Regatta Committee. Oliver was also an expert mountain climber, known for his many ascents in the Canadian Rockies. In 1972, Mount Cromwell in Alberta was named for him.

Oliver died in 1909 at the age of sixty-two, leaving Lucretia a widow with three almost grown children: Oliver Cromwell, Jr.; James; and Henrietta.[1] Left well provided for, Lucretia ascended further social and financial heights in 1912, when she married her second husband, E. T. Stotesbury, a Philadelphia multimillionaire and banking partner of J. P. Morgan. Ned, as he was known, had been a widower for thirty years at the time of his second marriage. His first wife, Frances Berman Butcher, had died in 1881 while giving birth to the third of their three daughters; the first had died as an infant.

Ned's career had begun at Drexel, the Philadelphia banking house

founded and directed by his uncle Anthony Joseph Drexel. Starting out
as a clerk, Ned was said to be on time every day and to keep meticulous
financial records of every cent he spent. In 1871, when Drexel went into
partnership with J. P. Morgan, Ned became a partner. By 1927, his fortune was estimated to be $100 million. His recipe for success was simple:
Listen, and don't talk much. When asked to move from Philadelphia to
New York, where J. P. Morgan was headquartered, he refused. His ties to
his birthplace were too strong. In 1882, he had founded the Stotesbury
Cup Regatta, a competition for high school scullers on the Schuylkill
River. He was also president of the Bachelors' Barge Club. Stotesbury, a
coal town in West Virginia, was named for him.

Ned was director of two railroads, a Philadelphia bank, an iron company, and two steel plants. He was also president of Philadelphia's Art
Jury and Fairmount Park Art Association (now the Association for Public Art), yet he was said never to read. F. C. von Hausen's portrait, painted
in 1936, shows a handsome, severe-looking elderly man, suavely outfitted
in his Florida resort clothes: white pants, white shoes, and a pastel jacket,
his straw boater resting beside him on a pile of books. He is seated on the
rim of a fountain at his Palm Beach mansion, El Mirasol.[2]

It does not require a vivid imagination to conjure the reaction of this
hard-nosed financier to Jimmy, his indulged and dependent stepson. At
one point, Ned wrote to Jimmy that he planned to spend his fortune on
himself, rather than on "your friend Roosevelt." This was after Jimmy
had changed his political allegiance in the 1930s, after the stock-market
crash reduced Stotesbury's $100 million to $4 million.

In 1912, Ned and Lucretia, now called Eva, had built three extraordinary mansions: the Beaux arts Whitemarsh Hall (145 rooms, forty-five
baths) in Wyndmoor, Pennsylvania, outside Philadelphia; El Mirasol
(thirty-seven rooms, with private zoo) in Palm Beach, Florida; and Wingwood House (eighty rooms, twenty-nine baths, fifty-two telephones) in
Bar Harbor, Maine. By the 1980s, all three would be torn down.

El Mirasol was the center of Ned and Eva's social life. His February
birthday party was said to be the apex of the Palm Beach season. P.A.B.
Widener, Andrew Carnegie, and Alfred G. Vanderbilt, as well as the art
dealer Joseph Duveen and the opera stars Nellie Melba and Mary Garden,
were just a few of the Stotesburys' guests.[3]

At one of their parties, the Ziegfeld Follies performer Dot King, dubbed the "Butterfly of Broadway," attracted the attention of Ned's son-in-law, J. Kearsley Mitchell, who had married Ned's daughter from his first marriage.

In 1923, Dot King was found murdered in her New York bedroom. Her maid had stuffed a pair of yellow silk pajamas under a cushion before calling the police. When the police searched the apartment, they found a letter to Dot from Mitchell, announcing that he was wild to see her and kiss her feet.

Called as a suspect in Dot's murder, Mitchell allowed that the yellow silk pajamas fit his style and that he liked Dot and sometimes tucked a thousand-dollar bill under her pillow, but he claimed that he and his attorney, after a night on the town with Dot, had separated from her at 2:30 a.m., some time before the murder. Mitchell was released to return to Philadelphia, and the investigation was never resolved.

Dot King, like many other women before and since, was possessed of a vitality and a bodily awareness that drew men: naked, high-kicking legs, breasts freed from restraints, hips with a will of their own. Dot may not have recognized the fragility of her hold—Broadway butterfly, then broken butterfly, as the newspapers called her—because she was freely availing herself of the power of the men who entertained her. Or so she thought.

Her freedom was an illusion. When Dot asked too much or gave too little, her man would destroy her. Dot could never have guessed how violent the man in the yellow silk pajamas could be, or how his attorney, his money, and his class would protect him.

It must have taken all of Eva's tact and charm to smooth over her son-in-law's scandal. Perhaps she and Ned escaped the inevitable gossip by concentrating on and moving between their three great houses.[4]

In 1917, after Buck Duke's architect, Horace Trumbauer, finished building Whitemarsh Hall, Eva Stotesbury wrote to him that she was enjoying the "majestic simplicity" of the house and had never been able to describe adequately its "thrilling loveliness." She found her eyes filling with tears when she contemplated the house in the light of the moon.[5]

El Mirasol and Eva figure in Stephen Sondheim's musical *Road Show*, which opened at the Goodman Theatre in Chicago in 2003. In the song "You," the character Addison Mizner (the architect of El Mirasol) talks Eva into allowing him to design her house. A later song, "Addison's City," touches on a real-estate plan similar to one that Jimmy would hatch after his first marriage, an ill-fated millionaires' colony at Boca Raton.[6] By then, Jimmy had seemed to answer the question of what he was going to do with his life; this had not been clear earlier.

In 1917, after apparently gaining a law degree from the University of Pennsylvania in an unusually short time, or from two lesser institutions (the record is confused), Jimmy joined the Navy. Not finding it to his liking, he transferred to the Marine Corps. His role in World War I seems to have been inconspicuous. Three years later, in 1920, he was honorably discharged.

That year, Jimmy was visiting his mother at El Mirasol when he met Delphine Dodge, daughter of Horace Elgin Dodge and Anna Thomson Dodge, who were vacationing at their own mansion nearby. Horace was cofounder with his brother, John, of the Dodge Motor Company in Detroit. Married in 1920, Jimmy and Delphine were divorced following the birth of a daughter, in 1922. From then on, the tabloids assumed that Jimmy would only marry for money. The real story is more complex.

Jimmy was a man of great charm, and charm not only covers many faults of character—which in Jimmy's case included self-indulgence, overweening ambition, and some degree of financial recklessness—it often compensates for those faults. A man who is a good dancer with a sense of humor and of occasion, who knows how to navigate the thicket of social conventions that govern upper-class life, and is, finally, a sportsman and a seasoned international traveler offers many distractions, especially to privileged women who are to a degree unformed. Jimmy was well suited to Delphine.

In 1920, Horace Dodge had commissioned a large yacht, powered by two quadruple steam engines that he himself designed. When launched in 1921, four months after Horace's death, the immense ship caused waves so large in Lake St. Clair that spectators had to dash for higher ground. It was moored at the bottom of the lawn at the Dodges' mansion, Rose Terrace, in Grosse Pointe Farms, Michigan. The yacht was christened *Delphine*.

When Jimmy met Delphine, the Dodge family had no way of knowing that Ned would cut him off. Whether on the lawn at El Mirasol,
under the palms, or on the terrace leaning against the stone balustrade,
or idling on the Dodges' private beach, Jimmy would have been an attractive sight, his dark hair side-parted and slicked down, his straw boater
decorated with a jaunty ribbon, his white pants impeccably creased. He
would have been matched by the charm of the ethereal Delphine in her
summer white silks, her dark hair elaborately styled around a face that
had a slightly blurred quality. They were immediately perceived as a
pair.

But, like Jimmy, Delphine had no income of her own; raised, like him,
to expect luxury, she suffered the indignity of depending on her mother
for every penny, because of the way her father's will divided his estate.
She seems to have had a difficult life, marrying three times and descend-
ing finally into alcoholism. Delphine died at age forty-four, in 1943.

There was another link between the Dodges and the Dukes. Horace
and John Dodge—"the poorest little urchins ever born," as they liked
to tell it—worked eighteen-hour days as teenagers in their father's Detroit machine shop. Henry Ford was so impressed by their skills and their
work ethic that he hired them to supply the Ford Motor Company with
parts. Paid partly in Ford Motor Company stock, the brothers became
in a decade major stockholders, worth more than $50 million. In 1914,
they broke with Ford to establish their own factory, building Dodge cars,
which threatened for a while to outsell Fords. They amassed a fortune of
$200 million, worth the equivalent of $2 billion today.[7]

In early life, Buck and Ben Duke reaped the rewards of a similar partnership, first as they labored in their father's tobacco fields and later as
they assembled the elements of the American Tobacco Company. Unquestioned loyalty bound each pair of brothers, contributing both confidence
and expertise to their joint ventures.

Jimmy never enjoyed such a partnership. Instead, he placed his confidence in women, beginning with his mother. Women, however, no matter
how rich or beautiful, did not at that time possess the technical expertise
and the access to capital that seed vast fortunes. Nor would Jimmy ever
encounter the kind of support Anna Dodge offered her husband. In later

life, a millionaire widow, she would remember how much she had enjoyed packing her husband's lunch pail in the early years.[8]

In 1920, when Jimmy and Delphine married, their future may have looked improbably rosy. Their reception at Rose Terrace was filmed by Pathé News and displayed before the feature in movie theaters across the country. The black-and-white newsreel showed bridesmaids in drop-waisted white dresses, white stockings, and white shoes, carrying white bouquets, ushering Delphine, nearly invisible in a nest of lace and tulle, down garden steps to a wide lawn.[9]

The Dodges, creators of thousands of jobs in their Detroit factories, were less afraid of exposure than the Dukes, whose cigarettes were already raising health concerns. As early as 1912, Dr. Isaac Adler had published the first book summarizing the results of research into the causes of the growing incidents of lung cancer, linking it to smoking as well as alcohol. The effect of Buck Duke's monopoly on North Carolina tobacco farmers had also caused an outcry, particularly in the jeremiads launched for a time by the newspaper publisher Josephus Daniels in the Raleigh *News & Observer*, accusing Buck Duke of robbing and oppressing poor farmers.

In a world far removed from the North Carolina tobacco fields, Jimmy had invested some of Delphine's money—or, more probably, persuaded her mother to become involved—in a proposed colony of luxury houses in Boca Raton. It never materialized. Jimmy had depended on his social connections with the likes of the King of Greece and the Countess of Lauderdale to invest in the project, but they apparently declined. The $3 million loss was made good by Eva Stotesbury and Anna Dodge.

Jimmy was employed at his stepfather's bank in Philadelphia. After that, he became president of the Peerless Motor Company, which promptly went bankrupt. Then he found a niche as partner in the advertising firm of H. R. Doughty and Associates. Later, it collapsed in scandal. His failures, however, didn't seem to limit his social options. Jimmy always seemed to land on his feet.

When Jimmy and Doris first met in Palm Beach, Jimmy was certainly attracted to her money. He needed it, after his 1928 divorce from Delphine, to support his way of life as well as his political ambitions.

Although later billed as a supporter of President Franklin Roosevelt, Jimmy was in the 1920s a radical right-winger, an ally of the rabidly anti-Semitic radio personality Father Coughlin. According to a *New Masses* article of 1942, Jimmy was a member of the "Washington Cliveden Set," who, like Mrs. Astor's Cliveden Set in England, opposed the coming war, hated Russia and communism, and were labeled appeasers for advocating a negotiated peace with the Axis Powers.

Jimmy responded to this article by bringing suit, telling *The Washington Post* and the *New York Herald Tribune* that he was determined to destroy the magazine. At this point in her life, Doris's troubles with the tabloid press, whose reporters had pursued her relentlessly since her father's death, would have made her sympathetic with Jimmy's outrage.

After they were married, Jimmy would persuade Doris to underwrite his entry into politics in New Jersey, undeterred by the fact that he was a political unknown with many opinions but no experience. Doris began her contributions with a check for $50,000 to the Democratic Party. In August 1936, she would write a flurry of checks to the chairmen of Democratic state committees in ten states, excluding New Jersey, where Jimmy planned to run for the U.S. Senate. Although it is not clear exactly how these $5,000 checks would have helped Jimmy in New Jersey, they established his right to claim financial backing from his heiress-wife for his future in Democratic politics.

At this point, Jimmy's political message was based on what he called "A New Deal for Money," which aligned him with the message of the Sound Money League. The league was organized to promote a return to gold as a basis for the dollar. Jimmy believed that Americans cared nothing about international events; he was pandering to the isolationist mood of the country.[10] His message would change with Roosevelt's successful run for a second term as president in 1936. Regardless, Jimmy failed to win a seat in the Senate.

Politics had mattered little to Doris when Jimmy began to court her in 1928. At that point, she seemed to him an innocent, "unscarred . . . by a sordid and callow world." When he first met her, he had found her charmingly "feminine" to the point of adoring her. He had worshipped her "little feet," almost as though she were a child.[11] That she wore a size eight shoe suggests that Jimmy valued romance more than reality.

By 1932, Doris was struggling to escape Jimmy, as his wounded and angry letters from June to September of that year reveal. Calling Doris, for unknown reasons, "Ambrose," Jimmy first apologized for losing his temper the previous evening. He explained that had been provoked by "your Mademoiselle" telling him that she, Doris, was too busy to come to the phone. He believed she had not been available because her mother objected. Jimmy complained that Doris had slighted him again when they met in Antibes, even though she had claimed that she wanted to spend more time with him. Then, when he stomped off, she had the nerve to scold him. Her ability to act as she wished without being intimidated by his outbursts of bad temper must have thoroughly disconcerted him. Few young women of this period—or, indeed, of any period—would dare to affront a clearly suitable and determined suitor. But Doris didn't need Jimmy to help her find her way, and she let him know it. This was also a part of the fascination she exercised over him.

After Doris snubbed him in Antibes, Jimmy complained that his pride had been "rolled in the dirt so frequently . . . that the good old worm has turned at last." He told her goodbye but still signed himself with her pet nickname for him, Maxie.[12] Doris may have based the nickname on Slapsie Maxie (Max Everitt Rosenbloom, 1907–76), a famous boxer who won the 1930 New York light-heavyweight championship. He was known for his open-glove style of boxing, which made his nickname suit the pugnacious Jimmy. Slapsie Maxie was also a great athlete, winning 222 of his 298 bouts, and in line with Doris's tastes, a very handsome dark-skinned man.

As before, so after their marriage, the social connections between Doris and Jimmy could not be ignored. A September 1939 handwritten note to "Liz" from "Becki"—apparently secretaries—accompanied a letter of introduction from Douglas MacArthur to the U.S. embassy in Paris. MacArthur had married Jimmy's sister, Louise Cromwell, in 1922. As a favor to his wife, General MacArthur was requesting that the use of the embassy's facilities be extended to Jimmy Cromwell and the rest of his party, including Doris, Marian Paschal, a chauffeur, and a chambermaid.[13]

Jimmy had all the proper credentials. Although they were encountering some reversals, the Stotesburys were still plenty rich. Jimmy mentioned that his stepfather slept in his own train car when returning to New Jersey from New York. Although Jimmy's grades at Lawrenceville, and later at the University of Pennsylvania, were mediocre, that was not a problem. Scions typically did poorly in school. More important than his grades, he knew people in New Jersey and New York and Europe who were Duke familiars. By now, Doris may have realized that for a wealthy single woman in an East Coast social world composed almost entirely of couples, ambiguously oriented bachelors, and widows, a husband did not need to supply the money. He needed to furnish the context.

While Doris avoided him, Jimmy taunted her with the fact that his ex-fiancée, Lydia, provided "plenty clever competition," decorating his apartment at 277 Park Avenue with flowers and bon voyage presents before he left once more for Europe. He expected that his letter of June 11, 1932, although scrawled in pencil on lined paper rather than on engraved stationery, would impress Doris more than love letters from titled European men, which often bore a make-believe coat of arms. Jimmy seemed to want to remind her that the titled men who might well be courting her in Europe were often as ersatz as the so-called Dollar Princesses sent from the United States to attract them. By contrast, he believed that his love letters would someday sell for a lot of money, because the next generations would be "ravenous for the mighty symposiums of that master mind" belonging to her future husband, Jimmy Cromwell. "Yassah— yassah—the old master himself."[14]

Often referring to himself in the third person as "The O.M.," Jimmy may have drawn his mock title from theosophy, a popular interest at the time. Madame Helena Petrovna Blavatsky, cofounder of the Theosophical Society, referred to her guide from the realm of the spirits as "the Old Master." Jimmy went on, teasingly, that he would have married the long-suffering Lydia in June, but after he told her that he loved Doris, or at least thought he did, Lydia looked at him as if he had hit her.

Jimmy was sixteen years Doris's senior. Perhaps she knew enough to be wary of an older man who called her "spoiled rotten" and who threatened to beat the resistance out of her "skinny little frame" once he had married her and had her in his grip. Doris could not have taken such a threat as only another example of the Old Master's peculiar sense of humor; the threat was too real. Perhaps sensing that he had gone too far, Jimmy ended the letter by admitting that he had to admire her "unlimited confidence." That same confidence may have led her to discount Jimmy's threats as bluster, which proved to be the right conclusion.

Jimmy wrote to Doris that Lydia had told her friends that their marriage had been indefinitely postponed. She was spending her time, he continued, bathing his handsome head with her tears. Admitting that he, too, was in pain, Jimmy assured Doris that his pain was nothing to what she would feel after he had beaten her until she would "look like a pretzel with the cramps."[15]

Two days later, Jimmy described taking his mother to the pier to sail for Europe. He had sent three motorcycle cops to escort her, which seemed to cheer her up: her world had been transformed by the stock-market crash, and her beloved Whitemarsh was now on the market, thanks to her husband's massive losses.

Doris, too, had been in Europe in 1932. Jimmy wrote that she should never have left home without his permission, adding that he sort of admired her for doing so, another example of his back-and-forth blaming and complimenting, which seemed to have its own peculiar power. Doris may have realized that if she gave in and followed his orders, he would likely lose interest in her. After all, the compliant Lydia hadn't succeeded in holding her mercurial suitor. When he and Doris were both back in New York, Jimmy wrote, he planned to get her in a taxicab careening around Central Park while kissing her "for 24½ hours without coming up for air," all in the hope of hearing her exclaim, "Aw, poor Maxie!"[16]

He'd been to the Atlantic Beach Club—with his sister, Louise; her husband, Douglas MacArthur; and the long-suffering Lydia—where, he claimed, a mob of people rushed up to ask when he was finally going to make an honest woman out of Lydia.

In September, Jimmy was in Venice with his mother. He wrote to Doris about her objection to his constantly "pecking" at her. She was far more at fault, he wrote, for deliberately interfering in his relationship with Lydia—he didn't explain how. Indeed, Jimmy may have been infuriated by Doris's reaction to her rival. In retaliation, he accused her of a total personality change from the sixteen-year-old girl with whom he had fallen in love, concluding that now Doris's "conceit and unutterable selfishness" had murdered his earlier adoration.[17]

Later that summer, at the Lido in Venice, Jimmy wrote Doris to excoriate her for her "impossible behavior," which he didn't describe. Probably, she was simply not paying him enough attention, although it would not have been unlike her to repulse his tiresome persistence by throwing sand in his face. He was furious that she was still encouraging her mother "to believe the most outrageous untruths" about what Jimmy would certainly have insisted was his sterling character, adding that, hard as it was for him to believe, Doris still seemed to believe that he was not up to her standards for a suitor.

He wrote that "a sweet and gentle girl" (the all-forgiving Lydia?) had given him a love as deep and sincere as his for Doris had been. He compared this love to Devonshire cream rather than the skimmed milk Doris offered. Claiming that Doris's money meant nothing to him, he stated that he was not willing to relinquish "a real chance for happiness" in exchange for the uncertain future Doris seemed to offer.[18]

Jimmy's next letter started out with a very different tone: he addressed Doris as his "Precious Little Sweetheart." But then he claimed to doubt her intelligence, apparently because she hadn't been writing him often enough: "Are you dumb darling?"[19] Could it be that she was an "authentic dumb bell" and that his strenuous efforts to educate her were useless?

Jimmy had found the chink in her armor: Doris's self-consciousness about her lack of formal education. There is something, too, in his skillful alternation of abuse and adoration that may have exerted its own attraction.

In January 1933, Jimmy seemed to be the one having doubts. Writing Doris that "General Blue Depression" had "an armlock on my skinny neck," he admitted that he felt like a failure after he and his friends failed to "flim flam the works of the Roosevelt steamroller"—referring to the tidal wave of public support that had swept Franklin Roosevelt to victory over Republican president Hoover in the election of November 1932. The Roosevelt ticket carried the country, and this landslide persuaded Jimmy to change his political allegiance: he would never willingly be stuck with a loser. He may have guessed that Doris, too, loved winners.

He opined that American women had lost their femininity (perhaps thinking of Doris, who certainly didn't fit the stereotype) because they "are so desirous of equaling masculinity in thought, word, and deed." This destructive "anomaly," he believed, would be rejected in time, because women knew that what the Bible said was right—"women's natural instinct is to give and to serve"—a belief that may not have appealed to Doris as she tried to shape her own life. Still, they had evidently been discussing marriage. Jimmy now advised her to be certain that she was ready to embrace "unforeseen sacrifices" by becoming responsible as "the guiding inspiration of his life."

Doris must have known the first sacrifice he would require would be of a substantial portion of her independence—and perhaps even of her income, which was much greater than his. Then he protested that in the last months she had written him only once, probably copied from "a Western Union 'thank-you' form"—not in the least what Jimmy would be willing to accept. Offended, he tried once again to say a final goodbye to his "precious hot and cold little girl." In rejecting her—or trying to—he continued his back-and-forth gambit: she was still precious.

Unable to let her go, Jimmy unleashed his anger at Doris's most recent display of "rude and indifferent behavior," which caused him to "want to squash you flat."[20] His rage was fueled by a conversation he had had with Elsa Maxwell, the gossip columnist, society hostess, and matchmaker. Maxwell described Doris in *Ladies' Home Journal* as a strangely pale, skeletally thin girl (her mother's insistence on a meager diet had paid off) who spoke in disjointed fragments, wore cheap department-store clothes—this must have astonished Maxwell's readers—walked as though she distrusted the floor, and wore so little jewelry that if she did put on bracelets it would seem as unlikely as the labor leader John L. Lewis's "joining the Union League."

In his letter to Doris, Jimmy wrote of his rage after Maxwell repeated the rumor that one British date had complained that Doris's car was equipped with a button to call for help. According to the baronet, Doris said she would allow him to accompany her home from a party, but only in *her* car. Then, Maxwell wrote, the British gentleman lunged at Doris in the car and paid no attention when she reprimanded him in no uncertain terms. The man seemed to believe, Maxwell implied, that for these notorious American girls, Dollar Princesses out to catch titled Englishmen, "no" invariably means "yes." When he lunged at her again, Doris pressed the button, the car screeched to a halt, all lights went on, and the doors flew open. The chauffeur and the footman jumped out and hauled the protesting baronet out of the car and deposited him by the side of the road. They then got into the car with Doris and drove off.

When he read this story, Jimmy's rage knew no bounds. He didn't stop to wonder whether Maxwell, whose trade depended on exaggerating rumors, had any real basis for her account. Instead, he wrote Doris that he was determined "to beat Sir Popadoop into a jelly." But his anger at the baronet also extended to Doris, who he seemed to imagine was somehow responsible. He was relieved, he wrote her, that "I didn't hurt you anymore than I did"—leaving the reader to wonder exactly what he had done. Claiming that her money had no effect on him except to make him extremely wary of slights, he repeated something that had become a theme in his letters—that he could never own Doris if he didn't own her body. Jimmy seemed to believe that marriage would confer that ownership.

His letters to Doris went on, recriminations and apologies alternating with expressions of passionate love, until it seemed unlikely that these two disparate people would ever come to terms. Doris was cool and aloof; Jimmy was all passionate intensity. He had already told her goodbye— definitively—infuriated that Doris would dare to offer him what he called "a clandestine affair." A week later he again professed that he loved her more than anything in the world and was waiting for her to answer his marriage proposal. However, he knew her mother's influence was still paramount, and at this point, Nanaline did not favor Jimmy Cromwell. Still, he insisted, he was the only man who could restore Doris to "health and peace of mind," which he seemed to assume she had lost.

In his next letter, Jimmy claimed a different view of their many squabbles: that they had in fact served to persuade him that they were right for each other, a conclusion difficult to understand. They had finally reached a decision to marry, although their differences remained.

Jimmy claimed that a primary one was her scoffing attitude toward sex, which she insisted on regarding as a form of amusement—an attitude that would have shocked many. He called her a Foolish Virgin—referring to the Bible story of the five virgins sent to meet Christ who forgot to bring oil for their lanterns and so couldn't see Christ when he appeared. He promised that the Old Master was planning a honeymoon Doris would never forget—perhaps meaning that she would never forget it because of his relentless assertion of masculinity.[21]

Doris never explained her reasons for finally accepting Jimmy's proposal despite their volatile relationship. It may have been the sheer force of his self-confidence that undermined her resolve to dismiss him. For, according to Elsa Maxwell, Jimmy outshone Doris in every way. He had no problem with spending money (in fact, she might have added, but didn't, he'd spent a large portion of Delphine Dodge's). In light of his extravagance, Doris's hesitation to buy even a ticket for a charity ball might seem bizarre. Jimmy had no time for doubts about anything, whereas Doris was apprehensive, full of hesitation. She hardly ever wrote a letter and was not much of a reader, but her husband-to-be read everything under the sun, or so he claimed, especially in the realm of economics. He would go on to write several books of his own.

Jimmy's first book was *The Voice of Young America*, published in 1933, in which he advocated guaranteed bank deposits, abandonment of the gold standard, compulsory unemployment insurance, and federal-aided public works, some of which would come to pass under Franklin Roosevelt.[22] His second book, published in 1937, was *In Defense of Capitalism*, in which he laid out a plan for tight control of money by the Federal Reserve System.[23] Neither of these books would have much appeal for Doris, or for the general public.

Maxwell's appreciation of Jimmy's virtues may not have been widely shared. However, she was exact in identifying an ideal that may have spurred Doris's decision finally to accept him. Maxwell believed that Doris and Jimmy were united by a single goal: to return her fortune—eventually—or at least a large part of it, to the American people. In this, Maxwell believed Doris was following the example of the Rockefellers. Of course, both her father and grandfather had established a clear family precedent of their own for charitable giving.

In fact, Doris was developing the philosophy that would shape her philanthropy. She was no longer giving in her earlier, haphazard, personal way, but in line with a belief in a moral imperium: "From everyone who has been given much, much will be demanded; and from the one who has been entrusted with much, much more will be asked" (Luke 12:48).

13 More clues to Jimmy's character are scattered through a series of letters, preserved in the Lawrenceville School archives, covering his years there, from 1913 until 1915. Lawrenceville, one of the oldest of the East Coast boys' college-preparatory boarding schools (now coeducational) sits on 700 acres, five miles north of Trenton, New Jersey, and about twenty-five miles from Duke Farms.

Jimmy's application for admission to the fourth form (tenth grade) on November 3, 1913, meant that he would arrive two months after the fall semester began. He had lived at boarding school since the age of twelve, at the West Miller School in Great Barrington, Massachusetts. These years covered the period of his father's death and his mother's remarriage. He seems to have emerged from West Miller just in time to cause his new stepfather perturbation.

In filling out his application for Lawrenceville in firm, dark handwriting, Jimmy's mother indicated that he should be prepared either for college or for a career in business. She answered the question about "religious affiliation or preferences" with "Protestant Episcopalian" and listed his home address as 1925 Walnut Street in Philadelphia, and his father's business address as Drexel and Company. Eva said her son's health was good even though he smoked, hardly a surprise for a boy of seventeen at that time; cigarettes were taking the country by storm. Half the U.S. population smoked, and there were no prohibitions against selling tobacco to minors.

For the school year 1914–15, "James" signed an agreement that may have signaled a growing uneasiness about the dramatic increase in underage smoking. He agreed to smoke in moderation, and to abstain from cigarettes in favor of cigars and pipes—both considered less damaging to health as well as carrying the seal of social approval.[1]

On November 8, 1913, Eva's secretary wrote the headmaster, Mr. McPherson, saying that Eva hoped he would not hold Jimmy's late application against him and asking him to be "indulgent" toward "James"—his formal first name now used, as though to indicate his admission to a higher level of maturity. Indulgence was a request Eva Stotesbury would make more than once. Her husband, Ned Stotesbury, eager to get his stepson out of the house, wrote the president of his alma mater, Princeton, to help get James into a congenial house at Lawrenceville. (The students at Lawrenceville lived in individual houses on the campus, each presided over by a teacher and his wife.)

Yet Jimmy was not, according to his mother, eager to go away to school again. She wrote to Mr. McPherson that James had pleaded hard to be allowed to stay at home after six (corrected in pencil to five) years at boarding school. But his stepfather was determined to send him off, "a bitter disappointment" to James. His unwillingness to leave his mother, who wrote that she had seen very little of him since her second marriage, was "assuaged" by his immediate liking for one of the Lawrenceville teachers.[2]

In the spring of his first year at Lawrenceville, a letter from the headmaster reassured his mother that he had made a lot of friends at school and had been working well until he fell sick with "a bilious attack" deemed serious enough to send him home.[3]

Jimmy's recuperation was slow. On September 19, 1914, Eva wrote Mr. McPherson that Jimmy was still not as robust as she would wish and was still plagued by what she called "auto-intoxication"—a polite term for constipation. As a result, his system was still invaded by the poisons from his burst appendix several months after it had been removed. She thought he looked too poorly to return to school but reported that he was determined to go back as soon as possible.[4]

Soon after Jimmy returned to school, his housemaster, Mr. Wheeler, wrote Eva that he had a "very unpleasant message to convey." Jimmy, along with two classmates, had escaped the campus in the middle of the night, planning to take in the attractions of nearby Trenton. At a time when trolleys ran at all hours, they were able to make their way to the house of one of the boys' parents, with the intention of borrowing the family car. When they couldn't figure out how to start the car, they roused the chauffeur, who, somewhat surprisingly, showed them how. They drove the car around Trenton, one of the boys wearing the chauffeur's jacket, rented a hotel room, and ordered three beers. After consuming the beers, they drove the car to the garage and hopped the late trolley back to Lawrenceville. The housemaster caught them creeping in sometime before dawn.

The escape alone could have caused their expulsion, but worse was to come. Mr. McPherson wrote to Eva that the boys were suspected of having been in Trenton, perhaps in search of entertainments beyond a glass of beer. The trio claimed, however, that they had only gone to visit the brother of one of them at Princeton, which they must have thought would seem a more respectable outing. One boy who was a repeat offender was suspended immediately. Jimmy was spared because his record up to that point was clean.[5]

As the two boys repeated their alibi, however, its cracks began to show. Finally, they admitted they were lying, having imagined that their lie would protect the boy who was already suspended. After the two miscreants told the truth, they were spared suspension but moved into separate houses and given demerits. The headmaster wrote Eva that the whole business had been "a very painful and unpleasant one." He was deeply disappointed to find that his faith in James's trustworthiness had been misplaced.[6]

Eva took it upon herself to argue her son's case. On November 3, 1914, she replied to the headmaster's letter "with a sinking heart." But she forged ahead: Jim (this was the first time she had dropped the more formal "James") had felt the full force of his stepfather's rage and disappointment, especially since the whole episode had been "uncomfortable." (The head-master had mentioned that the boys were cold, riding around late at night in an open car, which seemed to the Stotesburys to make the escapade even more bewildering.) Eva went on to say that she had felt the whole episode as a blow to her pride, and she was very grateful that the head-master had not suspended her son, because she had taken "such delight" in his placement at the school.

She went further, explaining that Jim was risk-loving and easily led into mischief, but she still believed he could become a "good man" under the proper influences. It was not entirely his fault that he had broken the school's rules, given that he had been raised by an invalid father—"a paraplegic"—a very unlikely excuse, since his father had been a well-known mountaineer. She blamed herself for allowing her son to become "her closest companion" but went on to confess that she had taken a good deal of pride in a companionship that was unusually close.

In a postscript, Eva added that Jim had told her he hated to lie to Mr. McPherson, who was such a brick.[7]

A school report listed Jim's "Mental Capacity" as "Good" but his "Studiousness" as "Inferior." He received 155 demerits in his second and last full year at the school. Already in September 1914, James had hoped to leave Lawrenceville before graduating, planning to complete his high school studies at home in Philadelphia.

Mr. McPherson had expressed some doubts about this approach, writing Eva on September 12, 1914, that to prepare for admission to the Wharton School (the college of business and commerce at the University of Penn-sylvania), James would have a very heavy load of schoolwork. In addi-tion to making up all his electives, he would need to pass English, Latin grammar, elementary composition, and algebra, as well as study the New Testament, memorizing verses of James, Galatians, Ephesians, and Peter. Apparently, he was able to fulfill these requirements and still leave be-fore graduation, although he is listed as a member of Lawrenceville's class of 1915.

Eva's wish that her son be treated with special consideration would be granted when the headmaster wrote one of Jimmy's teachers to ask that he be given a light load of schoolwork. In a letter thanking McPherson for his help, Eva admitted that she had been so busy with charitable work all winter that her husband had complained that Home Relief should begin at home. Home Relief, and General Relief, were the names of programs designed to serve destitute adults and children.[8]

Eva could hardly have imagined at this time the brilliant future that was to unfold for her son.

James Cromwell married Doris Duke in a quiet civil ceremony in the library of the Dukes' Seventy-eighth Street house on February 14, 1935. Nanaline had arranged for the marriage license to be issued at home rather than at New York's Municipal Building after Doris's doctor announced that he had been treating Doris for an unidentified nervous condition and that exposure to publicity might be dangerous. Whether Nanaline was being overprotective or the request reflected Doris's fear of public exposure, the maneuver worked. Only ten family friends and a few journalists were admitted to the ceremony. One of the journalists who had been present, Ralph Renaud, reported that the ceremony took place in front of a blazing fire and that the word "obey" had been cut out of the service.

Renaud went on to describe the lilies and orchids from Doris's greenhouses at Duke Farms that adorned the rooms—the first mention of the orchids that later became one of Doris's passions. According to *The New York Times*, Doris's wedding dress was a simple blue crepe.

Renaud wrote that Doris was as beautiful as a Greek statue, but very shy. Although she had been raised to have simple tastes, myths had already grown up around her. Renaud mentioned tabloid accounts of a solid-gold breakfast set and bathwater tinted to match her moods. Neither tale was true. The reporter also wrote that she was said to have worn a red bathing suit in Miami the previous winter. It had been described as an extremely provocative style that revealed her slender body.[9]

The brief ceremony was followed by a toast to the bride. After this formality, the bride and groom sped away to the ocean liner that would carry them to Monte Carlo on the first leg of their honeymoon. A news photo shows them running down the pier, arm in arm, smiling broadly.

The wedding sounds fairly stark in spite of the flowers and the roaring fire. Clearly, Doris, and perhaps Nanaline, who had for years objected to

Jimmy, wanted the whole thing over and done with as quickly as possible. Yet one of the very few unposed photographs of the occasion shows the couple with Nanaline, who gazes adoringly at her new son-in-law.

In a press photo shot shortly after the wedding on the deck of the Italian liner, the *Conte di Savoia*, a smiling Doris is wearing a dark suit, tailored in the extreme, with a small, close hat. As Elsa Maxwell might have predicted, Jimmy looked far more dashing, a white carnation in his buttonhole.

After eight days at sea, the ship's first stop was Monte Carlo. There the newlyweds would have enjoyed standard honeymoon fare: the beach, the casino, the satin sheets on the luxe hotel bed. On February 25, the couple boarded again and steamed toward Cairo and Petra. Their itinerary from February 27 to March 14 was duly noted in the local newspapers under "Richest Woman Visits" headlines. Jimmy carefully pasted the news stories into two large scrapbooks.[10]

From the beginning, Jimmy relished his status as the man who had married the richest woman in the world. A few of the news stories mistakenly credited Jimmy with the fortune, perhaps because reporters were unable to imagine that a woman in her early twenties could actually control so much money. During the trip, Doris paid bills with letters of credit from her New York bank, although Jimmy would have handed out the tips.

Here begins the painful confusion that often besets women who have more money than their husbands. The first impulse, born of love and gratitude, is to pretend that it is all his. She sets up bank accounts or gives him cash to pay the bills. (This was long before credit cards.) Then, as his sense of entitlement inevitably grows (for she has given him license to grow it), her generous impulse may fade as she realizes that he is taking over not only her income but also the status and power that go with it. There is really no such thing, in this scenario, as sharing, because, in terms of money, he has nothing to share.

Jimmy knew how to play the part of the husband of the richest woman in the world. He was always perfectly dressed, hovering protectively over Doris. In snapshots from their honeymoon, she wears her ambiguous cat-like smile.

It was inevitable, given her social status, that Doris would meet local royalty. In India, Princess Mdivani (Barbara Hutton) was waiting for the couple at Mena House with Princess Aga Khan. Doris may have noted certain similarities in her and Barbara's complicated histories. But Barbara, at four years old, had discovered her mother's dead body after she committed suicide, a family tragedy from which Doris was spared.

Barbara seems to have been exploited by at least some of her seven husbands. The death of Barbara's only child in a plane crash further darkened her life. Later attempts to link the two beautiful blond heiresses would spawn tales of catfights and parallel tragedies, but because of the way they decided to use their money, the two women would prove far more different than they were similar.[11]

As Doris and Jimmy plunged on through their itinerary, they made an unexpected stop to visit Mahatma Gandhi in his retreat at Wardha. Gandhi, however, was not eager to be met by yet another rich American couple. After traveling 470 miles by train from Bombay, Jimmy and Doris were left to cool their heels for two days. Finally, a United Press correspondent went with the couple to the All India Village Industries Association, where Gandhi granted them a brief audience with journalists present. Predictably, the following day's headline read "Richest Woman in the World Meets Holy Man."

Doris was genuinely interested in the extreme simplicity of Gandhi's way of life—the tent, the meager food, the whirring spinning wheel, and his message of the necessity of undertaking menial work. Indeed, her support of village craftsmen in the tile work for Shangri La, her house on Oahu, may have found its first inspiration at Wardha. The *Chicago Tribune* reported that Doris hardly said a word to the holy man. Instead, Jimmy dominated the conversation, with prognostications about the coming age of the machine. The reporter made much of Jimmy's handsome, well-developed body while describing his enthusiasm for the way machines were soon to transform the world, surely a message at odds with Gandhi's worldview. Later Doris told the reporter that she had felt as awed as she would have been in the presence of any of the great spiritual leaders, including Christ, the Buddha, and Muhammad.[12]

After visiting Gandhi, the couple went to Agra, and Jimmy wrote that Doris had been smitten by the flower designs, made with semiprecious stones, that they had both just seen at the Taj Mahal. On the spot, Doris commissioned local artisans to create tiles for a sumptuous bedroom-and-bathroom suite, copying details from the Taj, originally intended for Jimmy's cottage, which was situated next to El Mirasol in Palm Beach. Carved marble doorways, door and window screens, and floor and wall panels inset with delicate, bejeweled flowers re-created the patterns and motifs typical of Islamic art. The distinguished British architectural firm C. G. and F. B. Blomfield oversaw the plans as Doris and Jimmy hurried on through India, lunching with British colonial authorities and visiting historic sites.

Ptomaine poisoning in Agra—Doris would say she loved India but preferred American food—did not deter the couple from starting down the Ganges and visiting Kashmir. In early April, Doris was laid low by a troublesome wisdom tooth. She recovered in time to go over Blomfield's first drawings and estimates for the renovation of Jimmy's cottage, with the addition of her own Taj-inspired bedroom and bath. Eva sent along critiques of the architect's drawings, commenting that her new daughter-in-law wished to be a "lovely hermit" in Florida.

By May 1, Doris and Jimmy were in Darjeeling, and flew a few days later from Calcutta to Bangkok and then on to Rangoon. In Singapore in late May, there were more discussions of designs and estimates. Meanwhile, Eva took charge, commissioning Maurice Fatio, the Swiss-trained architect of estates in Palm Beach and Long Island. Calling him the only "capable" architect, Eva asked him to submit new drawings to replace those prepared by Blomfield. The cottage was to be expanded into a full-time residence, and Doris could hardly protest. She was in the hospital in Darjeeling at the time, recovering from what Jimmy called a "curettement,"[13] and what might well have been an abortion.

In June, the couple cruised around the Malay Peninsula on a yacht. From mid-July to mid-August, they rushed through Peking, Shanghai, Manila, and Tokyo. Jimmy had tried to arrange a few days of rest in a cooler climate, but that would have thrown off their Japanese itinerary, and so they plowed on in the greatest luxury the times allowed, nevertheless waylaid at various points by fatigue and illness.

In August 1935, they boarded the SS *Tatsuta Maru* for Honolulu, the last stop on what would be their nine-month itinerary. Luscious, overgrown, exotic, not yet an American state but a territory, the islands loomed in the Pacific. Disembarking at Pearl Harbor, Doris would have heard on the pier the soft, sliding syllables of the musical Hawaiian language. But everyone she needed to deal with would speak English, beginning with the functionaries at Bishop Bank. Doris and Jimmy settled into the big pink palace hotel, the Royal Hawaiian, at Waikiki, on the island of Oahu. They planned to stay two weeks before heading home in November to Palm Beach.

Through a combination of uneasiness with her mother-in-law's interference, apprehension about the inescapable social whirl at Palm Beach, and the irritation produced by nine months of living with Jimmy and his well-formed concept of the life they would lead as a married couple of extraordinary means, Doris reached a major decision, one that would rock the foundations of her marriage. In the spring of 1935, she decided to find land and build a house in Hawaii. On that land, the Taj Mahal–inspired wing, now called the Mughul Suite, would be incorporated into a new house, replacing earlier plans for Palm Beach. Eva must have been bitterly disappointed and perhaps a little annoyed: the change meant she would see less of her darling son.

Staying at the Royal Hawaiian while the plans for her house materialized, Doris made friends with the so-called Beach Boys, Hawaiian men who introduced the guests to surfing and outrigger-canoe racing. There, at the hotel and at the Outrigger Club, which she would later help finance, Doris met the band of five handsome brothers, the Kahanamokus, who would work to persuade her to extend her stay in Hawaii from two weeks to three months.

Jimmy soon returned to the mainland to work on another book, but Doris stayed on in Hawaii to search for the site on which to build her house and to install the Mughul Suite when it arrived from India. After weeks of roaming the island with Sam Kahanamoku, she discovered a craggy, wind-blasted promontory over the Pacific, near Diamond Head. When Sam announced the price—$100,000 for 4.1 acres of oceanfront— Jimmy vowed he would not pay another penny of Doris's money.[14] Sam received a 5 percent finder's fee.

Sam quickly became Doris's chosen companion. Later, when he traveled with her to the mainland, she confronted the fact that only her status as an heiress allowed him to stay in the same hotels and visit the

same nightclubs as she did. But nothing she could say or do would protect him from stares and sneers. On the mainland, native Hawaiians were
seen as "Negroes."

Sam's older brother Duke faced the same discrimination. In 1911,
when he broke the freestyle swimming record in the Amateur Athletic
Union in Hawaii, the judges claimed that the floats marking the course
had been moved closer together, and they refused to give Duke the medal.
But in 1920, in Belgium, Duke won two Olympic gold medals, for the
100-meter freestyle and the 200-meter relay, becoming the first Hawaiian
to do so. After retiring from competitive swimming, he supported himself by working at a gas station.[15]

Doris was soon absorbed in plans for her new house, the design of
which was influenced by the architecture she had recently seen in India.
Because of many changes to the plans, it would take 250 workers five
years to build the house, initially measuring about 14,000 square feet.
The design specified only one guest room, which aligned with Doris's notion of the house as her refuge rather than a site for massive entertaining.
Her desire to avoid all of that was one reason she had quit Palm Beach.

Still, Jimmy insisted on a guest suite, to be located in a separate struc-
ture, the Playhouse, which was across from the main house and separated
from it by the swimming pool. At that distance, Jimmy wrote, guests
would not "get into our hair."

Initially, Doris named her house Hale Kapu, meaning Forbidden
House. But by June 1938, when Jimmy wrote to his banker friend Bill
Cross, he referred to the house as Shangri La—certainly a more welcom-
ing name, but one with no connection to Hawaiian language or tradition.
Doris had named it for the mythical valley in the enormously popular
1937 film *Lost Horizon*, starring Jane Wyatt and Ronald Colman. Doris
had loved movies ever since childhood and would have seen this one as
soon as it appeared in the Honolulu cinema. Based on the bestselling
1933 novel by James Hilton, it featured a place of beauty and harmony
where people did not grow old.

In the movie's first shot, the Tibetan mission's façade previewed the
plain white concrete façade Doris would choose for her Shangri La. The
columns and stairs and pierced jali screens also appear at Doris's Hawaiian house, as well as the large pool and fountains. More important than

these details, however, was the film's message, that human beings can only find inner peace and happiness in a complete retreat from the world. The narrator intones at the start of the movie, "In this time of war and rumor of war, haven't you dreamed of a place of tranquillity? This place is called Shangri La." In renaming her house, Doris may have believed, at least briefly, that she would find there the perfect peace represented by the High Lama, a venerated spiritual master who advocated peace.

Today, the linked rooms of Shangri La gleam dimly, lighted by far-away chandeliers and sconces. The slightly stale smell of a house the owner has not lived in for more than two decades reminds one of forgotten closets with their dead sachets.

Swathed in protective coverings, Doris's bedroom and bathroom were almost completely hidden as they underwent restoration. The marble panels, designed and carved in India and inlaid with semiprecious stones, were visible only here and there, where a bright bit of color leapt out: a bud or leaf at the top of a tendril, the design beautifully simplified from what Doris had seen at the Taj Mahal. Silvery dolphin-shaped faucets and her mother's sunken marble tub, transported to Shangri La after Nanaline's death in April 1962, create the impression of a watery grotto. Doris hid her toilet at the back of her clothes closet, with a wall safe installed above it.

Shangri La would become, in time, the beautiful vessel for Doris's collection of Islamic art, ultimately one of the great collections in the world. (In 2014, select objects traveled to museums all over the United States.) Although several experts advised Doris as she assembled the magnificent tiles, ceramic vases, and textiles that would adorn Shangri La, their influence was minimal. She knew, from the beginning, what she wanted, based not on deep study but on a mysterious and intuitive sense of the beautiful. Creation of beauty, Doris believed, was the goal of her life.

An unattributed snapshot of Doris, her back to the camera, shows her studying a row of seemingly identical mother-of-pearl-inlaid bureaus in the courtyard of the antiquities dealers Asfar and Sarkis in Damascus in 1939. Would-be advisers stand at a distance as she makes her choice. On the receipt for her purchase of three of the bureaus, Sarkis wrote, "Only forty-three dollars!"[16]

The remoteness of Islamic art, in her eyes, from her own heritage may

explain her lifelong attraction to it. Islamic art lay far beyond the con-
fines of her upbringing and the conventional aesthetic of her family and
peers. In the case of the bureaus she acquired, although they were familiar items in the houses of her childhood, the exotic inlay of those she was
assessing in Damascus transcended the familiar.

Doris did not subscribe to the twentieth-century view of the Islamic
world as a monoculture. Her collection exhibits a great variety of styles,
from the seventh century to the twentieth, from South and Central Asia,
Europe, the Near and Middle East, and North Africa. She especially favored ceramics, which make up a substantial portion of her collection at
Shangri La.

In her Shangri La living room, plates, basins, and jugs in niches are
not glassed in, as they would be in other valuable collections, but are vulnerable to touch. Over the fireplace, the medieval shield and lances from
her father's collection, which should seem out of place on this tropical
island, join in the aesthetic dance.

In the early 1960s, Doris turned her Hawaiian-themed dining room
into a version of an Islamic tent. Egyptian and Indian wall hangings
blaze, and the ornate crystal chandelier, rather than looking as though it
belongs in a Paris ballroom, seems perfectly placed. In the Baby Turkish
Room (as Doris named it), Syrian-style niches combine painted wood,
marble, and ceramics that swirl together. Mosaic panels remind one of
the skirts of hula dancers. A throng of warriors, feasters, and dancers—
one of them cavorting upside down—turn the tile Playhouse fireplace
surround into a circus of brilliant color and energy. In Doris's life, as
in her collection, dynamism ruled; there was no room for stasis, for the
status quo. Everything was evaluated by her incredible eye. Earlier, at
Duke Farms, she had astonished a contractor by observing that one of the
walls he was building was two degrees out of plumb; he didn't believe her
until he measured it. At Shangri La, surrounded by a horde of workers,
advisers, contractors, and architects, Doris was, perhaps for the first time
in her life, firmly in control.

Doris left behind tape recordings of the music she played and sang at
Shangri La. These featured the Hawaiian musicians who were becoming
her close friends. The recordings are scratchy, the words hard to hear,
but the ambience is unmistakable: romantic Hawaii, her land of dreams.

After Jimmy left Hawaii in what would prove to be the first step in their ultimate separation, these songs were perhaps Doris's way of exploring her feelings. On one tape, she tells her guests, "I just had to play this number for you." She then launches into "He's the Healer of Broken Hearts" in her frail, silvery soprano, accompanied by her own piano playing and Sam Kahanamoku and one of his brothers on ukulele and guitar. The song ends with the promise that broken hearts would be healed by Jesus of Galilee.

After other voices sing traditional Hawaiian songs, Doris, now closer to the microphone, belts out "It Had to Be You," her piano thumping away in the background. The tape ends with Doris's wavering giggle and her childlike voice, saying, "Don't play it back, it's so flat. It's terrible."[17] Then, sounding more confident, she whistles another tune, though whistling was slightly transgressive for a woman of her time. Perhaps she heard her Southern mother comment, "A whistling woman and a crowing hen never come to any good end."

14 Being called the "Richest Woman in the World" meant there would always be a procession of money seekers— letter writers, doorbell ringers, and strangers—accosting Doris. Early on, she could ignore them; she had only pocket money, which her mother doled out in modest amounts. Then, on November 22, 1933, Doris turned twenty-one, and her trust disbursed $10 million, the first installment on her inheritance. That same month, she established her first foundation, Independent Aid, with an initial personal gift of $125,000. This was the first of the some twenty charitable organizations she would create during her lifetime.

Independent Aid financed the causes in which Doris was personally interested: the welfare of women and children, education, mental health, and family planning. Grants were also given to individuals for education or to relieve financial difficulties. In 1933 alone, the foundation gave away $2.6 million to, among other entities, New York City's Center for Self-Supporting Women and Students, Planned Parenthood, the Musicians Emergency Fund, and Duke University.

Now Doris began to search for a colleague who could help her sort out and fend off the endless requests for funds as well as organize Independent Aid. This is when she found Marian Paschal. Marian was born in Chicago on January 5, 1902. Doris may have first encountered her when she was working for a New York furrier, and they soon became close friends. This stout, black-haired woman, who had worked all her adult life and knew something about the complexities of business and the difficulties of social work, offered a counterweight to Doris's inexperience and untested idealism. Marian was also capable of the kind of devotion Doris had experienced with Jenny Renaud. Recognizing her merits, Doris rapidly promoted her, putting her in charge of Independent Aid.[1]

As their relationship grew more intimate, Doris persuaded Marian to sign a curious document laying out a legal plan for Marian, called "dear to the party of the first part," to become the beneficiary of a trust of $150,000 Doris planned to set up for her, but only if she could, within three years, reduce her weight to 150 pounds. The document further stated that the weight reduction was essential because Marian was now so heavy that she was jeopardizing her health. Marian never achieved the weight loss or the financial reward Doris was offering. Her failure to do so may have contributed to her early death, at the age of forty-four, in 1946.

Marian didn't hesitate to give Doris her opinion, even when it seemed it might not be welcome. She warned Doris not to let any man bulldoze her into marriage or anything else, reminding her that she had "limitless power" and should use it for her own benefit and for that of other people. She advised Doris that she should make it her goal in life to be not just beautiful but wise.

The early giving of women philanthropists—who would not at that point identify themselves as such—was often inspired by a misplaced sense of responsibility for the problems of friends. Small grants were given to ameliorate the effects of divorce and widowhood, with little recognition of the social issues these problems represented. In this kind of giving, each case is individual, disassociated from the larger injustices embedded in the culture. The impoverished divorcee is seen as the victim not of the divorce laws but of love gone wrong. The suddenly poor widow is viewed as the victim not of patriarchal practices governing inheritance but of personal tragedy.

Independent Aid was based on this familiar model, often called, de-
risively, flannel-petticoat charity. The term appeared in 1869, when some
New York ladies, members of the Ethnological Society, were disturbed by
accounts of the "Red Indians of New Mexico" who wore only paint and
feathers, or nothing at all. They decided to make red flannel petticoats
for these Indians, and thousands were stitched up and sent out west, to
the bewilderment of the Apaches, Arapahos, and Pueblos who received
them. After consultation among the elders, the tribes cut the petticoats
into strips and braided them into the manes and tails of their horses.

Doris's first efforts at philanthropy can be seen as equally well inten-
tioned and equally limited in effectiveness. Once the money Independent
Aid granted had been spent by the recipients, the problems remained.
For example, when Independent Aid tried to help a woman with two
children who had been deserted by their father, Doris was probably unaware of the legal difficulties abandoned wives faced in seeking alimony
or child support.

In the case of divorce, confusion regarding its causes and consequences had riled the United States since colonial times, leading to laws
that differed from state to state and created considerable hardship for
people seeking legal termination of their marriages. The 1906 Conference on Uniform Divorce Laws, although attended by representatives from
forty-two states and territories—and a minority of women—fell apart when
some states refused to follow its recommendations. It would be another
eighty-six years before the passage of the Uniform Interstate Family Support Act in 1992, which allowed for partial acceptance of the concept
of no-fault divorce.[2] All this lay outside of Doris and Marian's realm of
knowledge as they tried to help friends suddenly plunged by divorce into
severe economic need.

As for widows, Alice Paul's Equal Rights Amendment, which she wrote
in 1921, extended legal rights to them, including rights of inheritance.
Had it passed, no widow would have seen her dead husband's estate go in
its entirety to the children. Doris might have heard of Alice Paul, but in
her world, an unflattering light would have been shed upon this audacious
and remarkable woman. Paul's Equal Rights Amendment—"Equality of
rights under the law shall not be denied or abridged by the United States
or by any state on account of sex"—was introduced in every congressional

session after 1922. In 1972, it was finally passed by both houses and sent to the states for ratification, but it failed to achieve sufficient support, approved by only thirty-five states of the thirty-eight required—and died once again. Proposed in every Congress since, it has never been passed.[3]

Had Doris known of the effect that this amendment, if passed, would have had on the women Independent Aid tried to help, she might have been inspired to support it, as did Alva Vanderbilt Belmont. But Doris was still too young, at twenty-one, to separate herself from the prejudices of her mother's generation. Nanaline's generation, and many before it, endorsed private giving to relieve individual suffering but shied away from trying to change social institutions. That Independent Aid funded women in distress reflected Doris's empathy. Understanding of social causes would come later.

In 1934, for a salary of $6,000 a year, Doris named Marian Secretary (capital intended) of Independent Aid, in charge of "Contributions for Religious, Charitable and Philanthropic Purposes," a post she held until her death in 1946.[4] The organization had four directors: Doris; George C. Allen, dean of Duke's medical school; Duke University president Wilburt C. Davison; and Marian. The same group, with the addition of Stuart L. Hawkins as treasurer pro tem, served as the foundation's board.

According to a 1963 interview with Mary Duke Biddle Trent Semans, Doris's first cousin once removed, Dr. Davison enjoyed a special rapport with Doris, because he treated her with respect, always following up on money she gave with a report on how it was being spent. Dr. Davison was less conventional than the other men on the board, and he was not afraid to voice his opinions. Doris found his honesty refreshing, according to Mrs. Semans. Davison was Doris's likeliest ally on the Duke Endowment board, where Doris served as soon as she came of age.[5]

Although she attended Duke Endowment board meetings infrequently, because of her travels, Doris kept close watch over Independent Aid. One of its first grants went to Anna O'Grady, widow of a drowned baggage-handler. Consuelo, widow of the pilot Antoine de Saint-Exupéry, who wrote *The Little Prince*, had sued her husband's publishers for a share of his royalties; she also received help from Independent Aid. Edith Steckel, whose nephew was being treated at the Payne Whitney Clinic, was given a grant to help pay for his treatment. The Baroness von Klenner received one, but was removed from the Independent Aid list of those in need after Marian managed to sublet the baroness's Fifth Avenue apartment so that she could move to the country and, presumably, live more cheaply.[6]

Through a private grant from Doris, Independent Aid was able to take over the title to a plot in North Carolina's Woodlawn Cemetery, its purpose never revealed. The ruse was concocted to conceal Doris's name, thereby avoiding "some unpleasantness when the title is taken over," according to an unsigned letter to Marian. This is certainly not the first or the last time that a private foundation has been used to shield its founder from "unpleasantness." Such misuse of the foundation's funds for private purchases would cause future difficulties with the IRS.

The casual nature of grant giving is shown in Marian's letter to the Independent Aid lawyer Lee Baldwin in January 1937, recommending a loan to a promising young man proposed by a Mr. Hyde, as well as $300 to a Dr. Marion Kenworthy, who wanted to pay school tuition for a girl she knew. A letter stating, "I approve the above amounts," and signed "Doris," accompanied the requests. Her signature was now highly individual, a large, flowing "D" trailed at intervals by small printed letters.[7]

By 1935, Lee Baldwin had replaced Stuart Hawkins as treasurer pro tem and was issuing the checks. That year, a thank-you letter addressed to him from Mrs. Howard Paschal indicates that Marian's mother was involved with Independent Aid, too, picking up rent and telephone bills at the office, Room 2501 at 535 Fifth Avenue.

An earlier generation of philanthropists was setting the standard for responsible giving. J. P. Morgan, who had died in 1913, had given generously to hospitals and international aid. At his death, he left $80 million to his son, J. P. Morgan Jr., who triggered questions about tax law when he paid no taxes of any kind in 1931 and 1932. At risk was the tax-exemption status afforded not-for-profit foundations and charitable donations. Tax-exempt status was essential to the Morgan Library, opened to the public in 1920 and endowed by both father and son. In 1913, John D. Rockefeller donated $50 million to establish what would become, in 1920, the Rockefeller Foundation. Its mission was "to promote the well-being of mankind throughout the world." Like the Morgans and the Rockefellers, Doris moved from personal gifts to individuals to more organized giving through foundations.

Independent Aid was not granted charitable status and thus tax exemption until December 1937, and its failure to forward delinquent capital-stock tax returns in 1935 and 1936 brought a reprimand from the Internal Revenue Service and a request for this information within five days.

By 1941, Independent Aid was beginning to make the transition toward funding charitable institutions. This may reflect Marian's influence or the board's, or simply the inevitable shift in the world of philanthropy toward increasing impact. This shift was also a response to problems with the Treasury Department.

A 1945 inquiry from the Treasury Department addressed arrears of occupancy tax for 1942, 1943, and 1944 for its offices, now located at 595–599 Madison Avenue. Marian responded that the offices were not used for "gainful purposes" and therefore should be exempt from taxation and penalty for noncompliance. This seemed to end the problem. However, a certain informality and even disorganization continued, which was typical of first endeavors by young philanthropists.

In January 1941, Independent Aid granted $6,500 to the American Friends Service Committee, the same amount to the Center for Self-Supporting Women, an unspecified sum to the Child Placing and Adoption Committee—one of Marian's chief concerns—another, unspecified amount to a Judge Hill of the Manhattan Domestic Relations Court, as well as $3,000 to the Asborne Committee, which was conducting research on juvenile delinquency in the South. The Asborne grant was a result of Lee Baldwin's having had lunch with the director—"a grand chap," according to Marian.[8] Even with gifts to institutions, the chemistry of the personalities involved was crucial.

Marian knew the foundation would likely change its direction as Doris's views matured. She wrote Lee Baldwin in 1940 that probably there would be many changes over the years, though she hoped the changes would not be extreme. For example, Philip Kerr, eleventh Marquess of Lothian, a British politician and newspaper owner, was appointed ambassador to the United States in 1939. He told a group of reporters that Britain was bankrupt and would require large infusions of U.S. aid to fight Germany. Marian, who had reservations about this unsolicited grant, wrote to Baldwin: "We are trying to divert these funds to research and preferably to American institutions."[9]

But a check was written to Lord Lothian, showing how closely Doris was aligned at this early point in her life with the political views of her class. In 1939, many upper-class Americans who traced their ancestry to real or imagined British forebears believed that U.S. support for Britain was essential if Nazi Germany was to be defeated. They were eager to find ways around U.S. neutrality.

On October 10, 1940, in a letter addressed to Lord Lothian at the British embassy in Washington, Doris laid out her reasons for the gift. She wrote that for some time she had been looking for a way to help the British that "would at the same time, be of real benefit to my own country." She had first thought of assisting a plan to evacuate children from London to escape the Blitz, but wrote, "Now that this has been abandoned I am contemplating alternative action." It was abandoned after Congress defeated the Wagner-Rogers Bill in 1939, which had been designed to bring in refugee children with money already raised from private citizens, including Doris. She had previously donated $250,000 to bring British children to the United States, including Alec Cunningham-Reid's two sons.

She believed that, in order to· "maintain her position and defeat the enemy," Britain would need to depend on "munitions and war material from this country as well as Canada"—which were at that point illegal because of U.S. neutrality. The solution she proposed was for the United States to take as many British imports as possible in exchange for war material. This would be "of value in paving the way for the post-war collaboration which must be an essential part of the New World Order."

The New World Order was a conspiracy theory embodying the notion of a secret elite governing the world. Doris, imbued from birth with the idea of her class's superiority, might well have believed that such a system would be the best possible outcome of the conflict. She hoped to encourage interest in British imports and to fund "a permanent body which should devote itself to the formulation and execution of the necessary measures to ensure this." She pledged to Lord Lothian "to make an offer of financial support to this cause which will, I hope, meet with your approval."

Perhaps thanks to Marian's insistence, she added in the same letter that research would be needed before her foundation could fund such a project for the long term. In the meantime, "I should like to ask whether you would accept, on behalf of the British Government, a gift of $50,000 to be devoted to such war purposes as your Government may think best fitted." She added that the gift carried no conditions, although she would be grateful if the money could be devoted to the "campaign as I have indicated." The check, made out to the "British Ambassador" (unnamed), was signed by Marian Paschal and marked "special"—the last word handwritten and also typed.[10]

Since the legality of this check is questionable—a gift to an individual to purchase armaments forbidden by the 1935 Neutrality Act—it shows Doris's willingness to bend the rules in pursuit of an outcome she viewed as crucial.

To further these aims, Doris established, in 1940, her second foundation, the British-American Trust Fund, which morphed into the Doris Duke Fund. Much later, in 1979, the fund's original aims were questioned in a letter to Doris from G. Booth, director of the British Trade Development Office in New York. Apparently, the terms of the 1940 trust were so vague that Booth was writing to ensure that its funds were being spent as Doris wished.

He explained that interest income from the fund, $4,000 annually, had been used to train "Commercial Officers" all over the United States. Doris's then secretary, Elizabeth McConville, replied on Duke Farms stationery that Doris was quite satisfied with the manner in which the trust had been handling the money.[11]

Marian, who was acutely aware that Doris was constantly giving gifts, sometimes made small presents to her as gestures of affection. One of Doris's rare letters ends, "Thanks loads for the little blue slippers. They're awfully cute."[12]

But by late 1945, something had gone awry between Marian and Doris. Perhaps Doris was now taking increasing control of Independent

Aid and found Marian's advice an irritant. Or perhaps it was her weight. In a home movie, Marian sits stolidly in a black dress in the stern of a small boat Jimmy is rowing. When it docks, he leaps out and gallantly offers her a hand. Spurning his hand, Marian hoists herself out of the boat and then, in a touching attempt to prove her sprightliness, lumbers up the hill. In Doris's new life in Hawaii, Marian was an awkward leftover.

When Marian died tragically young, Doris's response was remarkably chilly. Writing from Rome to Independent Aid's treasurer, Stuart Hawkins, on September 6, 1946, Doris remarked that Marian's death must have created a lot of practical confusion in the office—ends that needed to be tied up, details to take care of. She directed that the fund's present commitments—some of which Marian had overseen—be honored at least until Doris came back from Italy. After inquiring about Marian's apartment and furniture and asking if she had left a will, Doris reminded Hawkins that the piano in the apartment belonged to Doris herself, and her name was on the lease. Marian was buried at Forest Lawn Memorial Park in Glendale, California.

On September 12, 1946, the day of Marian's funeral, Hans Staudinger wrote Doris from the Institute of World Affairs, headquartered in Geneva, Switzerland, that he needed to speak to her as Marian's closest friend. Staudinger reminded Doris that Marian had known how to create an atmosphere of "comfort and security," perhaps thinking that this would have provided Doris with a rare bit of ease. During her last years, Staudinger went on, Marian always spoke of Doris and confided that she had spent her best hours with the woman she called her "pet." He also mentioned that Doris had caused her beloved companion "deep worries." Summing up the woman he had known well, Staudinger commented on Marian's "explosive power," expressed in her work running Doris's foundation. Perhaps this was the very thing that eventually caused Doris to withdraw.

Finally, he apologized for failing to arrange a meeting between Marian and Doris the last time Doris was in New York, explaining that, toward the end, Marian had been afraid that her two friends would "conspire together" to have her taken to a hospital. She wanted to die in her own bed, which she in fact did.[13]

Doris's detachment contrasts sharply with the tone of her letter to

Marian a few months earlier. On May 7, 1945, Doris wrote "Marian dearest," enclosing letters for "the kids"—Alec Cunningham-Reid's sons, Noel and Mike.[14] In response, Marian wrote to Doris of the boys' recent visit to Duke Farms. They had brought three friends, and some discussion followed about drinking. Marian decreed that they must not exceed one daiquiri before dinner and one glass of red wine with the meal.

Mike called Marian often from school, writing her at one point that a cable from Doris had delighted him.[15] Marian may have garnered a similar joy from Doris's infrequent letters, but in the end, silence reigned, and the devoted friend was consigned to oblivion.

Doris never found another mentor to help her in the development of her philanthropy.

 Although Nanaline Holt Duke was left comfortably off when her first husband died, she never made philanthropy a priority. She did become somewhat involved in the early days of Independent Aid.[1] In 1920, she also served on the Board of Trustees of the Society of New York Hospital. She was the only woman on the board of the Duke Endowment until Doris was appointed in 1933.[2]

But, given the period, Nanaline may never have believed her share of Buck Duke's money was actually hers. She used it for clothes, but this was expected of the wife and later the widow of a rich man. To establish and fund a foundation, dealing with all the financial issues involved and deciding on its aims, may have seemed to this conventional Southern woman a form of hubris.

If Doris had succumbed to the same concern, she would have been disabled in her giving; if she had had children, she might have felt that she needed to preserve her wealth to pass on to the next generation. Yet inheriting money, as in the case of her half brother, Walker Inman, raises a difficult question: Was he blessed or cursed by the money he received from his family? Certainly, he resisted any attempt to push him into work. In 1947, he was invited to join the board of the Duke Endowment. In 1945, he wrote to Doris, whom he addressed as "Sis," that he had tried all his life to avoid work, but that now he couldn't refuse the trustees' invitation. He explained that he did not wish to commit himself to another business— taking care of Duke Farms during Doris's absence was job enough for him.[3] The focus and self-discipline required of one who must make money, and the evident rewards, are likely to evade those few who can avoid the necessity of submitting to routine, demands, and goals.

On June 7, 1945, in another letter to Doris, then in Rome, Walker enthused over his purchase of an old airplane. He planned to refurbish it, probably in the hopes that Doris, who was in the market for a private plane, would buy it.[4] But the plane Doris later bought was the Boeing 737-300 she used to transport her camels between Newport and Duke Farms.

Walker's tenure on the Duke Endowment board was relatively brief: he resigned in 1953, and Doris suggested that Kenneth Crawford Towe, an executive of the American Cyanamid Company, replace him, even though she had met Towe only at public events.

Once again, Doris's attitude toward the endowment and Independent Aid was, to say the least, informal. She chose friends or acquaintances, qualified or not, for positions of responsibility, perhaps with the notion that she could influence them more than she could better-qualified strangers.

Watson Smith Rankin, a member of the Duke Endowment board, re- membered in a 1963 interview that Doris, like her father, could speak decisively and did not hesitate to express her opinion at board meetings. Rankin recalled that, at one point, she was very concerned about the fate of forty thousand indigent children in North Carolina who were not in federal- or state-financed orphanages but were cared for in an ad hoc fash- ion by county welfare offices.[5] Marian Paschal, with her background in social work, had perhaps alerted Doris to the plight of these children. Grants for their care became one of the first priorities of the Duke Endowment.

The endowment proposed to "nurture children, promote health, ed- ucate minds and enrich spirits." It later provided funds for community hospitals in North Carolina, leading in 1931 to the opening of Duke's medical school. When her father signed the indenture papers for his endowment, Doris had been sitting on his knee.

Even as a child, Doris had clearly absorbed Buck's commitment to the stewardship of wealth, but she spread her gifts much more widely than he had. In 1933, she donated $100,000 to the First Methodist Church in Charlotte, perhaps to honor her father, but this was her last gift to that or any other recognized church.

From December 1933 on, Doris made personal gifts ranging from $1,000 to $10,000 to a broad range of charities, including the Citizens Family Welfare Committee, the Crusade for Children, and the Salvation Army, as well as organizations that sought to prevent blindness or improve the circumstances of the poor. These were anodyne gifts, reflecting no particular philosophy, made reactively as pleas for money poured in. If this had been the sum of Doris Duke's philanthropy, there would be almost nothing to say about it except that it reflects the standard giving of a woman of wealth of her period. But as she continued to develop as a philanthropist, her gifts began to reveal a less conventional and more individual point of view.

Some of Doris's philanthropy was institutional or became institutional, as in her creation of the Newport Preservation Society, which continues to support and expand her vision. Her more interesting and unusual giving was personal, largely to women of great talent, some of them African American. These gifts were affected by Doris's changing relationships with the recipients, and seldom continued after her death.

Katherine Dunham (1909–2006) was a beautiful African American dancer and choreographer whose skin was so light that she could have "passed"; whether she ever considered this possibility seems unlikely, since she was from childhood comfortable with her identity as a woman of color. Possibly, it was her radiant self-acceptance that first attracted Doris.

Born in Chicago, Katherine was sustained by her love for her family, especially her brother Albert—a love that Katherine later believed was incestuous, and that Albert finally rejected with seeming cruelty. Katherine's mother died when she was a small child. As an adult, she remembered her last moments with her mother as "so full of contentment" as she sat on her lap, sipping milk.

She studied anthropology at the University of Chicago, earning a Bachelor of Philosophy degree in 1936, and began her training in modern dance, with a focus on the dances of the Caribbean. Later, she formed her own company and toured the United States and Europe, introducing the rhythms and movements of African dance to her audiences.[6]

In vivid contrast to Doris, Katherine was able to bring into consciousness, and to express, her anguish at being born female. In one of her essays published in *A Touch of Innocence*, "The Rabbit Hunt," written in the third person, she remembered waiting for her father and her brother in a frozen field while they hunted rabbits. She could not move without "chafing her already raw thighs, where the hated gray-flannel long underwear hung sodden with urine." Had she squatted behind a tree like a girl, her father would have thought her weak and would never have taken her hunting again.

Katherine could bear this revelation because, as the daughter of a mixed-race marriage, she already faced a hard road.[7] In 1944, she danced in Louisville, Kentucky, where one third of the audience was black and restricted to the balcony. After her performance, she pointed out that people who shared her skin color were fighting and dying in Europe but were not allowed to sit with the white audience. Therefore, she continued, it would be impossible for her to return.[8]

At the beginning of her career, in 1935–36, Katherine had earned a fellowship from the Julius Rosenwald Fund, which allowed her to travel to observe dance in Haiti, Jamaica, Martinique, and Trinidad, studying native dances as both dancer and anthropologist. Later, she recalled that her curiosity had carried her into uncomfortable situations. In Haiti, in order to attend a Vodun ceremony, she was taken to a hut occupied by an enormous snake coiled in the rafters. She spent the night beneath the watchful serpent.[9]

Accustomed to luxury, Doris would never have subjected herself to sleeping in a hut under a giant snake. Nor could she have imagined being initiated into Vodun with a ceremony involving the sacrifice of a white rooster—or snapping chewing gum, as Katherine did, at moments of crisis. Yet the spirit of adventure that inspired Doris to explore the Middle East—while staying in luxurious hotels and being fêted by colonial authorities—corresponded to the spirit that drew Katherine to the Caribbean.

Katherine developed a technique she would teach for almost thirty years, from the 1930s, at her West Fifty-second Street studio in New York, where scores of students learned a form of ballet that adapted the movements of Caribbean and African dance.[10] It was called the Dunham Method.

Doris met Katherine during the popular 1941 Broadway production of *Cabin in the Sky*, which Dunham had choreographed. Doris immediately recognized Katherine's genius, and a close friendship and philanthropic relationship developed. An undated proposed budget from Katherine for "One Month Study and Teaching Assistant Grant" totaled $15,950. She also requested an additional grant of $41,524 for performance, travel, and study. Doris granted her the funds.

For a brief period in Los Angeles, Katherine taught Doris her method. On September 23, 1951, Katherine submitted a bill for $520, covering ten lessons, including three "native drummers" who accompanied the dancers. Then Doris asked to join the company. Dunham students were considered such proficient dancers that they gained roles in Broadway shows without auditioning. Aware of the damage that would be caused to her reputation if she hired a largely untrained thirty-nine-year-old heiress, Katherine had to turn her patron down. Doris responded by cutting off her funding, putting a fatal strain on their friendship.

On February 26, 1993, only months before Doris's death, Katherine wrote her that she had cried all night after Doris refused to talk to her. Nevertheless, Katherine thanked her for canceling the note on a long-term loan: "You know how much I've appreciated the loan all these years." On tour in Tokyo in 1957, Katherine finally shuttered her company, after twenty years, to save what was left of her self-esteem. She was in debt for $100,000.

Though Doris had not bailed Katherine out in the end, she had supported her at a crucial time in her career, when Dunham was still confronting the entrenched view that black dancers could not dance professionally unless they were trained in classical technique. As the dance critic John Martin explained in *The New York Times* on February 25,

1940, "The potential greatness of the Negro dance lies in its discovery of its own roots . . . exactly what Miss Dunham has done." This was the very work that Doris supported.

Martin continued that, since Katherine had the gift of creativity, she turned her dance research into art. Her objectivity and artistic instincts had enabled her to distinguish herself in the field. Though Doris may have believed that she, too, as an amateur dancer, had the natural instincts of an artist, she might have recognized that she had neither the sheer perseverance nor the creative genius that defined Katherine's mastery of dance.

In 1987, the Alvin Ailey Company performed *The Magic of Katherine Dunham* in New York, but the museum Katherine established in East St. Louis, which holds her paintings as well as her collection of more than 250 art objects from Africa and the Caribbean, is currently soliciting contributions and is open only by appointment.[11]

Doris's two large grants of this period stand out both because of their size and because they are not what one would expect of a typical donor to the New York Philharmonic Society or the Newport Police Fund.

In 1935, through Independent Aid, Doris gave $10,000 to Margaret Sanger's National Committee for Birth Control as well as $15,000 to Sanger herself. When Sanger retired, Doris continued to support her with small sums. In 1936, Doris gave $15,000 to the Birth Control Clinical Research Bureau, and, in a dramatic escalation, $1 million the following year to the Birth Control League. A year later, she gave another $15,000.[12]

Doris was crucial to the cause of birth control, although her role is seldom recognized. Early in her career, Sanger could not have raised these sums from any other donor or foundation for her controversial cause. What in Doris's privileged life caused her to care about birth control?

Early in her relationship with Jimmy, Doris inevitably had questions about sexuality that went unanswered. She would never have been able to discuss these issues with her mother, because of both prudery and ignorance. Becoming pregnant on her honeymoon and probably choosing to have an abortion suggest that Doris, and perhaps even Jimmy, lacked knowledge of birth control. As a wealthy woman with important connections, she would always have had access to abortion, but she may have recognized that this wasn't the case for most women during the decades when the procedure was illegal. Without access to birth control or a safe abortion, young women found themselves turning to back-alley abortionists. Doris would have never been forced to that extreme, but she may have felt an edge of panic when she found herself pregnant, creating empathy for other women, and thus her support for Sanger's mission.

Many years later, in 1951, Sanger began to promote birth control and legal abortion in India. She established the International Planned Parenthood Federation in London in 1951, writing Doris's then assistant, Georgea Furst, that the federation "has been growing, indeed popping up like mushrooms in the past year."[13] Sanger later described the columnist Walter Winchell's "whispering campaign" in the New York *Daily Mirror*, in which he had hinted that Doris was going to give $1 million to the federation. Sanger fell to her knees in thanks before realizing that Winchell's remark was a rumor, based on a casual conversation between Doris and Eleanor Roosevelt in December 1936. The meeting had happened after Doris made a personal gift of $50,000 to FDR's reelection campaign.

Sanger had hoped that Eleanor Roosevelt would promote her cause even after President Roosevelt failed to respond to Sanger's request that he include birth control in his public-health programs. Then, to her dismay, the president appointed a Roman Catholic, James Farley, as postmaster general; Farley maintained that it was illegal to send contraception information through the mail, severely limiting the Birth Control League's ability to communicate with its supporters. Mrs. Roosevelt had supported birth control when the Women's City Club of New York endorsed it, but she was unable to challenge Farley's rule.[14]

Sanger then wrote Georgea that sterilization should be a goal of the Birth Control League. Perhaps because of the criticism this goal was provoking, she qualified it as "part of the goal."[15] This advocacy would bring the whole birth-control movement into obliquity, linking it with the Nazi regime's use of sterilization to control those it, like Sanger, viewed as "unfit." She would go on to advocate involuntary sterilization of "imbeciles" and other outcasts, as long as the sexual urge was preserved. Sanger even believed the federal government should offer a pension to couples who accepted sterilization and pay for the operation. Repellent as these ideas are today, it is worth remembering that the NAACP cofounder W.E.B. Du Bois believed that eugenics, as this theory was called, supported his goal of "racial uplift."[16]

Sanger wrote to Georgea to ask about applying to the Doris Duke Foundation for a $5,000 grant. She sent congratulations to Doris for "bringing her name to this work." As Sanger recognized, Doris's decision to rename Independent Aid reflected her greater confidence in, and ownership of, her philanthropic work.[17]

Georgea promised to bring Sanger's request to the attention of the foundation board. The board was made up about equally of men and women, a rarity then as now. One of the men, improbably, was Mike Chinigo, the bête noire of Doris's work with the Rome *Daily American*.

Addressing Sanger as "Dear M.S.," Georgea reported on April 11, 1952, that the board had reviewed her proposal "without enthusiasm." She suggested a personal conversation with Doris when they were both in Los Angeles.[18]

Sanger replied on May 15, 1952, that she was "quite heartbroken" at the news. She added that at least there was good news from Doris personally, who had paid for one of the "colored nurses whom you have long supported" to go to Bombay for the upcoming population conference. With Doris's support, Georgea would also be able to attend.[19]

Almost four years later, in February 1956, Sanger once again asked Doris for a meeting in Los Angeles, to solicit another grant from the Doris Duke Charitable Foundation. To persuade her, Sanger reminded Doris that only her foundation's support had enabled "the colored (so-called minority group) people to learn of Birth Control."[20]

Doris, like many philanthropists, constantly faced the issue of whether or not to become friends with recipients of her generosity. Usually she chose to avoid engagement. Yet for Doris, as for most philanthropists, friendships with recipients could be very fruitful. She would certainly have enjoyed getting to know a woman as interesting and forceful as Margaret Sanger. But because there is always the pressure to give, and to give more, and because some recipients may consider such donations their due, the possibility of sustained friendship is often threatened.

Beginning in the 1920s and continuing to the end of her life, Doris supported many musicians, including Vincent Youmans, helping him to produce a ballet; the black jazz artist Bricktop, giving her money to open jazz clubs in Mexico City and Rome; and Mary Lou Williams, a black jazz pianist, who wrote a song in gratitude titled "Miss D.D."[21]

Thus Doris's early philanthropy significantly supported both birth control and jazz. Originally inspired by her father's example, she went on to transcend his accomplishments as a philanthropist through her wider-ranging imagination and her adventurous life. She may have hoped that marrying the cosmopolitan Jimmy Cromwell would give her access to a wider world. Indeed, her honeymoon helped to inspire her most ambitious creation, Shangri La.

 Daily life at Shangri La is laid out in colorful detail in the letters Doris's overseer, Commodore (as he was called) R. W. "Waldo" Swearingen, sent to Lee Baldwin, Doris's lawyer and financial adviser, at 30 Rockefeller Center in New York. Here again, one of the strange qualities of inherited wealth appears. James Duke left Doris's inheritance in trusts, to evade Internal Revenue rules and preserve the corpus. Trustees managed the investments and doled out Doris's income. The trustees' sole duty was to increase and protect the corpus of the trusts, not to satisfy the dreams and ambitions of the inheritor. The checks they mailed to Doris's account at Bishop Bank in Honolulu may have felt, to her, like undependable largesse.

Although Doris celebrated her twenty-fifth birthday on November 22, 1937, and received the second third of her inheritance, about $10 million, on that date, the corpus was still in trust, never to be released to her outright. It may have seemed to Swearingen that the trustees of Doris's trust, rather than Doris herself, were in charge of expenses and could object to bills. Accordingly, on June 30, 1940, Swearingen wrote to Baldwin, advising him to give a bottle of "heart tonic" to the trustees to fortify them before studying the month's expenses.

Swearingen admitted to Baldwin that he had persuaded Doris to lend him $6,000. He then attempted to reassure Baldwin that a first mortgage of $19,500 on the Commodore's house in Honolulu more than covered the loan. He went on to warn Baldwin that it would be difficult to anticipate how much more money would be needed to build Shangri La, especially since the owner was present, which meant the place was overrun with every kind of tradesman.[1] In these letters, the Commodore refers to Doris as "the owner," sometimes capitalizing the word. He does not mention Jimmy.

But Jimmy was by no means out of the picture. In March and April 1938, Jimmy and Doris traveled with five friends to the Middle East to buy art and furniture for Shangri La. Arthur Upham Pope, a scholar and an enthusiastic promoter of Persian art, was among them.[2] But after that trip, Jimmy became an increasingly infrequent visitor to Shangri La.

In a letter to Baldwin, the Commodore reported that the house was coming along beautifully, but that he had found it necessary to spend a lot of his own money correcting construction mistakes. He distrusted the others working on the site and suspected them of squandering Doris's money, which he said he would never do. He and Doris often shared a laugh at the expense of the various men trying to cheat her. Swearingen's letter to Baldwin also related that local tile workers were busy installing the Persian tiles, adding that Doris was pleased with their work, even though she had originally wanted to bring in tile workers "from the East."

On July 28, 1940, Swearingen told Baldwin that British captain Alec Cunningham-Reid, whom the Commodore called "Dapper Dan," and who had been staying at Shangri La, was about to leave Oahu. He had told Swearingen that he planned to bring out his two sons and his mother, but that plan was delayed.[3]

Earlier in July, Doris had been in the hospital, but she wanted no mention of it: "So I am omitting the listing of all vouchers pertaining to her hospital, nurse, and doctors' bills in the monthly statements that I give her." Swearingen was meanwhile taking her on "little picnics" to get her out of the house without "overtaxing her strength."

The unmentionable truth was that, on July 11, she had miscarried a premature infant, whom she named Arden. The baby girl lived only one day. If Alec was the father, his leaving Oahu seventeen days after the miscarriage might mean that he stayed long enough to see Doris through the worst of what was surely a wrenching loss. Doris might have imagined establishing a family with Alec, including his two sons, and cemented by the birth of their baby. Later, Jimmy would confirm that he was not the father, and the issue of the baby's paternity would be contested during his divorce proceedings from Doris.[4]

When she regained her emotional strength, Doris threw herself back into the perfection of Shangri La. The pursuit of beauty always cheered her up.

At Shangri La, she was constructing a museum-quality visual archive of Islamic styles and periods, from the thick green twelfth-century tiles in the entry to the delicate eighteenth-century Persian miniatures in the Playhouse. When she ordered tiles to be ripped out, as was her wont, it was because she recognized, on further study, a flaw in her design.

In his letters, Swearingen chronicled the changing scene at Shangri La. He enjoyed poking fun at Alec Cunningham-Reid, now back in London, claiming that the first part of his last name, "Cunning," represented his scheming character, while the last part, "Ham," referred to his theatrical duplicity: he was always acting a part. Relishing such gossip, Swearingen went on to report that Doris had fired Sam Kahanamoku—temporarily—because he and some friends threw a noisy party in the pool house after Doris went to bed. But Swearingen was too aware of Doris's affection for Sam to believe that he would remain fired for long.

Much as he enjoyed Sam's brief fall from grace, Swearingen must have been dismayed to find that his own relationship with Doris was deteriorating. He wrote Doris's lawyer Tom Perkins that he didn't feel welcome anymore at Shangri La, despite his involvement in the construction. Then, in August 1941, he reported to Perkins that he'd had to call a "conference" with Doris—now calling her "Mrs. Cromwell"—to remind her of a promise he claimed Jimmy had made to buy him (Swearingen) a car.

Doris was unaware of this arrangement. And Swearingen never received the car.

In a November letter, he wrote Baldwin of a row he had caused between Mrs. Kingscote and Mrs. Wisner, both of whom were caring for Alec's two sons, now in Hawaii. By telling Mrs. Kingscote, the boys' English grandmother, how fond they were of Mrs. Wisner, Swearingen had succeeded in poisoning the relationship between the two women, which led him to conclude that Mrs. Kingscote didn't want her grandsons to like anyone but her. Doris was well aware of this problem, Swearingen claimed. If so, Swearingen's faux pas may have been one reason Doris began to turn against her majordomo.

Doris now found a new friend in Johnny Gomez, who would live at Shangri La for the next seventy years, and died there in 1999. Although listed as a clerk on her payroll, Johnny was much more than that. He was her confidant, personal assistant, and right-hand man. His letter of May 31, 1949, to "Dorska," conveyed the tone of their friendship. He wrote that he was so happy to get her phone call, then told her that the willow tree she had planted was in an unsuitable spot and that he had it replaced with a small yellow Hawaiian shower tree just as tall as Iwani, one of her dogs. He hoped she would return soon, as she had promised, and sent her his love. This handsome, delightful Hawaiian was gradually replacing Swearingen as Doris's confidant and helper.

Doris had trusted Swearingen. In January 1941, she even delegated him to clear up issues around her payment of income tax to the Territory of Hawaii. She insisted that, as long as her dividends from the Duke Power Company were deposited in a New York bank, the income she drew was not taxable in Hawaii.

Swearingen wrote to Perkins that he was amused that the people at 30 Rockefeller wanted him to be "The Brains of the Organization" in Hawaii. He added that Doris always believed that the people back in the New York office were 100 percent right. This, he wrote, made him laugh. His bitterness was evident when he related to Perkins that Doris had "relieved" him of his responsibility for checking all the household bills. She had told him that all he needed to do now was to collect the invoices and turn them over to her, but he knew from experience that most of the invoices would be lost, and he would have to spend time getting replacements from various vendors.

In addition to running Shangri La, Doris faced the issue of what to do with Alec's two sons after the departure of their grandmother for England. During school vacations, they were with her in Hawaii, but now vacation was over and there was no question of returning the boys to their father in London. The Blitz, begun on September 7, 1940, dumped thirteen thousand tons of bombs on London. Whole blocks were still in ruins, and the population was bracing for what looked like a German invasion. Now Hawaii no longer seemed a viable refuge at any time of year: according to Swearingen's letter to Perkins on February 24, 1942, Shangri La, only 6.4 miles from Honolulu, had experienced a hit during the bombardment of Pearl Harbor on December 7, 1941. Fortunately, little damage was done. Doris had left the island, sending the two boys back to boarding school. She would return in 1945, after the war was over.

But Swearingen was still on the job. In mid-December 1942, he reported the arrival of twelfth-century "Nobby Tiles" without the papers needed to clear Customs. Doris would lay out the two hundred dark green Turkish tiles during her first visit after the war. Also, Swearingen expressed concern about the safety of the magnificent thirteenth-century Iranian mihrab Doris placed prominently on the east wall of her living room. As a religious niche, which is supposed to indicate to Muslims the direction of Mecca, it should have faced northwest, but Doris viewed the mihrab as a purely aesthetic adornment and placed it where it would show to most advantage.[5]

Doris's purchase of the mihrab, for $150,000, was the most important contribution of her friend and adviser Mary Crane to Shangri La. A young art student at New York University, Crane often traveled with Doris, offering her expertise.

On June 14, 1938, Mary had written to "Dear Dorjim"—this was the cable name Doris and Jimmy were using—to report about her research on the color used for columns in the Isfahan palaces. The columns were originally painted and gilded rather than inset with mirrors, but mirrors were Doris's first choice for the columns at Shangri La. Mary asked Doris to tear out the sections of her letter that required answers, mark them yes or no, and return them. She knew from experience that Doris would not reply to her questions with a letter of her own.

In June 1940, Doris had commissioned Mary to negotiate with the New York antiquities dealer Hagop Kevorkian for the mihrab. Though the Metropolitan Museum of Art also hoped to secure it, Crane persuaded the dealer to sell it to Doris.[6] In 1942, under Swearingen's supervision, the mihrab was packed up and stored until the end of the war.

In a letter to Perkins on April 23, 1942, Swearingen (still at Shangri La, perhaps because Doris could not bring herself to fire him) asked him to advise Doris to watch for news of Admiral Frank Jack Fletcher, who had been visiting Hawaii. During his visit, Doris and her friend Clare Boothe Luce were nearly drowned. Swearingen does not expand on his casual mention of this, but given the fury of the surf at Diamond Head and Doris's intrepid nature, it is easy to guess how such an accident might have taken place.

Clare Boothe Luce described her earlier visit to Shangri La in an article published in *Life* magazine, the publication of her husband, Henry Luce. After the fourteen-hour trip to Honolulu, Clare spent an evening at Shangri La, which she described as an exotic palace inhabited by a curious assortment of creatures in cages—flamboyant parrots and macaws whose ear-splitting shrieks rent the air, and monkeys adding their chatter, while fountains purled and tropical fish swam and glittered in pools.

In the midst of it all, Clare wrote, the most brilliant denizen was her hostess, Doris, her hair brushed up high on her head and her "blue Siamese cat eyes" sparkling as she performed "a remarkably fine hula for her guests." Clare recognized the difficulty of the hula, the "sweetly serpentine arms and mellifluous hips" Doris had mastered. Not all of her guests were as skilled. Lady Diana Cooper was able to perform the hula only "in a reserved kind of way."

On October 21, Clare wrote Doris a bread-and-butter letter, thanking her for her visit. She addressed her as "Doris, my sweet Shangrilan Houri," comparing her to one of the beautiful maidens who, in Muslim belief, lived with the blessed in Paradise. Clare wrote that she wished she were still by the swimming pool, admiring "your infinite variety of bathing costumes and the pulchritude therein incorporated."[7]

In Shangri La, music for dancing the hula brought Doris close to her Hawaiian friends. A snapshot shows Doris sitting cross-legged on a couch next to Sam Kahanamoku, her steel slide guitar on her lap. Sam, clearly in the role of instructor, watches her intently as he strums his guitar. Behind them on the wall, the red medallions of an Uzbekistan cotton-and-silk tapestry seem to dance like suns.[8]

 **17** Both before and after the war, Hawaii provided Doris with plenty of spirit-brightening recreation— swimming, diving, surfing, and outrigger canoeing— far from the ceaseless hounding of the press. Dedicated to long twice-daily swims at Rough Point and Shangri La, she adopted in the early 1950s the close-fitting two-piece bathing suits, often manufactured by Jantzen, that would become fashionable.

Doris wanted to share her passion. In 1960, as the United States became concerned about the success of Russian women athletes in the Olympics, she gave $500,000 to the Olympic Committee to investigate ways to improve the performance of American women swimmers.

Determined to improve her diving, Doris might have persuaded the Gold Medal swimmer Duke Kahanamoku to coach her, as he did many others, but instead he remained only a friend.

At Duke's sixtieth birthday party, Doris's lifelong friend Wilmer C. Morris remembered, Doris watched Duke with such admiration that Wilmer asked, "You really like Duke, don't you?"

Doris replied, "Duke has it all. He's known all over the world, and people admire and respect him, and with all that, he lives a very simple, uncomplicated life. He doesn't want a lot. Certainly, he's never asked me for anything."[1]

Instead of Duke, Doris hired an Olympic coach (whose name has not been recorded) to help her with her diving, using her swimming pool's retractable high diving board. (In a home movie filmed in 1960, the board is as tall as the surrounding palm trees. A male figure enveloped in shadow advances along it as if preparing to dive, then retreats.)

But Shangri La was not all about diving, swimming, learning Hawaiian music, and racing outrigger canoes, a sport in which Doris's proficiency is symbolized by a prize: a gold compact inscribed "Mrs. James C. Cromwell" above "Sam Kahanamoku," with whom she had won a race. The place also provided a secluded paradise for Doris and her friends until the aftershocks of the Japanese attack on Pearl Harbor began to affect her life there.

On December 19, 1941, the War Shipping Administration requisitioned for possible military use Doris's fifty-five-foot yacht, the *Lihi Lahi*, for $20,000. (The name of the yacht incorporates Alec's boys' nickname for Doris.) This was the first of many changes. But Doris was extremely patriotic. At the outbreak of the war, she had proposed temporarily turning Shangri La into a rest home for military personnel, but was persuaded that this would be impractical. Instead, she turned over the pool, gardens, and tennis court as a resort for officers on leave from Hawaiian military bases.

Lieutenant General Delos C. Emmons, military governor of Hawaii, wrote to Doris on August 19, 1942, thanking her for her contribution and agreeing to exclude "female visitors"—Doris may have feared an orgy. He had, meanwhile, invited Admiral Nimitz and Rear Admiral Bagley, along with their staffs, to visit Shangri La: "I am sure that they will also appreciate your kindness."[2]

On August 23, 1946, when Doris returned to Shangri La, she found it largely unchanged. For two more years, her arrangement with Swearingen seemed to hold. Then, on March 24, 1947, Swearingen wrote to Doris that he had become painfully aware that she had lost all faith in him and in his services, in spite of his years of loyalty and devotion. He had no idea what he had done or not done to earn her displeasure, and reminded her that he had once warned her that because of her prominence, she was certain to hear malicious rumors about him or anyone else in her household. He felt that this might lead her to misinterpret something he had done. She had promised that she would discuss any such rumors with him before taking action. That had happened several times in the past, and they had been able to work things out.

Swearingen continued that during Doris's visit in March 1947, she was never available to meet with him. The excuses were always the same— she was busy, or too tired, or sick. Now he wondered if she was angry with him about the way he had disposed of some of her possessions on her yacht. He had removed these things because he had heard from the army that they were about to requisition the yacht and that owners would not be able to remove anything once that happened. (He did not reveal what he had done with what he had taken.) Since then, his feelings had been hurt by everyone at Shangri La. The attitude there, he wrote, "fairly screams of my being in your disfavor."[3]

In May, Doris finally transferred Swearingen's authority to her new friend, Johnny Gomez. On May 17, 1947, in a letter to Johnny, her attorney Stuart Hawkins in New York relayed Doris's order that he become at once the superintendent of her estate in Honolulu. Doris went even further, executing a new power of attorney that named Johnny as her agent, and empowering him to make legal and financial decisions. Doris established her trust in new friends suddenly and completely, which sometimes led to her disillusionment.

Johnny accepted his role, as he explained in an oral history recorded in 1998, a year before his death. Going forward, he would serve as Doris's companion, shielding her from unpleasantness and providing her with the latest entertainment news (he said she never read political reports). Johnny provided this service not only in Hawaii but also at Duke Farms and Rough Point, as well as her various Manhattan apartments and Falcon's Lair, above Benedict Canyon in the Los Angeles neighborhood of Bel Air, which she bought in 1952.[4]

He traveled with Doris, often escorting her to concerts and gallery openings, and remembered accompanying her at the 1961 Newport Jazz Festival with Claiborne Pell (soon to take office as senator from Rhode Island) when a brawl broke up the concert. Doris supported the festival financially from 1957 to 1967, often bringing top jazz artists back to Rough Point for impromptu jam sessions. She recorded her own playing and singing on reel-to-reel audio equipment, still on display in the Pine Room at Rough Point.

Doris enjoyed the friendship of Mario Braggiotti, the well-known pianist, composer, and raconteur whose career had been launched in 1928, when George Gershwin asked him to play for his 1927 musical, *Funny Face*, in London. Mario and Doris met in Italy during the war. Through the Psychological Division of the Warfare Branch of the Office of War Information, he was supervising local and national radio programming. She was holding recording sessions with American GIs at that time.

Mario visited Doris at Shangri La. When he wrote afterward to thank her, he reminisced about seeing her working out with Eleanor Johnson Lawson (Doris's dance instructor and mentor in the psychic realm) on the beach, describing their routines as "tough." He added that he missed their times together and what he called the "beach mood" Doris created. Complimenting her on finding a completely balanced way of living, he promised to continue to write her while he went on with his career as a touring pianist.[5]

Eleanor, who through Doris's will would receive her largest personal bequest, was introduced to Doris by their mutual friend Katherine Dunham. Soon after they met, Eleanor gave Doris a set of crystals and instructed her on their use for divination. Eleanor also gave Doris dance lessons and served as a spiritual adviser.

Aly Khan (Prince Ali Salman Aga Khan, son of Aga Khan III) was another affectionate friend from the late 1940s, writing Doris in December 1949, seven months after his marriage to Rita Hayworth, that he didn't think she could understand how distressed he was at not seeing her—apparently, Doris, as was her wont, had canceled their engagement for a particular evening—and was devastated when he found out she was about to leave before he could see her again. He knew that when they did meet again they would not be alone. Still, he was grateful for the time they had had the previous week.[6] Aly Khan was one of a great many men and women who responded to Doris's distinctive blend of charm and energy, and were intrigued by her independence.

Alec Cunningham-Reid continued to be charmed by Doris even after their affair ended. He was one of the many friends Doris entertained at Shangri La after the war, renting an oceanfront villa for him and his mother. Tex McCrary and his then girlfriend, Ava Gardner, were also guests, as well as Elizabeth Taylor and John Warner.

Many years later, Jacqueline Kennedy recalled, in an undated letter, her visit to Duke Farms in the pouring rain. Doris had driven Jackie all over the farm, leading her to express both enthusiasm and astonishment that Doris didn't just keep the gardens for herself rather than sharing them. (The gardens were opened to the public in 1966.) This visit began a friendship that continued when Doris appointed Jackie as the first board member to the Newport Restoration Foundation in 1968.

On June 17, 1968, after Robert Kennedy's murder in Los Angeles, Jackie added a handwritten note to a typed form letter acknowledging condolences. "Thank you with all my heart and send you so much love at this sad time."[7]

Through it all, Johnny Gomez remained a loyal and accepting companion. Cautiously, he described Doris's new companion, Joey Castro, as just "a good friend." Joey, a jazz pianist Doris met in a Los Angeles nightclub in 1950, would become an important addition to her world. After she met the decorator Edward Tirella, who, according to Johnny, redecorated the kitchen at Rough Point with Johnny's help, he became "a good friend" as well.

In 1973, Doris would be a guest on Aristotle Onassis's yacht, cruising to the U.S. Virgin Islands and then on to Haiti. Jackie would write to thank her for putting down a deposit on a Haitian painting that Jackie's young son, John Jr., had admired. In another undated letter, Jackie wrote that she felt fortunate to find a friend like Doris, so spontaneous and sharing so many of her interests.[8]

Now that Johnny was officially in charge, Hawkins laid out a plan for handling Doris's expenses. He suggested making lists of all ongoing costs, believing this would be easier for Doris to read. These lists would cover repairs and expenditures, including staff salaries at her houses, as well as donations, real estate taxes, and a mountain of daily costs. Doris could not have anticipated, when she went to court at thirteen to gain ownership of Rough Point and Duke Farms, and then, years later, built Shangri La, and bought her Manhattan apartments and finally Falcon's Lair, that the result would be a dizzying accumulation of lists.

As Johnny's favor rose, Swearingen's fell. Back in Hawaii, he would be terminated because of the kind of misunderstandings that are inevitable when a woman of power and money believes that she is losing control.

Even after he'd been fired, Swearingen didn't give up. On March 27, 1948, he wrote to Hawkins that he continued to feel responsible for the stewardship of Shangri La, although Doris had turned the authority over to Johnny Gomez. He complained that he simply "could not tolerate" the way Johnny was handling the business of the estate.

At one point, Swearingen believed he had solved the problem by taking Johnny before a de facto jury composed of the housekeeper and the cook, where Johnny confessed to having made "mistakes." Swearingen didn't specify the nature of the wrongdoing.

On April 2, 1947, writing "Dear Boss"—a title he had never used before—Swearingen had complained to Doris that Johnny was stirring up the gardeners with accusations about thievery for which he had absolutely no evidence. He believed Johnny suffered from his lack of education but admitted that he was good at decorating—the reason Doris originally hired him. Now he was becoming far more unreasonable than Swearingen had expected, primarily because he would never admit to not knowing everything about everything. He was driving people crazy by telling them how to do their jobs. Doris's long-term staff resented this, as did various tradesmen brought in to make repairs. Claiming that Johnny had "no more tact than a jack rabbit," Swearingen needled Doris with the suggestion that her new superintendent was behaving so badly because she had made it obvious that she cared for him.

Just six weeks later, on May 17, 1947, Swearingen finally agreed to turn the management of Shangri La formally over to Johnny and made the announcement to the assembled staff. Although Johnny was completely unprepared for the job—bookkeeping, Swearingen thought, was a total mystery to him—he would begin at once to handle all business dealings, sending the vouchers and other documentation to Hawkins in New York. Swearingen proposed mailing Hawkins his own May accounts to compare with Johnny's.

In his penultimate letter to Hawkins, the long-suffering Commodore complained that "Mr. Gomez"—he had been instructed not to call him Johnny—had still not learned how to keep the books. Swearingen's last letter to Hawkins, written December 5, 1947, ended with a postscript asking to be told all the gossip. Then he disappeared from the scene.

There were often uninvited guests in the cove below Shangri La: the Hawaiians who swam and fished there, as was their right. The oceanfront was owned by the territory. During the construction of Shangri La in 1937, Jimmy had fought the authorities to gain permission to build their swimming pool cantilevered over the headland. His repeated requests, made through lawyers and often accompanied by veiled threats, were steadfastly refused. The pool was finally built in the garden between the main house and the Playhouse.

From the pool, Doris would often hear locals diving, swimming, fishing, shouting, and (presumably) making love below what she had originally planned as a private oasis. This unavoidable intrusion explains a curious feature of Shangri La: there is no direct access to the ocean. Instead, a locked door from the basement, where surfing equipment was stored, replaced the original design for a grand flight of marble stairs, which might have encouraged intruders.

Children rarely visited Shangri La, but two little girls lived there from 1938 to 1941. They were the daughters of Samuel Charlop, a skilled metalworker who helped maintain the place. Interviewed in 2009, Sam's daughters, Grace Cohen and Eleanor Freedman, gave glowing accounts of life at Shangri La, perhaps burnished by time. They described their apartment over the garage as "darling," with custom-made furniture. Their father, they said, always spoke highly of Doris, but without details, so that the little girls would not be able to answer impertinent questions at school. Doris offered to have their teeth straightened—a version of her effort to entice Marian Paschal to lose weight—but their father refused. Perhaps he did not share the mainland's preoccupation with straight teeth. Alternatively, he did not want to be further indebted to his employer.

The sisters remembered that Doris commissioned their father to make a dozen "bawdy" silver-plated nutcrackers in the shape of human legs, complete with male genitalia, bringing to mind a slur used against powerful women that was in parlance at the time: nut crackers.

Neither of the sisters remembered meeting Jimmy Cromwell, although they had heard that he was alone at Shangri La from December 1938 till April 1939. The two little girls could not have known about Jimmy's attempts to entertain two minor members of European royalty, whose names he didn't reveal. His elaborate plans for their reception, his expectations for their stay, and his attempts to shield them from the Hawaiian press show his always intense focus on enhancing his own status. Apparently, the couple never visited.

The sisters recalled that their mother's only role in Doris's household was feeding Doris's cats, which brought another, earlier memory: Jimmy had arranged to have two platters with silver dome covers presented to his wife at dinner. Under each cover was a Siamese kitten, and their offspring became the brood that Mrs. Charlop fed.[9] These kittens appear in the veterinarian Dr. Louis J. Camuti's book *All My Patients Are Under the Bed*.

Camuti remembered meeting Doris in 1936, a year after her marriage to Jimmy. Camuti recalled that he had felt some sympathy for the fix Jimmy Cromwell had been in when he had to choose a wedding present for his bride, who had everything. His gift of two Siamese kittens caused Doris to summon Camuti to make a house call. She received him at Duke Farms—rather to his surprise—"with her legs tossed over the arms of a chair." After he checked the kittens, Doris took him on a tour of the farm by car.

But first she called her two Great Danes into the rear seat of the car, warning the vet not to touch them. During the tour, the dogs licked the back of his balding head. When they returned to the house, Louis stripped to the waist in a bathroom to wash off the saliva. Doris knocked at the bathroom door and discreetly handed him a large towel.

After this strange initiation, Camuti visited Duke Farms regularly, driving out from New York to minister to the cats. Jimmy raised a fierce objection to his $385 bill, although Camuti explained that it took him a whole day to travel back and forth to Somerville. Not persuaded, Jimmy wrote him an indignant letter, telling him to suspend all future visits because of his outrageous charge. Finally, Camuti received a check for $100 from Doris. Nevertheless, he continued to take care of her cats for twenty-four years. Sometimes he was called in just to clip the cats' claws.[10]

After they were transported to Shangri La, the Siamese cats gave birth over time to an army of cats that, according to Grace and Eleanor, had the run of the estate. The girls may have noticed the paradox inherent in Doris's love of animals, which would sometimes be virtually abandoned when she moved on.

The sisters remembered Marian as Doris's secretary, a kind woman who weighed nearly three hundred pounds when they knew her. They added that Doris was very demanding of her staff. Some loved her; some hated her.

Passing over the presence at Shangri La of Johnny Gomez—"a kind of clown to keep her amused"—they remembered the Kahanamoku brothers as always being around to entertain Doris and her guests. They remembered that Sam sometimes escorted Doris, and his brother Sargent served as her liaison to Hawaiian culture, introducing Doris to local people and customs.

Throughout the 1940s, mainland reporters assumed that handsome, dark-skinned Sam was Doris's lover and read scandal into it. But in Hawaii, Doris's friendship with Sam seemed to arouse little comment. His role was familiar—the Beach Boy who taught the haole to surf and to race an outrigger, and who became a friend.

The sisters remembered Shangri La as a paradise. Eleanor particularly loved the animals, especially Tita'apa, the tame orangutan, who became her special friend. Thinking he was lonely, Eleanor said, Doris bought two large white rabbits to keep the orangutan company.

Both sisters enjoyed watching employees use nets to catch ocean fish to put in the dining room aquariums. At one point, a sixty-four-pound tuna was caught and sent to live in the saltwater swimming pool. The girls swam with it and tickled its belly.

Their father's chores were sometimes unexpected. Asked to pick up the actor Errol Flynn at a certain address, Charlop was met at the door by a man shouting, "He ran off with my wife and I hope they never come back."

One Christmas, the sisters were invited to the main house. Their mother dressed them in their best and curled their hair. Doris reportedly wanted some children to watch the opening of presents. Watch they did, sitting around a beautifully decorated Christmas tree as Sam and Johnny Gomez tore into their packages. Unfortunately, there was nothing for the girls. "I'm sure Doris meant well," Eleanor remarked tactfully.

After Pearl Harbor, their father told them he might be excused from the draft because Doris had written Eleanor Roosevelt requesting an exemption. But Mrs. Roosevelt refused, and they remembered their father then wearing a uniform and working for the Navy during the day and doing estate work at night. Soon afterward, the family moved to naval housing at Pearl Harbor.

After the war, when Doris offered Charlop his old job back, he instead went to work in Jimmy's paper mill in New Hampshire, one of several projects that Doris funded for her ex-husband.

Many years later, the sisters visited Shangri La with their children and remarked on the dense upscale subdivisions that now hedge the house. All of Doris's whimsies—the monkeys, the parrots, the tuna, the dining-room-wall aquariums—were gone.[11] Today the house is a museum, the Shangri La Center for Islamic Arts and Cultures, a showcase of the fine specimens of tiles, woodwork, and ceramics that Doris collected during her lifetime. Open to the public and offering fellowships to Islamic scholars, the house is beginning to realize Doris's purpose as expressed in her will: to promote the study and understanding of Middle Eastern art and culture, an aim even more vital today than it was at the time of her death in 1993.

Academic considerations were foreign to Doris, and she did not often seek the advice of experts. She bought objects because they attracted her and had meaning for her, which was usually how the rare women collectors of the period went about their buying. Louisine Havemeyer, whose extraordinary collection was assembled over a lifetime with her husband, Harry, wrote a lighthearted memoir called *From Sixteen to Sixty: Memoirs of a Collector*, in which she recorded amusing anecdotes surrounding their acquisitions—not the kind of detailed evaluations that would typically appear in a museum catalogue. Louisine also benefited from a long family tradition of collecting, and from a close collaboration with the Metropolitan Museum, where her collection resides today.

Unlike Isabella Stewart Gardner, whose Fenway Court in Boston is now the Gardner Museum, Doris left no travel diaries or correspondence with art-world authorities like Bernard Berenson. Insisting in her will

that her collection be hung as she had hung it—even when poorly lit—
Gardner would have expressed her aim, as Patricia Vigderman interprets
it in *The Memory Palace of Isabella Stewart Gardner*, as summed up
by the inscription over the museum's central entrance: "C'est Mon Plai-
sir." Doris, too, wanted Shangri La to delight, considering instruction
less important than the immediate aesthetic experience of the visitor. No
catalogue or appraisal is needed for that experience, although several now
exist.

If Shangri La had been her only notable achievement and donation to
the public, Doris Duke would still deserve to be remembered as a very
farsighted philanthropist. Equally important is her preservation work in
Newport, Rhode Island.

18 Thousands of miles from the promontory where Shangri La was built according to Doris's specifications, Newport, Rhode Island, exists in a mythic haze. The mansions, called "cottages" by the East Coast millionaires who constructed them in the late nineteenth and early twentieth centuries, set the standard for the Gilded Age.

In the early days, a long train ride and then an overnight ferry linked Manhattan with this spit of land extending into the Atlantic Ocean. The difficulties of getting to Newport were compensated for—at least in the eyes of some of its denizens—by the social rituals that defined summer life. These rituals—teas and balls, debutante parties and afternoon calls—had been initiated in Manhattan. But grass-court tennis matches, elaborate outdoor picnics, and excursions on private yachts were the particular pleasures of life "at the beach." Of course, many of the mansions' inhabitants never went to the beach at all.

The same architects—Horace Trumbauer, Richard Morris Hunt, Stanford White—whose work was showcased in New York designed the grand establishments along Bellevue Avenue, the tree-bowered road that runs from the little town of Newport to the end of the peninsula. Here Vanderbilts, Whitneys, and Belmonts, among others, displayed the fruits of fortunes made in tin, coal, gold, and cotton, as well as in the China trade.

At the Dukes' Rough Point, Frederick Law Olmsted's landscaping seems minimal. Lush green lawns and a few flower beds packed with blooms attempt to tame what must have been, before the house was built, a wild and woolly headland. Doris liked her sites to be challenging: on the Atlantic Coast, crashing waves and rough swimming; on the Pacific, wild surf and equally demanding swimming (one of Doris's maids drowned there). The point she made is not obscure. Life is threat, life is risk, and even a woman insulated by money is not exempt from its perils. Doris chose to expose herself to at least some of those.

Both in Hawaii and at Newport, weather was a constant hazard. These oceanfront estates demand constant battle by an army of gardeners to maintain a "civilized" lawn, trees, and flower beds in the face of winter winds and blasts of salt water. At Rough Point, the not-quite-complete attempt at taming seems appropriate to the site.

Below the bluff, a tortuous path called the Cliff Walk, a remnant of Native American days and always a public way, has crumbled until parts are no longer passable. The fact that this walk, which runs along the oceanfront, is public caused dismay to Doris and other householders. The most esteemed bits of coastal land nearly always remain at least partially the public's, an ownership that is never easily accepted by the builders of large houses.

Above the bluff at Rough Point, a statue of Cyparissus stands at one end of a formal flower garden. He was one of Apollo's lovers. The god, who must have been too busy for much regular companionship, gave the pretty boy a deer to keep him company. When a stray arrow killed the deer, Cyparissus asked Apollo to allow him to cry forever, and so Apollo, ever practical, turned him into a cypress tree oozing teardrops of sap. Probably the statue was not something the Dukes chose. It may have been bought by earlier owners, Vanderbilts or Leedses. However, Doris, who wandered everywhere on the property, would have seen it and perhaps wondered about the appeal of a story of eternal grief.

Today, the house's six gables cast sharp shadows on the grass, its granite walls seem to emerge from the rugged promontory, and its tall leaded casement windows, carefully curtained, hold a mystery. Before a climate-control system was installed, windows all over the house stood open; a net with a long handle was used to catch birds that flew inside and perched on the gilded picture frames.

The slight curve of the façade, embracing the circular drive, seems to offer a tentative welcome, contradicted by the embellishments on the front doors. Fierce bronze animal heads grasp the handles with their teeth.

Rough Point's construction began in 1887. Frederick W. Vanderbilt, seventh son of William and great-grandson of the dynasty's founder, Cornelius, hired the firm of Peabody & Sterns to design and build a version of an English country manor on the headland known as Rough Point. The house was for a while the largest of the "cottages" at Newport. It replaced two modest structures, and yet it seems neither as overwhelming nor as ostentatious as later Newport houses. As a setting for Doris's early years, the house could not have been more appropriate, providing as it does stability and proportion, as well as the possibility of adventure.

The house did not suit its first owners. In 1906, the Vanderbilts sold it to William Leeds, the Tinplate King, who left it to his wife, Nancy. She, in turn, sold it to James Buchanan Duke in 1922. Under his command, the house took its final form.

In 1915, Buck and Nanaline had begun renting houses in Newport. Nanaline loved the area and had found her place there, which was no mean feat. Ward McAllister, nicknamed "Mr. Make-A-Lister" because of his lists of those who had arrived socially, warned that newcomers should not be afraid of sitting "on the stool of probation" for a minimum of four seasons before they were accepted by the more firmly established inhabitants.

While renting, Nanaline waited out her probation, following the established rituals, giving tea parties, card parties, and frequent dinners for large groups of her friends, many of whom she knew in New York. No one could resist her combination of Southern charm and social acuity. At Rough Point and in New York, she entertained guests who would provide entrée to Newport's elite society as well as amusement. Buck, traveling by train and ferry late Friday and returning to his New York house on Sunday evening, was a quietly genial but often absent host.

In 1922, after buying the thirty-one-year-old house, Buck hired the New York architect Horace Trumbauer to alter it to fit the family's needs more closely: to entertain, and to display the paintings and tapestries Buck had acquired in Europe while traveling on tobacco business. Trumbauer lightened up the dark-wainscoted interiors, redesigned the great hall to provide wall space for Buck's French tapestries, plastered the ceilings, and replaced the dark flooring with white marble. He also added a solarium that faced the precipitous drop to the Atlantic, with a bedroom above it, surely the choicest room in the house. Doris loved the solarium and filled it with plants. In 1924, Trumbauer finished his improvements, shortly before Buck Duke died.[1]

Nanaline spent the year shortly after Buck's death draped in widow's weeds, touring Europe with her thirteen-year-old daughter. Upon returning to New York, she and Doris established what would become the pattern of their life until Doris married. They spent most of the year at the Seventy-eighth Street house, with weekend visits to Duke Farms. In July, they moved to Rough Point for the six-week summer season; the house was closed up for the rest of the year.

Gradually, Rough Point became Nanaline's domain. Once her teenage years had passed, until her mother's death, Doris appears to have visited rarely. Although she loved the rugged oceanfront, the excruciating details and conventional expectations of social life in Newport would have bored her.

But as a girl, Doris had found her place in Newport. A 1923 life-size portrait of her by John Da Costa, hanging on the grand staircase at Rough Point, shows a pretty, bored-looking blond girl in a long white dress with a blue sash. She hated the sittings, longing instead to escape to Bailey's Beach to play with her friends.

A snapshot taken in 1924 shows a broadly smiling little girl standing with her close friend Alletta Morris. They are holding the small silver cups they won in a sand-modeling contest. Two years later, Doris won a cup for tango, and shortly afterward, another small trophy for tennis. At Newport she developed the passion for sport that would run like a bright thread through the rest of her life.

The three modest trophies, enclosed in a glass case, still rest on her bedroom desk at Rough Point. They communicate much about the broad

ABOVE: Doris Duke swimming, Rough Point, 1968

ABOVE LEFT: Doris Duke with a member of the U.S. Seamen's Service
in New Orleans, Louisiana, 1944

ABOVE RIGHT: Doris Duke with an unidentified man in front of the Colosseum, Rome, 1944

LEFT: Doris Duke with unidentified men, Sicily, 1944

RIGHT: Doris Duke with Alec Cunningham-Reid in Europe, ca. 1940

Doris Duke with Michael Cunningham-Reid, ca. 1940

Doris Duke with Tex McCrary (left), date unknown

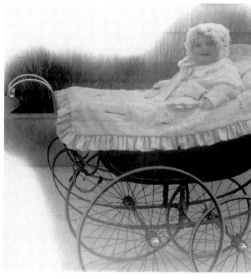

Baby Doris, 1913

Infant Doris on Nanaline Duke's lap, 1913

COSTLIEST HOME OPENED ON 5TH AVENUE WITHIN A YEAR.

LEFT: *The New York Times*, January 4, 1914, Picture Section, p. 1

RIGHT: Doris Duke and Alletta "Leta" Morris, ca. 1923–24

LEFT: Doris Duke on the beach, ca. 1923

ABOVE LEFT: Doris Duke (right) with Alletta "Leta" Morris, ca. 1923–24

ABOVE RIGHT: Doris and James B. Duke, ca. 1923–24

Portrait of Doris Duke,
ca. 1924

ABOVE LEFT: Doris and Nanaline Duke in Piazza San Marco, Venice, ca. 1923–24

ABOVE RIGHT: Doris Duke laying the cornerstone of the West Union building, Duke University, June 5, 1928. Also pictured are the chief engineer, A. C. Lee, and the Duke Endowment chair, G. G. Allen.

BELOW: Doris Duke with Marian Paschal, ca. 1935–40

TOP LEFT: Wedding portrait, 1935

TOP RIGHT: Doris Duke and James Cromwell at Wingwood House, the Stotesbury summer estate in Bar Harbor, Maine, 1936 or 1937

ABOVE: Doris Duke at the Moti Mosque, 1935

TOP: Doris Duke with Charles Asfar, ca. 1950

CENTER: Doris Duke in Damascus, Syria, 1938

ABOVE: Doris Duke and James Cromwell, ca. 1936–37

Sam Kahanamoku, Doris Duke, James Cromwell, and William "Chick" Daniels in Waikiki, ca. 1935–37

Doris Duke and crew sailing off Waikiki, ca. 1937–41

Doris Duke with Sam Kahanamoku, 1939

Doris Duke leaning on Sam Kahanamoku, ca. 1937–38

Doris Duke with Nana Veary, ca. 1937–38

Shangri La under construction, 1937

TOP LEFT: Doris Duke and crew, sailing, ca. 1936–37. From left: Sam Kahanamoku, Doris Duke, Bill Kahanamoku, and Sargent Kahanamoku
(Courtesy of Hawai'i State Archives. Photograph by Nate Farbman)

TOP RIGHT: Doris Duke on diving board, 1939

BELOW: Porfirio Rubirosa playing polo

Duke Farms main residence

Greenhouse at Sarah P. Duke Gardens, in Durham, taken by Johnny Gomez, 1964

Formal gardens at Duke Gardens, 1964

TOP LEFT: Doris Duke with a fellow member of the Nutley First Baptist choir, ca. 1971

TOP RIGHT: Johnny Gomez at Falcon's Lair, ca. 1953–60

Rough Point, Newport, Rhode Island, 1968

ABOVE: Doris Duke with Duke Ellington, ca. 1955

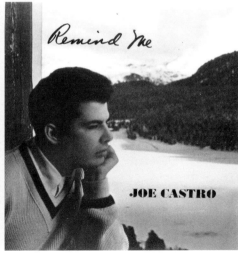

ABOVE LEFT: Joey Castro, 1961

ABOVE RIGHT: Joey Castro, cover image for unreleased album, *Remind Me*, 1965

Doris Duke, Bernard Lafferty, and Nuku Makasiale
(Bernard Lafferty Papers, David M. Rubenstein Rare Book & Manuscript Library, Duke University,
Durham, North Carolina)

Bernard Lafferty, ca. 1991–92
(Bernard Lafferty Papers, David M. Rubenstein Rare
Book & Manuscript Library, Duke University,
Durham, North Carolina)

Portrait of Doris Duke by Cecil Beaton (© The Cecil Beaton Studio Archive at Sotheby's)

outlines of her early years in Newport: physical freedom, such as she also enjoyed at Duke Farms, but with the addition of the ocean and all its possibilities, and friends. A neighborhood child in New Jersey once saw three-year-old Doris clinging to the other side of a boundary fence, weeping with loneliness. That would not happen at Rough Point, where she could walk to Bailey's Beach to meet Alletta.

Alletta recorded the friendship between the two lively, athletic girls in her diary for 1925, in her assured dark script. A student at Miss Hewitt's, a small private girls' school in Manhattan, Alletta began her diary by recording that, although she was only twelve at the moment, she would turn thirteen before the summer was over. Her excitement at the prospect of achieving her first teenage year is palpable.

Alletta, her sister, Betty, and their mother traveled by train to the riverboat, the *Commonwealth*. They got off the boat at 3:30 a.m. at Fall River, Massachusetts, having slept the best they could, and were driven to Newport.

Alletta unpacked her things and looked around the house her family had rented. She liked one small pink room but was really delighted by another room, which was painted blue. Doris telephoned her almost as soon as the family arrived and said she couldn't wait to see her.

The next day, Alletta went to the beach and was reunited with Doris. The two girls swam out to the raft; they would swim together almost every day. In the afternoon, Alletta went over to Rough Point to play with Doris. The girls were soon deeply involved in their summer activities, climbing on rocks at the beach to look for snails, and dancing in the late afternoon in "Dorrie's" living room. Often they went to the casino and played tennis on the grass, one of the many sports at which Doris excelled.

The six weeks passed quickly, with French, drawing, and pottery lessons. The friends also played croquet and hide-and-seek and had lunch parties. They enjoyed riding the waves, particularly when they were roughed up by an Atlantic storm. Calm days were dull in comparison, but the girls were seldom bored. Vacant hours were filled with the tennis tournaments their mothers organized. They were especially excited about the sand-castle contest and practiced at the beach for two weeks. Alletta wrote in her diary that they hoped to make an American Eagle with the flag, admitting dubiously that it was "very hard to do." After another practice session, she noted that their design was beginning to take shape. The girls won that pair of silver cups, perhaps more for their patriotic sentiment than for their creation. In one photograph, it looks somewhat shapeless.

Another afternoon, Alletta dressed up and went to play mah-jongg at a friend's house, where she won a gold-and-carnelian bracelet. Each girl received a charm, reminiscent of an adult Newport party where jewels were hidden in sand in the middle of the dining table and each guest was given a silver trowel for digging; this led to a furious competition.

The girls loved getting into messes. At one art class, they enjoyed mushy paint fights. They also had mud fights. No one seemed concerned about their dirtying their clothes.

There were many gatherings. "Mrs. Duke gave a supper party for six girls," Alletta wrote, adding, "She was very nice." At one party, where there were twenty boys and girls, they all danced and walked around in the moonlight.

Alletta's diary paints a picture of Nanaline Duke as an engaged and accessible mother, at least during the summers in Newport. From Alletta's point of view, Mrs. Duke was just like the other mothers, intent on keeping their daughters busy and out of mischief. Alletta liked her.

Doris tried to teach Alletta how to dive, but Alletta couldn't master it; she wrote that she could only "go straight" into the water. Their days were so full of vigorous physical activity that Alletta's report that they went to a haystack and sat for a while, talking, seems unusual.

As summer was drawing to a close, the weather turned wet and foggy and the temperature of the ocean cooled. Alletta wrote, "I did not get wet all morning." After lunch, they went to the final day of the tennis tournament, and Doris won another cup.[2]

Alletta remained Doris's friend for life, although they were often separated geographically; the only letter from her in the archive (she addressed Doris as "DeeDee Dear" and signed herself "Leta") conveys great affection. She suggested that Doris practice her letter writing: "Grit your teeth & start!"[3] Alletta persuaded Doris to support various animal-welfare organizations and to include support for this cause in her will. In fact, animal welfare always mattered to Doris, who from childhood on was often surrounded by dogs, particularly at Rough Point.

As the New York veterinarian had noticed, Doris did not discipline her dogs, treating them more like beloved children. When she got older, it must have seemed easier to enjoy close relationships with her pets than with complicated human beings.

Rough Point is rich in symbols, some mysterious, others giving up their meaning easily. For example, the place of honor over the dining-room mantel is taken by a painting of the Annunciation by the sixteenth-century artist Palma il Vecchio. Its message of acceptance of divine will was one that Doris would seldom acknowledge. But the Annunciation, like much of the art in the house, was purchased by Buck Duke. When he died, the contents were exactly what Bellevue Avenue would have expected.

After Nanaline's death at age ninety-two, on April 12, 1962, Doris began to reclaim the house, acquiring new pieces and adding others from her own collections. The changes are subtle. She rearranged the heavy furniture in the dining room to reflect her wish for more intimate gatherings: the big dark mahogany table, moved to the windows from the center of the room, now provided seating for eight, whereas Nanaline had usually had it extended to seat sixteen.

To her father's three exquisite sixteenth-century tapestries, gentle scenes of courtly life displayed in the Great Hall, Doris added three Flemish tapestries depicting the Roman general Scipio's furious battle to conquer Carthage. Next, she hung tapestries of allegorical scenes from the fables of La Fontaine, one depicting an elegant waistcoated fox.

Nanaline's taste is most clearly revealed in her daffodil-yellow morning room with its dainty upholstered furniture. She used her houses less for showing off collections than for entertaining; the paintings and tapestries were incidental, although necessary to create the proper atmosphere. Nanaline's large, elaborately carved desk testifies to the numerous invitations, notes, and letters she must have written there. Doris preserved the room, which she seldom used, as evidence of her mother's exquisite if conventional taste and her dedication to hospitality.

The Vanderbilts' billiard room became Doris's sitting room, used for after-dinner gatherings. Because she was very thin, Doris was always cold, and so open fires blazed under the marble mantel, especially after she began, in the late 1960s, to extend her summer visits to Thanksgiving.

Her great friend Oatsie (Marion) Charles remembered coming into this room with its roaring fire to find the after-dinner chocolates molten in their silver dish. Oatsie also remembered that there were dogs everywhere in the house and outside—not pedigreed creatures, but rescue animals. One evening, she was driven round and round the circular driveway, unable to leave the car because of the pack of barking dogs.

On another occasion, when Doris invited her for tea, Oatsie encountered not a pack of dogs but a pair of camels on the terrace outside the solarium. The camels accepted handfuls of graham crackers. Oatsie thought they were absolutely charming. During a hurricane, Oatsie remembered, Doris had the furniture taken out of the solarium; straw was strewn on the floor, and the camels were sheltered there. They often followed Doris from Newport to New Jersey, in a cargo plane outfitted with protective wrestling mats.

Oatsie remembered that everything Doris did worked out—from her investments, which, with good financial advice, she tripled during her lifetime, to how she made Rough Point truly her own.[4] Doris's adaptation—not transformation—of Rough Point showed her respect for the past. Her alterations are most obvious on the second floor, not so much in her frilled and flounced bedroom, with her silver cups, as in the paneled, informal Pine Room, surely the smallest in the house, where she kept her piano, equipped with a study light, as well as pencils and paper for composition. Here she practiced for two to three hours every day, recording her work on a big reel-to-reel tape deck.

As so often in the case of women like Doris, defined, almost entirely, by money, her seriousness as a pianist has never been credited. Yet anyone who practices for several hours a day deserves to be taken seriously, not as a dabbler or a professional who must play to eat, but as that rarest and most precious phenomenon, the true amateur. Equal consideration should be given to her dedication to learning various forms of dance.

At first glance, Rough Point, like the Seventy-eighth Street house, seems to discourage physical movement—large, stately rooms often repel exuberance. But outside the house, Doris had the ocean as playground and challenge. Into old age, she swam twice a day in the surf below Rough Point, disdaining the rope let down to help her from the top of the steep bluff. The member of her staff who went out to the bluff in case she needed rescue was warned to hide behind a tree.

Doris refused to spend her time organizing houseguests, preparing lists for enormous formal dinner parties, or participating in the social rites of the other inhabitants of Bellevue Avenue. She did entertain, though on a smaller scale. Her guests at Newport were eclectic. Jackie Kennedy and Martha Graham might sit next to black musicians whose performances Doris attended every summer at the Newport Jazz Festival.

Established in 1954 by Doris's Newport neighbors the tobacco millionaire Lorillards, the Newport Jazz Festival signaled the arrival of the modern age, at long last, to the enclave. The festival was much resisted, not only by old-time Newporters, who disliked the crowds, but also by jazz musicians like Charles Mingus, who objected to the low pay. Doris was one of its original supporters.

Doris's friendships with the black musicians she met at the festival would have raised many eyebrows among her neighbors. Indeed, she insistently and regularly crossed "the color line" that defined propriety for Bellevue Avenue. In addition to supporting the jazz festival, she sang in the choir at a Nutley, New Jersey, Baptist church. A 1971 photograph shows her in her choir gown surrounded by black singers, one of whom is touching her shoulder.

Doris never spoke or wrote of what her open-mindedness meant, or what it cost her in terms of opprobrium; certainly, some of her contemporaries' gossip, and some of what has been written about her, rests on the buried bone of racism.

Yet she had long since adopted her father's code of silence in the face of criticism. Nor would she have become a spokeswoman for the civil rights movement. Her preoccupation with creating beauty was in accordance with her highly individualized taste. A tiny medieval child's chair sits by the vast fireplace in the Great Hall at Rough Point. The bust of an unknown queen, bought cheaply at a Newport junk shop, sits in a place of honor under the great stairs. Tour guides today call the bust St. Cecilia, after the patron saint of music, on whose feast day, November 22, Doris was born. Possibly seventeenth-century Spanish, the bust is just as likely to be a nineteenth-century reproduction, but its provenance is not what matters. What matters is that it appealed to Doris. Set among expensive examples of her father's taste, the unattributed bust could as easily have been an ordinary stone, a common seashell, or a broken branch.

A Tiffany silver swan, the only one ever made, sits in the middle of the dining room table at Rough Point. This is the very silver swan that often traveled with Doris during the last decade of her life, along with her camels. Stranded at Rough Point when Doris died in 1993 at Falcon's Lair, the swan strikes a plaintive note, as in the seventeenth-century madrigal by Orlando Gibbons:

> The silver swan, who living had no note,
> When death approached, unlocked her silent throat . . .

Doris left no note, either, and her musical compositions are now forgotten, but Rough Point, Duke Farms, and Shangri La attest to her creativity and originality, none more clearly than Rough Point, where the past is subtly influenced by the present.

Ming dynasty porcelains, a magnificent wine jar, a sleeping bronze putto—everything in the Great Hall and throughout the ground floor reflects the established taste of nineteenth-century American plutocrats. But, thanks to the inpouring of ocean-infused light, the overall effect is warm, comfortable, golden. Still, nothing golden lacks for shadows: the mahogany doors leading from Nanaline's morning room to the Great Hall were salvaged from the Fifth Avenue house next to the Dukes' mansion. Designed by Stanford White, the house was never completed. In 1906, White was murdered by Harry Thaw at Madison Square Garden, because of White's affair with Thaw's wife, Evelyn Nesbit. That death was witnessed, but the death that damaged Doris's reputation had no outside observers.

In 1962, in Hollywood, Doris was introduced by her friend Peggy Lee to the thirty-seven-year-old decorator Edward Tirella, who had redesigned Lee's garden. Impressed by his work, Doris engaged Tirella to redecorate her houses and to work on her gardens. They became close friends, with Edward often visiting Rough Point.

On the evening of October 7, 1966, Edward was driving Doris into Newport for dinner. When he got out of the rented car to open the tall wrought-iron Rough Point gates, Doris slid over into the driver's seat and, by her telling, her foot slipped onto the accelerator. Suddenly the car plunged forward, and Edward was crushed.

On October 12, 1966, Police Chief Joseph A. Radice referred to Edward's death as "an unfortunate accident" in an article in the *Schenectady Gazette*. According to the *Newport Buzz*, the local newspaper, Doris told the police chief that all she could remember was that "the car sped forward and Edward was standing in the center of the gate."

Chief Radice announced, "There is no cause to file charges against Miss Duke and as far as this department is concerned, the case is closed."

Immediately after the accident and before the police arrived, neighbors saw Doris wandering, disoriented and weeping, on Bellevue Avenue. She was hospitalized for shock and lacerations to her face.[5] Within days, vague and ruinous hearsay had so soiled her reputation that some in Newport still believe she murdered Edward Tirella.

Edward had "a really jubilant attitude and personality," according to Fred Sopko, who created the Japanese and English gardens at Duke Farms. Sopko learned that Edward was born in Dover, New Jersey. A handsome man, after high school he went to New York to get into show business. He traveled to Hollywood and accompanied Mae West to entertain the troops during World War II. Later, he began to specialize in garden design.[6]

While Doris was recovering in the hospital, her lawyers decided to pay off Tirella's family, but this only increased the sense of scandal. If Doris had been able, she might have questioned whether it was wise to use her money to silence the Tirella family, with the inevitable implication that she intentionally caused Edward's death.

Some of Doris's friends acknowledged her grief. The textile designer Kaffe Fassett, who had worked with Tirella on the film *The Sandpiper*, wrote from London that he shared Doris's grief, for he and "Eduardo" had been close companions. Understanding her trauma, he expressed deep sympathy.[7] Another friend, perhaps from childhood, wrote in an unsigned letter that Doris must wish she could still turn to "Ninnie"— her beloved governess, Jenny—for comfort. But by then, Jenny was dead.

David Rimmer, Doris's longtime friend and assistant, who had known her well since he worked on the design of all her houses and gardens, testified in his 2003 and 2004 interviews with Joseph Ciccone, of the Columbia University Library, that Edward and Doris always got along very well; sometimes, David remembered, when Edward was staying at Duke Farms, the two would get up in the middle of the night and go to check the greenhouses, where they would talk for hours.

David explained that the car that had killed Edward was an Avis rental that Edward had arranged because the only car kept at Rough Point was "an old clunker." As always, Edward drove when he and Doris wanted to leave Rough Point for dinner in Newport. David explained that the rental car's engine tended to accelerate due to some unspecified problem with the automatic choke. David believed this was what had caused the accident.

The interviewer interrupted to ask if the impact of the car had crushed Edward. David replied that it was worse than that: the car had shoved Edward at full force through the iron gate and across the road, crushing his body and the car against a tree.[8]

Attempts to prove that the automatic choke of the rental car was the problem failed, despite Doris's statement to the police chief that the car had "jumped forward" when she slid into the driver's seat. Doris's lawyers sued Avis's insurance company for damage to the gates at Rough Point. They did not win the suit.

Immediately after the accident, there were stories in the press, and since the Tirella family continued to push for a settlement of $1.1 million to compensate for the income they claimed Edward would have made during his lifetime, a court trial seemed inevitable. In fact, a jury was chosen to ascertain whether Doris had been guilty of negligence in Edward's death, but before it could meet, the case was dismissed, the prosecutor declaring that the cause of death was an accident. After another year of legal struggles, the Tirellas agreed to accept $200,000 as compensation, but the clouds of rumor around the incident never fully dissipated.[9]

Perhaps the most credible explanation of the accident comes from David Rimmer's oral history. Since the gates to Rough Point opened inward, Tirella might have realized when he got out of the car that Doris needed to back up so he could unfasten the padlock and open them. Driving a car she had driven only once before, with an unfamiliar gearshift,

Doris might have failed to get the car into reverse, stepped on the ignition, and plowed forward.

Since she walled herself off from the press, refusing interviews that would have given her a chance to explain what had happened, the easy animosity and fascination that often color our perceptions of rich women controlled the story of Edward's death.

**19** Although Rough Point was opened to the public shortly after Doris's death—as was stipulated in her will, which left the estate to the Newport Restoration Foundation— the house retains few signs of her life: no photographs or books, no letters arranged artfully on a desk, no breakfast trays resting on satin-sheathed beds. The most potent evidence of her ownership is her piano, her closets, and the gallery once devoted to her philanthropy and then used for other, temporary exhibits.

At her death, Doris owned ten thousand pieces of clothing, all worn. At Rough Point, this collection was edited down to about two thousand items. The closets are not enormous—many well-off women would find them small—but they are seemly and well organized, with the dresses hanging in serried ranks. And what dresses they are: dozens of dahlia-colored silk caftans sweep the floor over a few pairs of size-eight shoes—Doris always preferred to go barefoot. Most remarkable are the Schiaparelli-pink two-piece bathing suit she wore into old age and the wet suit for surfing; these items would not have found a home in any other middle-aged woman's Newport closet.

Jet Set to Jeans: The Wardrobe of Doris Duke, 1930–1990, the catalogue for the 2005 Rough Point exhibit of Doris's wardrobe, states that
her clothes not only represent every decade between the 1930s and the
1990s but also make up "her most complete collection," and represent her
"spectacular eye for quality." Her slenderness and height made her the
ideal model for both new trends in fashion and classic design.

Her clothes run the gamut of twentieth-century couture: a short black
lace evening dress from Balenciaga, an Yves Saint Laurent (for Christian
Dior) cocktail suit with a boxy jacket and a mink collar, and a Hattie
Carnegie silk velvet suit, decorated with metallic embroidery. Before her
death, she gave pieces from her couture collection to the Fashion Institute
of Technology in New York and the Costume Institute at the Metropolitan Museum, indicating her appreciation of the historical significance of
the clothes she had worn with such flair.

Since she was always fascinated by shifts in fashion, Doris's wardrobe included a cream wool pantsuit with a windowpane jacket in André
Courrèges's androgynous style and a Pierre Cardin vinyl dress printed
with symbols of the 1969 Apollo 11 space flight to the moon. She also
bought Givenchy and Halston, Saint Laurent and Oscar de la Renta, Valentino and Chanel, but was not above shopping at chain stores for the casual
clothes she most often wore, especially blue jeans.

Nearby was the gallery that used to exist at the end of the second
floor at Rough Point, and that symbolized something transcendent—
the power of her generosity. The red entrance walls of the gallery were
inscribed, in white, with the names of the hundreds of not-for-profits
she supported, often anonymously. Sometimes she sent small checks,
sometimes large ones. She would give away $400 million during her
lifetime. The amount she spent on her own indulgences is small by
comparison.

Prominently displayed on a mannequin in the middle of the gallery
was the beaded white leather dress Doris had worn at her naming ceremony on the Rosebud Reservation in South Dakota on November 26,
1958, another indication of the range of her giving. There is an irresistible
connection linking her bright pink bathing suit, her surfing outfit, and
the leather belt inscribed, in beads, "Doris," by members of the Rosebud
Reservation.

The preservation and enhancement of Rough Point fit the typical narrative of conscientious inheritors: to conserve the visible record of privilege in the houses and artifacts that expressed it. Even here Rough Point is unique: it is the only one of the great Bellevue Avenue houses now open to the public that was occupied in recent history. But Doris did not limit her scope to Bellevue Avenue, where restoration and preservation of the "cottages" were probably assured. As she came to know the rest of the town, she realized that its considerable colonial history—the period when, as a harbor, it was vitalized by seagoing trade—survived in blocks of deteriorating eighteenth- and early-nineteenth-century wooden frame houses in downtown Newport.

Walking the narrow sidewalks, she would have seen ragged one-story cottages that once housed sailors, sea captains, harbormasters, craftsmen, and tradespeople. Built cheek by jowl on busy streets, and lacking gardens and gates, these houses were too small to interest the wealthy as summer homes.

Other individuals had saved a few houses, but Doris's vision was larger. In 1968, she founded the Newport Restoration Foundation, aiming to restore and preserve whole sections of two neighborhoods on the down-sloping streets that lead to the harbor. Once established, the Newport Restoration Foundation bought, restored, and saved seventy-two houses, a remarkable achievement that stands out in the history of American preservation for its scope and prescience. Jacqueline Kennedy Onassis was the first board member of the organization.

In these small houses lived the people who in the eighteenth and early nineteenth centuries practiced the essential crafts of a thriving harbor community. Often built around a central chimney, which was the only source of heat, these small, low-ceiling structures were compact and efficient.

Doris bought the little houses for about $10,000 apiece and restored them, using local craftsmen. She hired literally hundreds of workers to uncover the clapboard and repair chimneys, paying for all labor, construction, and materials. She supervised details like the choice of exterior colors herself. All these houses, painted in the somber eighteenth-century palette of greens, dark blues, and browns, with their small, regularly placed windows and their simple entries, speak of dailiness: the hard work of surviving in that earlier world, where women hauled the household water in buckets and did the laundry in steaming outdoor kettles, where chamber pots had to be emptied every morning and the freezing out-houses visited on winter nights—the extreme opposite of Doris's world.

In all these houses, the work of restoration began with tearing down walls, revealing earlier woodwork—floors, beams, and mantelpieces. How rewarding it must have been for Doris to see these period features revealed.

Her work from 1968 to 1986 was unique not only in scope but also because of her decision to rent out the finished houses, another truly innovative stroke. She did not design colonial Newport to be another Williamsburg, a dead assemblage of artifacts from the past, with costumed reenactors, where only tourists roam. Today, seventy-two of the meticulously restored houses in the Historic Hill neighborhood and in the Point may be rented. The leases are for a year, with renewable options, and the rents run from $1,050 to $4,000 a month, with the foundation providing maintenance. The turnover is low, the waiting list long. Interestingly, the tenants are not just renters. When signing leases, they are asked also to sign a stewardship agreement that may be unique in real estate. The tenant must recognize and accept that "the needs of the house supersede your own." To acknowledge that as a tenant one is less important than the house one inhabits demands a certain degree of humility.

These small houses exact other concessions. Heating bills are high (the frame walls are not insulated), there can be no air-conditioning, no window screens, no visible satellite dishes: "In signing the lease you take responsibility for preserving this unique part of our American heritage." The Newport houses represent "a nationally significant collection" as one of the very few wooden enclaves left in the United States.[1]

Throughout the winding streets that often yield a glimpse of the harbor, there are several plaques bearing Doris Duke's name. One is on the Buffum-Redwood house at 74 Spring Street, built around 1700. The house is chocolate brown; its windows are somewhat disfigured by storm windows; the glass lanterns by the front door are fitted with spiral energy-saving bulbs.

Grants for restoration, awards for worthy projects, a Historic Home-owners tool kit, and information on how to research old houses support followers of Doris's vision. The foundation excels in attracting volunteers, training them in preservation skills, and creating the little communities that women involved in handwork seem expert at assembling, if only for a brief time.

Doris finally stopped buying houses for the Newport Restoration Foundation when the number reached seventy-two. According to her friend Oatsie, she balked when homeowners, seeing the possibility of commanding higher prices from the tobacco heiress, raised their asking prices from around $10,000 to $30,000. That was more money than Doris was prepared to spend.

Eventually, the foundation acquired a total of eighty houses, but this is not its only accomplishment. The foundation also owns a handsome brick house, Whitehorne House, which Doris bought for the collection she was assembling of the distinctive eighteenth-century furniture Newport cabinetmakers produced by hand. The foundation also owns Prescott Farm outside of Newport, where the agricultural lifestyle of the eighteenth century has been re-created and the 1812 windmill restored. These properties are all open to the public.

In addition to preserving the past, the Newport Restoration Foundation recognizes the need to address contemporary problems. The foundation offers workshops in protecting historic properties from the rising seawater caused by climate change. It also offers hands-on learning experiences. If Doris were alive today, she would be astonished to see how her original idea, the preservation of small, decaying houses, has grown and blossomed into an in-depth introduction to the life that predated the building of the grand houses on Bellevue Avenue.

Doris would have been one of the first to recognize that the era of private mansions was coming to an end. Real estate taxes, water issues, the cost of converting coal-heated furnaces and installing air-conditioning, as well as the reluctance of contemporary owners to deal with dozens of bedrooms without the benefit of live-in staff, checked the impulse toward grandiosity. Doris might even have welcomed the change.

 "Bring out the racks!" Doris would call to her maid when she was ready to pack for another trip, and racks of clothes for every occasion would be wheeled out of closets and parked beside her cluster of suitcases.

Her seasonal peregrinations from New York to Duke Farms, Rough Point, Shangri La, and Falcon's Lair, along with European and Asian forays, made for complicated logistics. She depended on a legion of supervisors and workers as well as her half brother, Walker, to keep things running smoothly in her absence.

Doris's most demanding property was Duke Farms, the expenses for which were paid by the Doris Duke Foundation, incorporated in June 1958. Its single board member was Doris's childhood friend Alletta, now Leta M. McBean. Buck Duke had begun to assemble the 2,250-acre estate in Somerville, New Jersey, in 1893, when he bought the Sophia Veghte farm. In the following years, Buck purchased forty adjacent farms, finally totaling 2,700 acres.[1]

He used the farm for his herd of 250 Guernsey cows and for his racehorses, which were exercised on a half-mile track. By the turn of the century, he had decided to create at Duke Farms a magnificent parkland. Unfortunately, the soil was sandy, and there were few natural features such as hills, lakes, valleys, or forests to provide visual interest. Buck remedied this as best he could with gardens, artificial lakes, bridges, waterfalls, and thirty-five fountains, one a copy of the great fountain at the center of the Place de la Concorde in Paris. The water for all these features was drawn from the Raritan River and an adjacent canal. It was then filtered and pumped into a private reservoir that held forty million gallons. Lawns were laid down, separated by forty miles of macadam roads, bordered with rustic stone walls covered in summer with crimson rambler roses. The Veghte farmhouse was buried deep inside a vast addition, to which Doris later added even more rooms, producing a huge house, almost as long as a football field. It is the antithesis of Shangri La.

The house included a multitude of large rooms and, perhaps its only charm, a taproom with 1930s murals of cocktail glasses and hands of playing cards. A 1920 inventory lists each room: drawing room, grand hall, library, staircase hall, dining room, entrance hall, telephone room, servants' dining room, kitchen and butler's pantry, Mrs. Duke's bedroom and bathroom, colonial room, mauve room, French room, pink room, blue room, halls, and eleven servants' rooms. In 1932, Doris added an indoor tennis court, and in 1938 the "Hollywood Wing," which included an auditorium/theater and a shooting gallery. There was also a palm court.

The farm seemed to breed projects that were doomed to failure. After his honeymoon in 1909 with his first wife, the *New Jersey Union Gazette* reported that Buck wanted to replace the old farmhouse with a stone mansion based on English, Italian, and French models. In 1909, Buck hired Horace Trumbauer to design the mansion in imitation of François Mansart's 1642 château at Maisons-sur-Seine. Perhaps Trumbauer persuaded him that a model from one European country was sufficient.

But the house was never built; the steel beams it would have required were needed for World War I. More pertinent, after the the British-American Tobacco Company was divided among other companies by court order in 1911, Buck shifted many of his investments from tobacco to hydroelectric power and began to spend more time in Charlotte, where, in 1919, he bought the big white house called Lynnwood.

At first, Doris used Duke Farms on weekends just as her father had, making few changes and improvements. But when the lakes became home to thousands of snapping turtles, Doris had them removed, fed a diet of cornmeal, then killed and cut up to make turtle soup. Disliking the appearance of some massive eight-foot boulders her father had had placed in the waterways, she decided that they should also be removed, which required a crane and jackhammers. She purchased Jersey and Angus cows and a prize bull to improve the existing herd, hiring George LaFever to care for the animals. He had previously worked at the Biltmore Estate in North Carolina.

Doris fired LaFever in 1948. Later, he complained in a letter that he didn't know what her intentions were for the farm.[2] Neither did she. As a showplace for exotic animals—including two Humboldt penguins and three sea lions that succumbed to the New Jersey heat—the farm was not really suitable. According to Doris's original plan, the eleven linked greenhouses contained plants representing those found in France, England, China, and Indonesia. Expensive to run and inefficient, too hot in the New Jersey summers, and leaking heat in the winter, the greenhouses were torn down in April 2008, as part of ongoing changes to make Duke Farms an example of conservation techniques and practices. A large solarium was preserved, called the Orchid Range.

Doris had enjoyed planning and working in the greenhouses at Duke Farms in New Jersey. As she became expert in cultivating and hybridizing orchids, she produced a variety, the Phalaenopsis, which is relatively easy to grow. This orchid became the ancestor of those that now abound in upscale food shops and hotel lobbies.

In 1964, Doris hired Robert Dingwall as assistant gardener, and soon promoted him to chief grower and managing director. He explained Doris's involvement in an interview with Joseph Ciccone. Dingwall met with her every morning when she was at Duke Farms to consider changes in garden design. He remembered her requesting that he find a more successful way to include red and white tulips as well as lilacs, which had not done well previously. When she traveled, Dingwall remembered, he sent her Polaroid photographs of the gardens so she could comment and send suggestions about changes. Dingwall said some others on her staff (unnamed) wanted her to be less involved, leaving decisions to them and simply supplying money, but that was not Doris's way.

Preparing Duke Farms for expanded public visits, as required in Doris's will, took nearly ten years after her death. Issues of access, questions about promotion, and decisions about fees to be charged needed to be addressed by the Duke Farms board. As stated in a brochure, the farms were to "serve as a habitat for native plants and animals." Programs offered to the public included "Moth Night," workshops on orchid cultivation, tree-identification walks, and lectures on raptors.

While decisions were being made about the ultimate use of the house, there were no signs outside the gate identifying the property, and no trash cans—visitors were expected to carry out everything they brought in. But visitors were welcome and had the unusual opportunity to wander the grounds without a guide. An orientation center provided a history of the place.

To bring the property in line with Doris's interest in environmental conservation, the showplace indulgences—Buck Duke's ponds, fountains, and statuary—have been replaced with a community garden and solar panels. The cows, corn, and hay that occupied the fields before 2004 are gone, and invasive plant and tree species have been removed, yet the place still seems much as Doris would have experienced it as a child.

Arriving from Manhattan on spring and fall weekends, she would have sniffed the soft, sweet smell of clover and heard birds out-chorusing one another. Here she could run and jump as she never could in the city, but here, too, she was lonely, an only child who at this point had few friends. As she grew older, she might have realized that her father's dream, to build an estate rivaling North Carolina's Biltmore, had never materialized.

Biltmore was begun in 1889 by George Washington Vanderbilt and finished in 1895 on more than ten miles of land on the outskirts of Asheville, North Carolina. Seeking the very best, Vanderbilt hired Frederick Law Olmsted to design the grounds and Richard Morris Hunt to decorate the interior of what was then the largest house in the United States. By comparison, Trumbauer's vision of a house for the New Jersey flatlands was far less exalted.

In 1969, Duke Farms planned to draw approximately one million gallons of water per day from a canal fed by the Raritan River, and to return 925,000 gallons by pump to the river (which was unlikely, given the high rate of evaporation in summertime). This usage alarmed the New Jersey Water Council, empowered in 1958 to control "the use and disposition of water released into the Raritan River" to meet the needs of neighboring towns.

Ten years earlier, Doris had secured an exemption from the water council's rule. At the same time, she bought "536 shares of capital stock of the Raritan Water Power Canal Company" and donated them to the Somerset County Parks Commission, which then granted her the right "to draw water upon and use water from the Canal." The parks commission agreed "not to interfere with or impede the flow of water in the Canal" but did not "obligate itself to supply future water." In return, Doris secured access to and responsibility for the repair of "the Filter House and/ or Power House," a substantial savings for the commission.

In 1964, Doris gave $493,000 to the commission to improve waterways around Duke Farms and to install a head gate in the river. This island, which Doris had given to the county in 1960, was reserved for public access to boating, swimming, and fishing.[3]

As the state's population soared and water use increased, the New Jersey Legislature jumped in, mandating by statute that no one could draw water from the river at more than seventy gallons per minute, which was insufficient for Duke Farms' fountains and lakes. In 1969, a hearing was held before the water council. Duke Farms was drawing more than its allotted share of water through two intake pipes siphoning from the river, not the canal; the canal was already being emptied by heavy use.

If the canal fell to an even lower level, "notwithstanding the adverse publicity to Miss Duke," the parks commission or surrounding towns might file a complaint, resulting in a fine of fifty dollars for each violation and fifty dollars for each day the violation continued. The reference to adverse publicity would have irked Doris far more than the minimal fine.[4] In response, and over the course of several years, Doris had more ponds and lakes filled in and fountains turned off, altering Buck's vision of a baronial estate.

Then, in 1971, Tropical Storm Doria destroyed parts of the head gates, and an uncontrolled surge of water carried mud and debris into the canal and the island park. Now unattractive and unsanitary, the island would no longer appeal to visitors. Naturally, Doris was solicited for funds for the necessary repairs. But, as the *Somerset Gazette* reported, according to Doris's manager, she was no longer interested in the restoration. This was due either to the fickleness of an inheritor or to an investor's right to withdraw support from a project she no longer deemed sustainable. As she became increasingly involved in other projects, her fondness for Duke Farms may have waned.

The future of Duke Farms was to be decided after Doris's death. In her will of April 1993, unspecified funds were to be provided from the Doris Duke Charitable Foundation "if necessary to offset justified operating deficits or to make capital improvements or major repairs." However, the enormous mansion, whose future use and purpose were not defined in Doris's will, soon became financially untenable. Since the aims Doris had outlined for the land were that it should be used for the development of various conservation programs, the trustees of the foundation were faced with a difficult decision. Should they devote what might turn out to be a major portion of the budget to repairs and maintenance of an enormous house, emptied of all furnishing, deteriorating, and of little historical value? Or were they to use the majority of the budget for the development of conservation programs, as Doris's will stipulated?

Doris's will also made provisions for a separate foundation for New Jersey farmland and farm animals, designed to prohibit "the use of animals as part of any agricultural or horticultural research." Presumably, this indicated a desire to preserve the land on which these animals resided.

Her will created another foundation, for the preservation of endangered wildlife. It calls for her trustees to designate in the "parks area" of Duke Farms "an enclosure to protect endangered species of all kinds, both flora and fauna, from becoming extinct." Doris left it to others to define which endangered species needed protection.

Her will also stipulates that "a certain portion of my real property located in Somerville, New Jersey," should be leased for a dollar a year to "a college or university specializing in farming education." She directed that the Delaware Valley College of Science and Agriculture in Doylestown,

Pennsylvania, "be given the first right to lease such property, providing that such college pay all of the expenses of operating such property." Finally, the development of Duke Farms as a major educational enterprise is ensured by funds allocated in perpetuity by the Doris Duke Charitable Foundation, currently holding $2.1 billion in assets.[5]

When Duke Farms was first opened to the public in May 2012, it may have seemed that the place would only provide the relief of open space to residents of one of the fastest-growing states in the country. But the breadth of Doris's intentions for the farms allowed its trustees and managers great opportunity for inventiveness and collaboration, as glowingly described in the May 3, 2012, edition of *The New York Times*.

The header, "An Oasis, Once Gilded, Now Greened," expressed the change in Duke Farms since Buck's day. Doris would have enjoyed reporter Kate Zernike's enthusiasm as she biked around the park and the farmland, admiring the Greek statues Doris had placed in the shell of the burned hay barn, and recognizing the importance of projects like the floating islands—actually specially designed floating planters that absorb algae, replacing chemicals such as copper sulfate often used for algae control but damaging to the environment.

Doris would have welcomed having university projects make use of the farms to grow a hybrid American chestnut tree resistant to blight, or to study recontouring and planting along the banks of the Raritan River to control flooding. However, no university took up the challenge, probably because of the expense involved. Meanwhile, the mansion remained a problem. Its contents had already been auctioned at Christie's after Doris's death, the proceeds going to the Doris Duke Charitable Foundation.

In 2016, the trustees of the estate made a difficult but necessary decision. The mansion was demolished that spring, so that the site could be used for conservation projects more compatible with Doris's vision. Some New Jersey citizens expressed their fury at the destruction of a house that they admired, and that they may have believed contributed to the prestige of their community.

The house had contained some prized ceramics. Doris, who was said to have never reprimanded a staff member for breakage, repaired any broken items on Thursdays and Saturdays in a room set aside for this purpose, with the help of a professional ceramicist.

One of the most remarkable features of Duke Farms had been the Thai Village, bought during Doris's 1957 visit to Bangkok. Disassembled, shipped to Duke Farms, and later stored on the indoor tennis court, the village was paid for by Doris's Thai House Foundation, renamed the Southeast Asian Art and Culture Project in 1961.[6]

Since Doris had no immediate heirs, she may never have been tempted to leave Duke Farms, Rough Point, Shangri La, and her other properties to relatives. Often when the wealthy do bestow vast properties on their descendants, the gift proves to be a burden, especially when no endowment for ongoing expenses is included. Besides, Doris may never have felt the urge to preserve the houses she loved as monuments to her taste and her way of life.

Her view was larger. Each of her properties exists now as a well-endowed gift to a public that, though they may come to gawk at "the way things were," may take away an entirely different impression. They will have learned something about conservation at Duke Farms, a bit about tapestry and painting at Rough Point, a sense of a humble past in the restored cottages at the Point in Newport, and a glimpse of what is meant by Islamic art and culture at Shangri La.

**21** In 1941, having heard of Doris's work at Duke Farms, Louis Bromfield asked her to visit his Malabar Farm. Louis was a successful writer with a mission: to restore to fruitfulness his farm in central Ohio, and to spread the gospel of good land use.

In *The Heritage: A Daughter's Memories of Louis Bromfield*, Ellen Bromfield Geld wrote that her father as a young man was "headstrong and gay," qualities he preserved into middle age. Ellen adored him and shared his mission, eventually transplanting it to her own farm, near São Paulo, Brazil.

Louis's background stands in sharp contrast to the playboy politicians, part-time diplomats, and expensive sportsmen Doris knew. Born in 1896 in Mansfield, Ohio, Louis studied agriculture for a year at Cornell, and then transferred to Columbia to study journalism. After the outbreak of World War I, he went to France to drive an ambulance. Later, he enlisted as a soldier in the French Army, fought in seven major engagements, and received the Croix de Guerre for bravery. A tall, somber-looking man with penetrating dark eyes and a receding hairline, he exuded confidence born of his early achievements. After the war, he lived in France for thirteen years with his wife and their three daughters, getting to know Ernest Hemingway, F. Scott Fitzgerald, and Gertrude Stein. In 1931, he met Edith Wharton, who was living in her eighteenth-century farmhouse north of Paris. The two shared a love of gardening and began a correspondence that lasted until her death in 1937.[1]

One of Louis's thirty-six books, a novel called *The Farm*, was published in 1933. The book is full of nostalgia for his earlier life in unspoiled Ohio. It was also an indictment of contemporary farming practices. Rachel Carson's *Silent Spring*, published in 1962, is sometimes credited with starting the conservation movement, but *The Farm*, which appeared twenty-nine years earlier, tackles the same issues, its message arguably more important today, and as frequently ignored, as it was all those years ago. Louis linked bad farming practices to the decline of civilizations, writing in his 1942 *Primer of Conservation*, "The oldest nations' decline lies at the root of soil and water destruction."

In 1939, the Bromfield family left France to move back to Ohio. They found the wild country Louis remembered replaced by ill-managed, unproductive farms. Louis bought an old nine-room farmhouse in Pleasant Valley, near the town of Lucas in Richmond County. He then bought four adjoining farms and began to research and experiment with ways to reform the agriculture of the valley.

Eventually he built a thirty-one-room mansion and lived there with his family and with the forty or so members of the other families who lived and worked on the farm. He named the farm Malabar, in homage to a coastal city he had visited in India. His 1937 book, *The Rains Came: A Novel of Modern India*, had earned him the money for the down payment.[2]

As the Malabar horticulturist David Rimmer described in a 2004 interview, Louis introduced the use of organic fertilizer, planted cover crops in winter to hold the soil, and used the Graham-Hoeme plow. It went much deeper than standard plows, which merely scraped off the topsoil, causing it to blow away.

David met Doris on her first visit, in 1941, and found her very shy and distant, an impression that would change when she invited Louis and David to tour Duke Farms. David recalled that, though the farm area was in good shape, the gardens and park were severely overgrown and running wild, which indicated Doris's priorities.[3] The ornamental park and gardens had been her father's passion. She was moving toward using her land to produce food.

After his first visit to Duke Farms, Louis wrote Doris to thank her for their delightful time together. He referred to David as his invaluable assistant, who would be sorely missed now that he had been drafted. Hoping they could visit Doris again before David left, Louis wrote that this time they would like to stay longer and even spend the night. He'd been thinking a lot about Duke Farms and had many ideas he wanted to discuss with her.[4]

In the preface to *Malabar Farm*, Louis presented his belief that people must begin again to rely on the basic principle of farming: the preservation of soil itself and of its fertility. So much had been wasted through erosion and ignorance of best practices. Good soil, he wrote, was washing away at alarming rates.

Dividing his farm into areas suitable for woodland, cattle grazing, and crops, Louis proved in a few years that he could make a modest profit by planting the kind of crops that attracted birds and game and tending to the purity of his streams, so that the fish were abundant. The "Plan" Louis designed for his farm was based on the fundamentals needed to create an ideal community, with hard work and cooperation being two critical factors.

The four families who shared Malabar Farm were not in the usual sense employees or tenants. They were equal to the owner in their responsibilities, and perhaps even in their enthusiasm. After eight years, Louis could claim that he had achieved a life built on shared goals and soil sustainability. His method, which he called "trash farming," included planting, and plowing under, cover crops, as well as the careful use of planned crop rotation.[5]

Doris had probably not noticed the depletion of her land, because during her father's ownership the management of Duke Farms had emphasized its decorative aspects. Elaborate formal gardens, greenhouses full of orchids, vistas across artificial bodies of water, fountain plumes, the Greek statues—it all conveyed a European ideal of beauty, without reference to utility or conservation. Changing Duke Farms to accord with Louis's vision meant changing Doris's own values and purpose.

For example, she had bought a prize purebred bull to improve her cattle stock, but purebred cattle caused a great deal of trouble and expense; Louis thought they were a waste of money. Mixed breeds were sturdier and did not demand the same level of care. He concluded that purebreds were largely bought for show. Thanks to Louis's influence, Doris eventually sold her herd.

Louis worked in his fields himself, alongside volunteer and paid hands. Based on practices he had learned while living in France, he planted soil-enriching cover crops, such as clover and alfalfa, on the contour and in narrow strips. This helped to control soil erosion. Corn and wheat were grown in rotation. Doris enjoyed participating in the work at Duke Farms, but she lacked Louis's knowledge of farming practices as well as the education in correct land use that Louis promulgated during his many years on the Ohio Conservation Commission. He drove thousands of miles in all sorts of weather to provide the instruction essential to changing the practice of agriculture, meanwhile writing thirty-six books in thirty-three years. His novel *Early Autumn* earned him a Pulitzer Prize in 1927.

In the 1940s and 1950s, Louis Bromfield was beginning to teach Doris Duke a new way to live, despite their distinct differences. And not only Doris—thousands of visitors came every Sunday to visit his farm, which is something Doris might have shunned at Duke Farms as a frightening invasion of her privacy.

In September 1952, Louis's wife, Mary, died at the age of sixty. With a weak heart, she had become, according to her daughter Ellen, a pitiful woman, living on the fringe of an active family. Her youngest daughter, Ann, who was later diagnosed with schizophrenia, attended her.[6]

Immediately after Mary's death, rumors began to circulate about a romantic relationship between Louis and Doris. In 1956, a reporter told Louis that newspaper stories were coming close to claiming that he and Doris were married. Louis answered that this could be a possibility, but only in the distant future. He added that they were very fond of each other.

Also in 1956, the Carroll Pontiac Company in Newark, Ohio, gave Louis a new Pontiac in recognition of his service to agriculture. On January 16, using Carroll Pontiac Company stationery with the printed motto "Dollar for Dollar, You Can't Beat a Pontiac," Louis's assistant, C. J. Solomon, known as Bill, wrote to Doris to thank her for an enjoyable visit at Duke Farms the previous weekend. Then, after apologizing for what he was about to write, saying he didn't want to seem too personal, he explained that he felt compelled to tell Doris that although, during the twelve years he'd known Louis, there had always been a widow or divorcee at the door, vying for his attention, this was different.

For the past month, he went on to confide, Louis had talked a great deal about Doris, admiring the way she handled her position in life and her commitment to new ideas about agriculture. Finally, one evening when no one was around, he'd confided to Bill that he was interested in Doris as a woman.

Not wanting to miss the opportunity, Bill wrote that he had pressed Louis to reveal his feelings. Louis had become frank, admitting that Doris had touched his heart. Bill felt that Doris should know that now Louis was motivated to lick the cancer he had been battling, and live a long life. If she had any interest in sharing his life, she should strike while the iron was hot.

He went on to ask Doris to urge Louis to go to the New York hospital where he was being treated for cancer and to stay there a month, as his doctor wished. In a postscript, he added that he wanted Louis to have some of the happiness Doris had given other people.[7]

Whether Doris and Louis ever discussed marriage is unknown. He died two months after Bill's letter, on March 18, 1956. Doris, at Duke Farms at the time, cried bitterly upon hearing the news.

After Louis's death, Malabar Farm was in serious financial straits. Ellen wrote that her father, like all American farmers, had been bedeviled by taxes that made it impossible for him to break even on his crops. Ellen admired her father's determination to continue to farm in a sustainable way, though she admitted that he was never able to turn a profit. In desperation, he had sold some of the farm's woods to a lumber company, which meant that a wasteland of tree stumps replaced what once had been green and lush. Doris came to the rescue, buying back the timber rights, so that over the course of the years saplings began to replace the devastation. There is still a worn sign at Malabar, "DORIS DUKE WOODS," probably to the bewilderment of visitors.

Ellen was immensely grateful, writing that Doris, aware of Louis's cancer, had given him "refuge" while he was being treated in New York. In addition to buying back the timber rights and restoring the woods, she had done all she could, Ellen felt, to comfort Louis in what would prove to be his last illness.

But by May 1957, Ellen wrote Doris that Malabar Farm was again in financial difficulties. Ellen was desperate to buy the farm but didn't have enough money to finance the purchase. Instead, it was about to be sold to a developer who planned to turn it into an upscale riding academy and housing development. Next, Louis's friend Ralph Cooley wrote to Doris to thank her for providing an infusion of cash to the newly formed Louis Bromfield Malabar Farm Foundation, which allowed the foundation to buy the farm as a permanent memorial to Louis. In this way, Ralph wrote, Louis's vital work in soil conservation would be carried forward to influence the next generation of farmers.[8]

Doris's gifts to Louis's family in his memory continued for years after his death. From Brazil, Ellen wrote to Doris on November 10, 1957, expressing her gratitude for Doris's help in saving the farm and also in covering Ann's psychiatric treatment.[9]

In 1968, A. W. Short, director of what had become the Louis Bromfield Malabar Farm Foundation, wrote to Doris that he hoped she would take some personal satisfaction in learning that more than fifty thousand visitors had come to the farm the previous year, and that, as a result of their entrance fees, the farm was no longer losing money.[10]

This stability, however, did not last long. Facing foreclosure in 1972, the foundation donated Malabar Farm to the State of Ohio. It is now Malabar Farm State Park, its fame perhaps increased by the fact that Humphrey Bogart and Lauren Bacall's wedding took place there in 1945. Louis had known them years before, in Paris, and had been one of Bogart's close friends. The restored main house, now an inn, serves French food, and the spring-cooled roadside vegetable stand Louis built as a memorial to his wife offers fresh produce to visitors and passersby.

After Louis's death, David Rimmer took on the job of managing Duke Farms. Doris had told him that she was thinking of selling all but a few hundred acres of the property, but that seeing the work at Malabar had ignited her interest in horticulture. She became fascinated by garden design and created new plans for the property, including the Japanese gardens that became her signature. She also knew how to roll up her sleeves. On one incredibly hot day, David remembered, when the old wooden benches in the greenhouses were being torn out, Doris worked alongside her employees, who wanted to quit but, because Doris was undaunted by the heat, felt compelled to stay.

David supervised the park crew at Duke Farms who tended the water and security systems, oversaw thirteen other employees, and managed the reconstruction of an ambitious dam project, at a cost of $100,000, to secure more water from the Raritan River for the fountains and lakes. David also cleaned up Doris's lakes by killing invasive weeds; he sent numerous photographs of his work to Doris when she was away.

In addition, David oversaw the removal of thousands of trees that had been killed or blighted by Dutch elm disease. By 1989, 75 percent of North America's seventy-seven million elms had been destroyed. There was no cure; dying elms had to be chopped down to prevent the spread of the disease. It took David's crew many years to get rid of all the elms at Duke Farms.

When Doris was in residence at the Farms, David would load Doris and her dogs into her old Buick and drive her around to see the various projects under way. She always had many questions and suggestions. At one point, she asked David to write up an account of what each of the staff was accomplishing each day. Fortunately, she later dropped that demand.

By 1966, David was running all of Doris's houses and supervising the staff in each place. He also oversaw the moving of furniture and various paintings from house to house. He liked Doris, felt honored by the amount of responsibility she gave him, and had gained her trust, perhaps because he never asked her for money beyond his salary.[11] But in 1974, he resigned from the board of the Duke Farms Foundation for unspecified reasons, and vanished from Doris's life.

David's abrupt unexplained disappearance followed the pattern of many of Doris's close relationships. A volatile mixture of sexual attraction, affection, and economic dependency could blow up when Doris lost

interest, focused on someone else, or suddenly felt exploited. These end-
ings, brutal as they were, do not change the fact that many of the people,
men and women, who worked for Doris became her close friends or
lovers, and that they wrote letters of great tenderness and appreciation,
even after the relationship dissolved. But she kindled in everyone who
knew her well an emotional intensity almost certain to erupt in expulsion
at some point.

In the 1950s, Doris embarked on a spree of real estate buying, adding
to what she already owned at Shangri La, Rough Point, and Duke Farms.
In 1950, she bought a large penthouse at 475 Park Avenue renovated by
the architectural firm of Shreve, Lamb and Harmon, which had been responsible for constructing the Empire State Building. It had seven rooms,
thirteen closets for her considerable wardrobe, and a large terrace. In
1952, after selling her first apartment, Doris acquired the penthouse at
3 East Eighty-fourth Street, with a view over the roof of the Metropolitan Museum to Central Park. This apartment, twelve blocks from the
grand house she grew up in on Seventy-eighth Street, had three bedrooms,
three baths, and a large terrace. The society decorator McMillen Inc. furnished the apartment, which Doris donated to New York University in
1967. In 1998, the apartment sold in two days for $1.35 million to Dawn
Mello, president of Bergdorf Goodman.

Increasing her real estate holdings and accelerating her travel may
have been attempts to distract herself from the turmoil in her personal
life as a result of Edward Tirella's death, or, in the case of her Hollywood
purchase, to recapture an old dream.

In 1953, the year after Doris bought Valentino's old house, Falcon's
Lair, Tony Duquette, a friend and well-known L.A. designer, helped
her with its redecoration, as well as with parts of Shangri La and Duke
Farms. At Falcon's Lair, he installed a muslin-draped Palladian window
with a view of the Pacific, and a multitude of gilded and crystal candelabras and wall sconces. He also used exquisitely colored and textured
fabrics, including specially printed silks, lush velvets, and finely woven
Lyon damasks and brocades.[12]

It is hard to know what Valentino would have made of this décor.
Falcon's Lair was said to have been haunted by his ghost. In fact, Doris

had at least one séance there, a frequent event when Valentino owned the house.

Doris had met Tony at the first solo show of his fanciful designs for gardens and home furnishings, which was held at the Mitch Leison Gallery in Los Angeles. She was introduced to him by Cobina Wright, an opera singer turned gossip columnist for the Hearst newspapers. Doris and Tony became fast friends, inventing together an amusing decorative style they called Chow Fun, a play on the name of the Chinese dish. (This later evolved into what Tony described as Hollywood Chinoiserie.) Doris and Tony often traveled together to Rough Point, Duke Farms, and Doris's Manhattan apartments. He was charming and adaptable, and his companionship meant a great deal to her.

Tony orchestrated every detail of the interior design of Falcon's Lair. Small by mansion standards at 4,700 square feet, it was somewhat overwhelmed by the elaborate furnishings that were Tony's trademark. He covered walls with printed taffetas, and added gilded lambrequins, Chinese Coromandel screens, and rock-crystal chandeliers.[13]

Of all Doris's houses, her Hollywood estate may have been the one where she had the most fun. From the recording studio over the garage, to lavish Hollywood parties attended by stars, to the whimsical collaboration with Tony and playful imaginings of Valentino, Falcon's Lair was a kick-up-your-heels kind of place. Still, Doris's wanderlust had not diminished.

**22** In 1953, Doris visited Lebanon for a second time, the first time having been on her honeymoon with Jimmy Cromwell. In Beirut, she reconnected with the Asfar brothers, antiquities dealers from whom she had acquired many of the objects at Shangri La. She now began to spend time with the younger brother, Charles Asfar, who promptly fell in love with her.

His first archived letter to her, dated June 16, 1953, addresses her as "Guita, Dearest." He went on to say that her leaving had upset him deeply, far more than he had anticipated. He felt that he'd spent "the most beautiful moments of his life" with her, and he appreciated their time together enormously. Still haunted by the memory of her caresses, he regretted that she had only written him a few letters.[1]

Business problems complicated Doris and Charles's relationship. The wooden lattice Charles had designed for her bedroom at Shangri La did not fit the altered floor plan, and she had to have it shipped back for changes. Her lawyer, according to Charles, refused to pay the $650 shipping fee. Meanwhile, Charles asked Doris not to send him a Christmas present: she had already overwhelmed him with her lavish gifts, and all he really wanted was her news. Her two most recent letters from early June had "warmed his heart," which, he wrote, had "badly needed reheating."

A few weeks later, after Doris returned to Lebanon, Charles wrote that he was reassured by her demonstrations of affection. She had bewitched him again with her "sweetness," which seemed to have left a delicious perfume behind her. Astonished by her eagerness to accept him as he was and to forgive his faults, he wrote that he regretted having failed to thank her adequately.

During her travels in Syria, Doris had intensely admired various architectural features, as proved by her acquisition of "the Damascus Room" for Shangri La. In his letter of June 30, Charles wrote about his immersive work on decorative panels of eighteenth-century painted wood for Shangri La.[2] Charles created a mock-up of the Damascus Room, sending Doris more than a dozen photographs for her approval. She bought from him everything needed to furnish the room: hanging lamps, braziers, small tables, and textiles.

When it was all installed at Shangri La, the room dazzled with its intricate painted, gilded, and carved surfaces, its ceiling copied from a Persian carpet, and its vitrines holding blue glazed porcelains. It was a riot of color and detail, with no surface undecorated. Because of Doris's choice of lighting, the room shines with a magnificence that was not in evidence when the decorative panels were photographed in Damascus, with a somber-looking Georges Asfar, Charles's brother, seated in a corner, cigarette in hand.

That July, Charles wrote that although her most recent letter had eased his worries about their relationship, he sensed in it a sorrow that he had seen in Doris, a sadness that concerned him.[3] Charles was one of the few whom Doris allowed to see her melancholy. It was a rare mood, usually hidden, revealed only to those to whom she felt closest.

On April 30, 1954, he wrote that her latest letter had been a painful surprise. She had accused him, along with his brother, of belonging to the "profiteers" who were only interested in her money and who sometimes tried to cheat her, something he and his brother would never do, he claimed. Deeply wounded, he surmised that the real trouble was caused by Hagop Kevorkian. He apologized for the inconvenience he had caused her with "the Kevorkian affair" and promised never to mention her name in this context again.[4]

Hagop Kevorkian was an Armenian American antiquities dealer and archaeologist who in 1929 had acquired at auction the Mughal album of calligraphy and painting that became known by his name. Charles Asfar may have dropped Doris's name in an attempt to secure a business connection. This, of course, would have seriously offended her.

In the same letter, Charles wrote that he had faith that the misunderstanding between them would be cleared up. He continued to believe that Doris cared about him, despite reading in the newspapers about her rumored marriage to Charles Trenet. Not having heard from her, he was assuming the rumors were true, adding magnanimously that he had always believed Doris should marry again. (However, she did not.) He seems never to have dreamt that she would choose him, contenting himself instead with an on-again, off-again relationship that her marriage to Trenet would not preclude.

In September 1952, Charles Trenet, a French songwriter and performer, reignited his career at the Paris Théâtre de l'Étoile, where Katherine Dunham, Doris's protégée, was also performing. The most famous of the nearly one thousand songs Charles wrote and performed was "La Mer." But Trenet had a complicated personal life. In 1963, he would be arrested for "corrupting the morals" of four young men and would spend twenty-eight days in prison.[5] Until then, he was closeted, although it is unlikely that his homosexuality would have fazed Doris. It did not bother her in other friends.

On August 9, 1954, Charles Asfar wrote that he had been delighted by Doris's latest letter. Rather than finding it boring, as she had expected, he had been fascinated. Once again, he noticed how practical she was, and how well organized, strengths he found rare in women.[6] But it was her enthusiastic collaboration that most of her architects and designers and artisans missed when a project ended. Doris treated most of the men who worked for her as collaborators, rather than as hired help. Because she often worked alongside skilled craftsmen, especially those who laid tiles at Shangri La, she knew firsthand the meticulousness of their efforts.

After describing his purchase of a small piece of land near Beirut, which he was turning into an orchard, Charles asked, perhaps jokingly, if he could present himself as a permanent guest at Duke Farms, which had looked "magical" to him in photographs. He promised he would behave well and be an ideal houseguest.

Missing Doris keenly, Charles disclosed that he had gone to a night-club to think about her. He wondered if she remembered the evening when he'd first realized that she was drawn to him. They had been sharing a table with two other people, but Doris asked them if they would mind moving farther away. Then she'd whispered to Charles that she really liked him. He hadn't taken it seriously, but now their love had grown and come into full bloom. He begged her to write him and send him her photograph. Certain that he loved her, he believed he always would. Now he wondered whether she would come back to him if he asked her.

During her latest visit, he confessed, he was concerned that her love had faltered. He was hardly able to believe that the passive woman he held in his arms was his passionate Dorishka. She seemed so changed from when they had first fallen in love. Though she kissed him, her kisses were tepid. He was terribly disappointed and angry to find her so indifferent.

For a while, he had wondered whether Doris's withdrawal had been all in his imagination. But then, in Isfahan, she had told him things that nearly broke his heart. Now he begged her to write him what she really felt about him. Maybe all they had left was the memory of a great love. He'd prefer to know the truth right away than to be upset by later revelations. Really, it would be better to commence his suffering, if he had to suffer, at once.

Then, sharply changing the subject, he told her that the woodwork she had ordered was about to ship. The rest of Charles's letter moved smoothly into a discussion of his commission, ending, "A thousand affectionate kisses from C.A."[7]

Charles later mentioned two more letters from Doris, but then he began to suffer her silence once more. He wrote her that his nights were troubled by the memory of her in her nightgown, which put him into a state of feverish excitement. Waxing lyrical and explicit, Charles described kissing Doris all over, and lapping up the nectar that flowed between her thighs. But he had a question: Why had she asked in Tehran whether what he was doing was for his satisfaction alone? Why was it so

difficult for her to believe that her lover was invested in giving her pleasure as well as in pleasuring himself?

Charles wrote that his fantasies of lovemaking wore him out as much
as the real thing. He also realized that he ought to be ashamed to write to
Doris in such frank detail—perhaps she would be offended.[8] In fact, his
explicitness may well have offended her, because almost two years passed
before her next letter. On October 24, 1957, Doris wrote to Charles in
Beirut. He responded that he appreciated her writing to him when she
was so busy in Paris, and wrote that the political situation in the Middle
East was ruining his business. Because of the Suez Crisis, initiated in
1956, when Israel invaded Egypt to gain control of the Suez Canal, American and English tourists were no longer admitted to Egypt or neighboring countries. For Charles, the palmy days when rich tourists traveled
and bought antiquities freely were over.

Charles acknowledged that on her most recent visit, he had observed a
degree of closeness between Doris and her guide. His tone conveyed that
he was amused rather than troubled by this flirtation. Charles claimed to
understand that this man must have assumed that Doris was unattached.
He knew from experience that sitting together in a café drinking every
evening could lead to familiarity. His sympathy for a man he might have
resented as a rival reveals a detachment that may have annoyed Doris.

Charles went on writing with a calm maturity that Doris probably
found at odds with his passion. He admitted that he did not and could not
possess her, and that their love was essentially free. They were spending
most of their time apart, and obviously other relationships were likely, if
not inevitable, for both of them. But he still believed in their love.[9]

Doris kept Charles's intimate letters for the rest of her life, eventually
consigning them to her archive. By doing so, she is telling us something
about herself, memorializing her erotic power and the enchantment of the
men who fell in love with her—but also her frequent remoteness, which
she clearly considered her prerogative.

 From her earliest days as a philanthropist, Doris had avoided those who had wanted to involve her in big social betterment projects. An exception had been her trip, with First Lady Eleanor Roosevelt, in November 1937, to Elkins, West Virginia, where the Depression had hit especially hard.

Together, they had visited the Tygart Homestead, the largest and most successful of ninety-nine subsistence communities built by the federal government to mitigate the dire effects of the Depression. The Tygart Homestead offered opportunities to 198 unemployed men to build their own houses and work at furniture making. Eleanor's own furniture-making enterprise—at her Hudson Valley retreat, Val-Kill—may have inspired this project.

Though the Tygart Homestead created jobs, it also stirred animosity in the community, by competing with local furniture-making businesses. This may explain a curious photograph in the Library of Congress in which two out of three Tygart Homestead women are hiding their faces with sheets of paper. Other news photographs from the visit show Doris, like Mrs. Roosevelt, wearing a severely tailored suit, gloves, and hat with no visible jewelry. Scurrilous rumors had Doris going around in furs and diamonds. Although there are no letters documenting her friendship with the First Lady, Doris's reputation as a philanthropist drew the two women together, at least briefly.

Eleanor had suffered in 1918 on discovering the affair between her husband, Franklin, and her social secretary, Lucy Mercer. She had eventually made her peace with the situation, but her sexual relationship with Franklin had ended, and Eleanor turned more and more frequently to her women friends for companionship and emotional support, especially the journalist Nancy Cook. Doris may have noticed Eleanor's hovering sadness as well as the reassurance she gained from her relationships with her women friends. This was the path that Doris, too, would follow in the last years of her life. And although she would never rise to Eleanor's level of social activism, Doris saw in West Virginia what poverty looked like and what could be done by the federal government to relieve it. But this revelation was an exception, not an awakening.

Many years later, on January 22, 1974, Arnold Miller, president of the United Mine Workers of America, wrote to Doris to enlist her help in mitigating the suffering of mine workers during a prolonged strike at the Duke Power Company's Brookside Mine, near Evarts, Kentucky, in Harlan County. Miller's letter began, "As a trustee of the Duke Endowment, you are involved not only in the Endowment's philanthropic work, but in the policy and practices of Duke Power Co." The endowment was the controlling stockholder in the company, with over thirteen million shares, and most of its income came from this mine and four others like it.

Miller assumed that Doris, as a trustee of the endowment, was familiar with the source of its funds, which may not have been the case. Though she had attended a few board meetings, she may not have read the daunting financial summaries she would have been sent. If they had been mailed to the Duke Business Office, she may never even have seen them.

Miller's letter continued that he was sure Doris would not approve of mining conditions in Evarts, where Duke Power Company employees were mistreating miners in contradiction of the values the endowment supported, violating federal mine-safety laws, and allowing harsh tactics to be used against the strikers and their families. Although the Duke Endowment was committed to children's health and well-being, the miners' children at Brookside lived in broken-down shacks without indoor plumbing, running water, or central heat.

The six-page letter went on to cite the disparity between the Duke Endowment's dedication to improving education and the $81,000 in county property taxes it avoided paying annually by lowballing the value of its Kentucky mines—funds that would have supported local schools. Describing the brutal working conditions in the mine, Miller noted the irony that prisoners of war who had worked there during World War II were protected by the Geneva Convention, but Kentucky miners had no such safeguard.[1]

At the time Miller sent off his letter, the Brookside miners had been on strike for six months. Early in the strike, Miller explained, Duke management had photographed the miners "on duty" on the picket line and threatened to blackball from future employment those who continued to strike. Then the company had hired a security guard with a criminal record, unnecessary, Miller wrote, since he had ordered the strikers not to react violently to any attempts to provoke them. Still, rifle shots were fired and lighted dynamite was thrown at the strikers.

The strike was inspired by, among other factors, the high rate of disabling injury in the mine—two to four times the national average, Miller wrote—because of violations of mine-safety laws. Further, the region had been drained of much of its mineral wealth, leaving behind slagheaps, abandoned mines, and miners, he wrote, who resembled impoverished Native Americans on a reservation.

Miller concluded that a small group of the Brookside miners would like to meet with Doris at the next trustees' meeting to discuss their plight. He quoted the mission statement of the endowment's 1972 Annual Report: "To make provisions in some measure for the needs of mankind along physical, mental, and spiritual lines."[2]

Doris was a woman of her times, for whom duty meant faithfulness to family, friends, and country, and to causes supported by her peers that did not threaten their investments. That miners on a picket line could be described as "on duty" might have seemed strange to her. Surely, men protecting their own interests were not "on duty" in the same way as soldiers protecting their country.

Still, aroused by Miller's letter, Doris wrote him, "I was horrified to hear of the appalling conditions at the Brookside camp." She added that she was only one of fifteen trustees of the endowment and had "very little influence." This last assertion, given her name, was hardly the case, but may have reflected her marginalization as one of only two women on the board. She wrote that she had telephoned her cousin, fellow trustee, and friend Mary Semans, who was "extremely distressed to learn of these conditions," and who planned to ask an unnamed trustee to visit the mine, promising to let Doris know what measures were taken "to alleviate the situation."[3]

Unfortunately, Doris did not visit Harlan County herself, and Miller probably realized that a less powerful trustee would not be as likely to bring about change. The conditions under which the miners lived and worked were not addressed. Had she traveled there and herself witnessed the human suffering of the miners, she might have been spurred to action.

Doris's behavior stands in vivid contrast to Teddy Roosevelt's personal intervention in the United Mine Workers strike of 1902. Negotiating with both sides, he was able to bring about a resolution that reduced the miners' hours of work and increased their pay, while allowing the owners to avoid officially recognizing the union. Later, Alva Rockefeller convinced her husband to visit, with her, miners who were striking at his Colorado mine. The result was a temporary amelioration of their conditions.

In April 1974, student activists at Duke University began to protest the situation at the Brookside Mine. News photos showed them marching with anti–Duke Power placards, which would have startled and offended Doris, who was always respectful of her father's name and legacy. At the same time, Carl Horn, another endowment trustee who was also the president of Duke Power, wrote to Doris that he would gladly meet her at any time or place that was convenient to discuss the labor situation at the five Duke Power Company mines. Horn believed that settling the strike was possible. He had met with Miller, and they were working on an agreement that would include upgrading the miners' living conditions. He added that Duke Power Company had invested in a chronically distressed area, inheriting run-down shacks, which the company was improving or planning to replace with mobile homes.

Doris did not reply to Horn or involve herself further in the Kentucky mine situation, but Miller's letters may have caused her to question, if only fleetingly, why her enormous financial donations went largely to arts organizations run by and for the upper class.

During the years 1971 to 1975, Doris's giving did not depart from what would have been expected of most inheritors of her period. Her Newport Renovation Society was overseeing the creation of Storer Park in the Point neighborhood as part of its commitment to restoring the colonial town. She contributed to the Broadway singer Jane Pickens Langley's run for Congress as a Republican from New York, and also supported the patrician New Jersey Republican Millicent Fenwick during her four terms in the U.S. House of Representatives. She invested in the London stage production of *Gypsy*, provided space at Duke Farms for the local 4-H Club, and donated generously to Big Brothers Big Sisters of New Jersey.

Her support of two women politicians may have signaled a change in her point of view as the second wave of the women's movement pushed for passage of the Equal Rights Amendment. In addition, her gifts to benefit people she and other inheritors would probably have called the underprivileged included Hale House in Harlem and the St. Labre Indian School in Ashland, Montana.

All philanthropists face serious questions about the effectiveness of their giving. One of the most difficult to answer satisfactorily depends on one's willingness, or unwillingness, to move outside of one's comfort zone when considering causes that are foreign to a preferred point of view or are run by unfamiliar people. But Doris did manage to push into that realm.

For instance, Doris had supported African American artists for years, but in 1958 she turned her attention to the needs of Native Americans, after she visited the Rosebud Sioux Reservation in South Dakota.

In a December 2, 1958, letter to "Dear Madam," Antoine Robideaux, secretary of the Rosebud Sioux Council, wrote that he was sending her a tribal certificate, adopting her as a member of the tribe and giving her the name Wa-cantiki-ye-win, or Princess Charity. This name would celebrate her as a generous and caring woman who helped one of the poorest Native American tribes in the country.[4]

Moved by their appreciation, Doris decided to visit. At her naming ceremony, she wore her beaded doeskin regalia, the belt embroidered with her first name. A blurred snapshot shows her smiling broadly.

Doris's curiosity about the tribes may have been aroused decades earlier, when her beloved half brother, Walker, sent her an undated post-card from a summer trip to Yosemite. The postcard shows a tepee with several Indians lying around it. Walker's message read that he'd felt sorry for the Blackfoot Indians he had met; they had told him they had no blankets for the winter.[5]

What would Doris have seen when she arrived, after a long trip, at the Rosebud Reservation in South Dakota? Bleak government housing, wrecked cars used as bedrooms, clean-swept dirt yards, and outhouses. Her reaction was doubtless influenced by the John Wayne movies of the late 1940s and 1950s: *Fort Apache*, *She Wore a Yellow Ribbon*, and *Rio Grande*. The romanticism of these films would have made the reality of what she saw at Rosebud even more shocking.

Still, Doris would have been insulated by the trappings of her class. A big car would have met her at the tiny Rapid City airport for the drive to the reservation, though it would not have been allowed onto the reservation without an escort of elders.

Rosebud had been settled in 1876 by the Brulé Lakota leader Spotted Tail's band of Sioux after the United States instituted its extermination policy to avenge the Army losses at the Battle of the Little Bighorn. Doris might have heard that the Black Hills were sacred to the tribe, and Paha Sapu was the site of the four-day vision quest demanded of young warriors. Miners and the railroads had already pierced the Black Hills in spite of the Sioux's passionate resistance.

By 1883, U.S. destruction of the buffalo, essential to the tribe's survival, was complete. The Sun Dance and other sacred rituals were banned by the Episcopal Church, and Native American children were forced into boarding schools to learn English and become "civilized." Deprived of the horses that had been essential to their warrior lifestyle, the Sioux were expected to become farmers on land so arid there was little chance of success.

Now, as the Sioux poured from their houses, their sheer number— each family seemed to have many children—may have alerted Doris to the presence of a people determined not only to survive in the harshest of circumstances, but to flourish. If she expected to find victims, the dispossessed broken by poverty, she would have been proved wrong by their vitality and resilience.

Traditionally, a naming ceremony would have begun with a religious rite. Doris would have found herself closed up for several hours in a lodge made from bent saplings and covered with tarpaulins. Red-hot stones would have glowed in a central fire pit, and water thrown on it from time to time would have produced loud bursts of steam. In the hot, damp space, she would have heard chanting and prayers in the darkness. After several hours, she would have found herself purified, yet depleted, and barely able to crawl out of the lodge.

There is no record of Doris experiencing a sweat lodge ceremony, and it is difficult to imagine her—in her traveling suit, girdle, stockings, and high heels—enduring this ordeal. According to custom, she would have stripped first, covering herself with a towel. Her athleticism and comfort with her body and the barefoot, unconstrained physical life she led, at least at Shangri La and Rough Point, might have helped her to crawl, nearly naked, into the sweat lodge.

After all, she had come to Rosebud to learn, as she had years earlier, when she visited the souks in Beirut and traveled long distances through the desert to meet Gandhi. Earlier in life, she had not been deterred by strangeness or allowed herself to be inhibited by her own ignorance. But by middle age, her obsession with privacy, even secrecy, tended to limit her experiences. However, here in remote South Dakota, she had been out of reach of the gossip columnists who plagued her with the kind of scrutiny that often made her want to hide.

Contrary to her custom, she made friends there with Bob Burnette, the tribal chief. Writing to Doris on October 31, 1968, Burnette asked her to help him find a way to thank her for her generosity; words did not seem to be enough. He was hoping to give her something that even with her fortune she would not be able to buy. Probably, his expression of heartfelt gratitude was the reward Doris most appreciated.[6]

Born on January 26, 1926, in Mission, South Dakota, Burnette had devoted his life to advancing the aims of his tribe. At the time of his first letter to Doris, he was about to go to federal court in Washington, D.C., for a hearing on abuses perpetrated on his tribe by the Bureau of Indian Affairs.

He expected to win a settlement for the tribe of $35,000, and he planned to give Doris a token amount of this sum if his suit was successful. The settlement was to cover the misappropriation of federal funds by his own tribal leaders, although Burnette had trouble believing they could be so dishonest. He wrote that Doris's faith in him was strengthening him to deal with the many legal details of his suit, as well as the resentment of his various tribal members. He signed off by once again thanking Doris for her generosity and explaining that it was still hard for him to believe that a woman of her standing cared about poor Indians.[7]

Ten years later, Burnette wrote to Doris again. By this time, he had visited her at Shangri La and Duke Farms, and their friendship had flourished. He was mailing her a package containing a pendant, made by the same person who had made the moccasins she had worn at her naming ceremony. (These were later on display at Rough Point.)

Burnette, by this time suffering from the heart problems that would eventually kill him, asked to meet with Doris. Apparently, he was now being persecuted by his own tribal officials, for attempting to shed light on their corrupt practices. Voicing an opinion common in Native American country, although one that Doris had probably never heard, Burnette wrote that federal subsidies were ruining his people, undermining their ambition, and turning them into dependents and victims. Then, abruptly, he described the respect he felt for Doris and the comfort and relief he experienced in her presence.[8]

Four years later, on July 14, 1982, Burnette wrote to inform Doris that his tribe had won their suit to reclaim the Black Hills, and called this success the high point of his life.[9]

The court had ordered the federal government to pay the Sioux reparations of $106 million, but the tribe refused the money. Placed in an interest-bearing savings account, it had grown to $757 million by 2012, but the impoverished tribe still refused payment. The Rosebud Sioux were determined not to surrender their claim to their sacred Black Hills.

One year later, on July 28, 1983, Burnette wrote his final letter to Doris, thanking her for a recent loan. Addressing her as "Princess," he shared his delight at the way his lawsuits were turning out. His success was arriving at a time, he wrote, when orchards on the reservation were bearing fruit, and he was confident that everything he had worked to accomplish was also coming to harvest.[10] Two months later, Bob Burnette died, ending one of Doris's most rewarding personal and professional friendships.

**24** In 1958, Anne Morrow Lindbergh, wife of the aviator Charles Lindbergh and author in 1955 of the mild, wildly popular spiritual tonic *Gift from the Sea*, wrote several letters to Doris and paid at least one visit to Duke Farms. Anne wanted to interest Doris in the work of Dr. John N. Rosen, in the hopes that she would want to fund it. Dr. Rosen had developed a method of treating schizophrenia through what he called "direct analysis," which meant diving directly into the patient's subconscious. Making an unexplained connection between the doctor's deep dive and his ability to re-create the crucial relationships of his patients' childhoods, Anne hoped to convince Doris that this radical method dissolved the feeling of doom that separated schizophrenics from normal life.[1] Doris did in fact become interested in Dr. Rosen's approach to mental illness for a time.

The Rockefeller Brothers Fund had set up a small institute where Rosen's work could be studied scientifically and where doctors could be trained in his method. Anne served on its board of directors, confiding to Doris that her interest in this work came from the fact that she had felt "at times in my life separated from others—who hasn't?"[2]

After visiting Duke Farms in May 1958, Anne wrote that she had found it refreshing to talk with a friend like Doris, rather than to strangers. Their communication about Dr. Rosen's work was, Anne felt, even more exciting than her adventures flying an airplane solo or earning a glider pilot's license.[3]

On June 18, 1958, Anne thanked Doris for visiting some of the residences for schizophrenic patients. Anne wrote that she had spent a lot of time trying to persuade skeptics that Dr. Rosen's method was worth their consideration. She expressed the relief she found in talking to Doris, who not only understood but also was able to ask the right kinds of questions. This was something that Anne prized.[4]

Doris's friendship with Anne Morrow Lindbergh would be brief, perhaps because she did not sustain an interest in financing Dr. Rosen's work. Instead, Doris's search for spiritual nourishment intensified through her acquaintance with Ruth Elwell, a psychic and marriage counselor who was often invited to Shangri La.

Ruth wrote to Doris in 1958, during the early days of their friendship, that the mysteries of the human psyche had always fascinated her. She introduced Doris to a mystic named Fred, who, Ruth said, was adept at bringing together past lives. During Fred's séance with Doris, he brushed her hair into a new style—not as a superficial maneuver, Ruth explained, but as a way of restoring Doris to her true self, the majestic being she had been in her previous lives. Ruth added that when Doris had danced the hula that same evening, she had seemed transformed.[5]

With the instruction and encouragement of her Hawaiian friends, Doris had become an expert hula dancer. Probably the form she learned was the modern, or auana, version (the word means "to drift"), sometimes danced to the accompaniment of Western instruments. Even in this modern form, however, the hula is regarded by those who know its long history as a form of prayer. Doris probably felt its spiritual power. But by moving in a way her white friends might interpret as erotic, Doris also presented herself as a confident, vibrantly sexual woman. She continued dancing the hula well into middle age.

In 1963, in Paris, Doris continued a friendship begun some years earlier with the yoga master Sri Ananda. As a young man, he had become acquainted with Swami Kuvalayananda, founder of the Institute of

Yoga Research in Lonavala, India. Under Swami Kuvalayananda's guidance, Sri Ananda began to learn the therapeutic aspects of hatha yoga. He went on to found the Indian Yoga Center in Paris, which was where Doris met him.

On September 4, 1963, Ananda wrote to Doris from his Paris headquarters, acknowledging that she almost never wrote to him but that he hoped at some point she would let him know where she was and what she was planning to do. He went on to say that he was thinking seriously of getting married, since his work was hard and he was tired of always having to eat in restaurants. The girl he intended to marry was not rich but came from a good family, spoke four or five languages, knew yoga, and could help with his work. The marriage would take place in Paris in three weeks. He hastened to reassure Doris that his marriage would have no effect on their relationship, and that she would always be his cherished friend.[6]

Friends, acquaintances, lovers, business associates, even spiritual advisers seldom kept their distance emotionally. These personal letters penetrated the wall that often isolates women of great wealth because of their own suspicions or the uneasiness of the people who approach them.

Ten years earlier, Doris had developed a friendship with Bhikkhu Auruddha, who wrote her on New Year's Day of 1953 from his forest hermitage in Kandy, Ceylon, attempting to persuade her to visit him with some of her friends. He felt sure she had learned a great deal from her sessions with Yogi Rao. (Yogi Rao had attempted, in front of an audience, to walk on water. Sinking, he had to be rescued from drowning by his disciples, but blamed his failure on the fact that he hadn't had his morning bowel movement.)

The Bhikkhu continued that since Doris had already mastered the disciplines of meditation and breath control, he felt sure she was ready for more elevated practices. Although only a low-level follower of these practices himself, he was presuming he had something to teach her.

He promised Doris not only that she would attain peace of mind and perfect health but also that her face would develop an extraordinary brightness, as if her skin was lit from within. No cosmetic could bring about this transformation, only a higher understanding of the mysteries of the universe, which would make all worldly sensations seem trivial.

Still hoping to persuade her to visit, the Bhikkhu wrote that he lived alone in a beautiful spot in Kandy, surrounded by trees. He hoped to hear that she was coming to see him, with her friends. Three weeks later, on January 25, 1953, the Bhikkhu (now calling himself Ba) sent Doris another copy of his New Year's Day letter, since he had not heard from her.

Though Doris continued her search for spiritual guidance the rest of her life, she did not go to the forest hermitage. Decades later, in 1983, a psychic named Ruth Montgomery wrote to her from Washington, D.C., relaying information that had come to her through her gurus. According to these guides, in her earlier lives Doris had been a figure of some importance in classical Athens and had even studied with Socrates. She had been transported at a later time to the American West, where she had taken part in the Indian Wars. At an earlier period, she was a Puritan embroiled in England's religious struggles, and had to escape, with her family, to Holland. She had died aboard a ship headed for the colonies, then reemerged as a scientist in modern France. Ruth concluded that Doris had been well occupied in her previous lives.[7]

Doris had already found a teacher who would give her much more than Ananda, Ruth, or Ba: the mystic Nana Veary. One of Nana's basic tenets was that spiritual teaching should not be encumbered by payment, although she accepted donations. This would have been a welcome message to Doris, for whom financial relationships were inevitably complicated. Over a period of years, Doris came to trust Nana as spiritual mentor and traveling companion.

Nana's emphasis on forgiveness proved healing for Doris. She advised reconciliation through asking to be forgiven for slights and injuries, intended or unintentional. Doris also admired Nana's close connection to disappearing Hawaiian beliefs such as lokahi—unity and harmony that arise from diversity. In Nana's teaching, Doris found a little of both.

In her book, *Change We Must: My Spiritual Journey*, Nana laid out an informal, mild, and humorous account of her own spiritual journey. She first joined the Pentecostal Church, but found she couldn't accept its belief that God would save only 140,000 people. Then came two years of largely unsatisfactory study with Ernest Holmes and the Science of Mind; she found his abstractions, such as "Mind is mind. Mind is both universal and individual," difficult to grasp.

After initially rejecting the chance to attend a séance in Hawaii, Nana went, and was convinced of its authenticity when the spirit knew her Hawaiian name, which meant "petals of the marigold." Soon Nana herself became a medium, advising and counseling others. In a vision, she saw the image of an Indian imprinted on the screen door. His name, she discovered, was Thundercloud. She called him Grandfather Thundercloud, and said she was guided and protected by him.

In 1963, Nana was invited to a dinner party at Shangri La by a Hawaiian kahuna called Daddy Bray. She knew only that she would meet a woman who had inherited a lot of money.

Entering the front hall, Nana would have encountered a burst of filtered light through pierced wooden screens. As she passed under an arch adorned with aquamarine tiles, she would have glimpsed an interior courtyard with a fountain. When she reached the living room, she would have waited for a while. At last Doris would have appeared in one of her brightly colored caftans, extending her long, well-manicured hand.

Nana may well have been dazzled by the brilliant light, radiant color, and her hostess's shimmering appearance. Doris must have melted in Nana's enveloping embrace.

In his introduction to *Change We Must*, Mike Sayama, director of the Institute of Zen Studies in Hawaii, remembered that Nana hugged everyone, hugs that opened their recipients' hearts. Nana was described as the very embodiment of pure love. This would have been powerful medicine for Doris, a woman of her time, for whom hugging—indeed, any physical expression of affection—was usually sexualized.

Nana realized that Doris, whom she called Ruth in her book to protect Doris's privacy, was not only an heiress but a woman important to Nana's own spiritual journey. Yet, at that first dinner, she remembered, they had sat across from each other without speaking a word.

Dinner would have been served in the deep blue dining room at Shangri La, redecorated to resemble a Moorish tent, with draped curtains, red fringe, and niches set with precious porcelain under an enormous four-tier glittering crystal chandelier. Later, at Nana's house, while she and her friend Sheila were eating poi, the mashed taro root that was a staple of the Hawaiian diet, Nana had another vision, this time of a huge black dog. Next to the dog, Nana saw an odd black table with elaborately carved legs. She told Sheila what she was seeing, but her friend saw nothing.

Three days later, Doris called Daddy Bray to ask him to invite Nana again. Nana wrote that at first she hadn't wanted to go, but that Sheila persuaded her. They drove out to Shangri La, and the maid showed them into the living room. Then Ruth came and took them out to the Playhouse, on a bluff over the sea. Nana sat down and Sheila took a seat near Ruth.

Before a minute had passed, Sheila began shouting that she saw a big dog. Nana wondered what dog she was talking about, but then she, too, saw the dog, the very same one that had appeared in her vision. Next to it was the odd-looking table, but now it was white, not black. Nana told Ruth about her vision, and Ruth said it must be the same table—she'd recently had it painted white. She tried to give it to Nana, but Nana told her she had no place for it.

Doris and Nana became such good friends that Doris invited her to go with her to Seattle for sessions with a medium. Ultimately, Nana accompanied her on half a dozen trips, some of them lasting months. For the first time, Nana visited France, India, Thailand, and England, always staying in the very best hotels, where Nana, with her dark skin, would have been seen as Doris's servant.

During the 1970s, Nana became more and more essential to Doris's comfort and peace of mind. She went with Doris to Egypt in 1970 to look at the temples that were going to be flooded by the building of the Aswan Dam.

On that trip, Doris had hired a tour guide, but he was a reckless driver, and Doris didn't seem able to get him to slow down. Nana's response was to meditate, as was her habit when riding in airplanes, trains, or cars. She wrote in *Change We Must* that the spirit guide she called Grandfather Thundercloud soon began insisting that the driver slow down or there would be a wreck. Doris was still not able to get the driver's attention, but Nana told him so firmly that he was endangering their lives that he finally did slow down—just before a tire blew. At the next village, they were able to find a spare and continue on their way.

The driver didn't know the way to the dam site, and, after wandering about for some time, was stopped by soldiers who told them the bridge ahead was out. Nana and Doris were both put out by the delay, but Nana persuaded Doris to take a nap in the back seat. Suddenly they heard someone shouting at them to get out of the car. They jumped out and found that an Egyptian woman had been murdered by unknown assailants just a few feet away. Nana began to say prayers of gratitude to God for saving them from catastrophe.

Eventually they arrived at a small inn, took a room, bathed, and lay down to rest, but no sooner had Nana closed her eyes than Grandfather Thundercloud ordered them to leave. Moments after they departed, the inn collapsed, killing two guests.

Immediately upon arriving at the temples that would be submerged when the Aswan Dam was completed, Doris fell in love with their beauty. In fact, she tried to buy them to save them from destruction. She wanted to transport each temple to a different U.S. state capital, but the price President Nasser demanded was simply too high.[8]

It was perhaps through Nana that Doris found her way to the Self-Realization Fellowship in Los Angeles. That Doris left the fellowship $500,000 in her will suggests that she found something she was looking for there. The Pacific Palisades Lake Shrine Temple and Retreat is very beautiful, with its ornate temple, lake, windmill, and carefully tended gardens.

Perhaps Doris drew some comfort from the writings of Paramahansa Yogananda's still widely read *Autobiography of a Yogi*. The swami's "Law of Abundance" was particularly apt for Doris. God, he preached, created wealth and saw its potential for good.[9] Since Doris must have known that a large part of her fortune was based on tobacco, causing disease and death all over the world, Yogananda's faith in the potential goodness of money may have offered her a bit of solace.

**25** Doris's search for inner peace became more urgent as the serene atmosphere she had hoped to establish at Shangri La was disrupted by Joey Castro. He had once brought her pleasure and companionship through their shared love of jazz, but his behavior became increasingly disturbing because of his alcoholism, which Doris tried, fruitlessly, to mitigate or even cure. In addition, Doris struggled with the behavior of her troubled nephew, Walker Jr.

In 1965, the thirteen-year-old had been sent to live with her in Hawaii, and she would become his legal guardian. Since Walker was too much for his parents to handle, they sent him to Shangri La in the hopes that the atmosphere there and the presence of his aunt would calm him down.

Unfortunately, the arrangement was a disaster. Walker was a handful. He shot Doris's Christmas-tree ornaments with a dart gun, set fire to crates of expensive teak, and threw a cherry bomb into her swimming pool, followed by tampons dipped in ketchup. Doris finally sent him to a wilderness camp, admitting in a letter to her cousin Angier Biddle Duke that she was too preoccupied with her own life to pay enough attention to such a difficult child.[1] But at least she had tried.

Writing from Teton Valley Ranch in Wyoming, Walker prefaced his letter to his aunt Doris by explaining that he was writing only because the campers were required to compose one two-page letter a day. Describing how the boys caught snakes and put them in a camper's bed, Walker claimed that the screams he heard were not because of the snakes but because the boy was being tortured by having his fingernails pulled out. Another camper, Walker claimed, had died the day before from food poisoning. And there were snakes in the swimming pool.[2]

Much later, an August 13, 2013, article by Sabrina Rubin Erdely in *Rolling Stone* argued that Walker Jr.'s problems—and, later, his children's—were caused by their having too much money. Apparently, Nanaline had left her entire fortune to Walker, which, added to an inheritance from his mother and from Doris, amounted to approximately $65 million. But it is simplistic to think that money was the cause of the entire problem. It surely resulted instead from the denial of his unaddressed psychological problems.

Tragically, Walker Jr. grew up to become a heroin addict who abused his twin children, locking them in the cellar of his enormous Wyoming house, exposing them to freebase fumes, and terrifying them with the types of destructive acts he had practiced at Shangri La. He threw dynamite in the water when he went fishing, blasted holes for the pecan trees he wanted to plant, and put on firework displays that had the spectators running from falling embers. When his first wife left him, Walker shot up the horse track he had built for her in South Carolina.[3]

Walker Jr.'s disastrous visit to Shangri La was only one of the events that disrupted Doris's life at this time. By the 1950s, the shield constructed years earlier by advisers and lawyers to screen her had begun to crack. In 1951, the "Duke 'n' Duchess" issue of the Duke University humor magazine ran a series on a plutocrat named Buchanan Littleworth, his promiscuous daughter, Diana, and her Latin American gigolo. The administration condemned the piece, Dean Herbert J. Herring writing that the satire did not live up to the ethical standard established by the *Duke Magazine* Publication Board. The fallout caused Walt Wadlington, the student editor, to resign, and the magazine to cease publication.

An editorial in *The Daily Tar Heel* opined that the magazine had only itself to blame.[4]

In a seeming attempt to bring closer the advisers who had to some extent protected her, Doris suggested moving her business office from 30 Rockefeller Plaza in Manhattan to Duke Farms. In his carefully reasoned response of October 3, 1973, A. E. Searles, one of her newer advisers, reminded Doris that it had always worked well to have the office in Manhattan, where the staff could coordinate all of Doris's personal and philanthropic business. The oversight they provided was essential, especially in view of Doris's complicated tax situation, with the IRS still occasionally questioning the validity of her tax-exempt charitable contributions. Also, Searles wrote, it might be hard to find the same caliber of professionals in Somerville, and there might be additional security issues if the office was at Duke Farms rather than in a well-guarded Fifth Avenue tower. Searles also reminded Doris that since the staff sometimes received requests to handle her shopping, Manhattan was clearly more practical.

Eventually Doris prevailed, and the office did move to Somerville. Around this time, she must have changed the rules governing the decades-long screening of her mail. She began to read her own letters, even those conveying threats, which may have increased her sense of vulnerability.

On October 17, 1966, a man identifying himself only as "Jay" wrote Doris, his letter beginning with an apology for disturbing her. To reassure her, he wrote that he had no connections with the press or with any of her relatives or friends. He went on to commiserate with Doris for having been taken in by unscrupulous men, which he felt was the fate of women with a lot of money. Doris may have wondered exactly which men he was referring to, and why he seemed at ease asserting that she was a victim. Jay presented himself as an option for romance she might want to consider. He was about her age, in good shape, without any obvious disabilities, well educated, with a comfortable and reliable income. His traffic offenses were minor and constituted his only encounters with the law. He was not an alcoholic—she could take his word for that—nor was he a joiner. He had little interest in religion or politics. In short, Jay was a completely unencumbered man unless she took exception to his love of dogs. This may have been the one and only feature of Jay that could have appealed to Doris, who was often trailed by her pack of beloved dogs.

Jay proposed a meeting, at a time and a place of Doris's choosing. To protect her anonymity, and his own, he suggested that she pay for an unsigned ad in the personal column of *The Philadelphia Inquirer*, simply replying to his proposal with a yes or a no. Jay enclosed a ten-dollar bill to cover the cost of the ad, suggesting that if Doris chose not to reply, she should donate the money to the Society for the Prevention of Cruelty to Animals.[5]

Doris may have laughed at Jay's letter. She may also have been ever so slightly unnerved by it. That someone who revealed neither his full name nor his address knew how to reach her, and also possessed details about her life, might have brought home once more how exposed she was to strangers. Even though Jay would have been immediately dismissed as a potential suitor, as an infiltrator of her personal life he might have been harder to forget.

On April 12, 1968, Doris received a six-page handwritten letter from one Joe Cahill, who wrote that he remembered Doris as an eleven-year-old girl riding her bike.

Joe had been fired from employment at Duke Farms ten years earlier, after thirty-four years of service, without ever being given a chance to explain himself. He was furious at Johnny Gomez, and wrote that Doris should never have listened either to Johnny or to the other malefactors of what Joe called "the gang from Ohio." He claimed that the staff at Doris's business office in New York had warned him against these men, especially Ralph Cooley and Reamer, whom Doris had met through Louis Bromfield.

Doris could not have been pleased to read that Joe claimed to have pictures of her and other members of her family, or that he had turned down large sums of money offered him by *Look* and *Life* magazines for his collection.

He griped that Doris's father would never have permitted the kind of men she was now employing, and asked that she grant him the authority to fire members of the "gang." He objected to having Duke Farms open to the public for a fee, something he believed Doris's father would also never have allowed. And he claimed that Buck Duke had promised him lifetime employment at Duke Farms.[6]

On March 10, 1975, a woman who called herself Ann sent Doris a

Mailgram from Baltimore, warning Doris that her money did not excuse or disguise her bad behavior with men. And as for her greenhouses at Duke Farms—they did nothing for the world! She suggested that Doris cozy up to Howard Hughes, who was cut from the same bolt of cloth as she. And she should immediately break off all contact with Ann's husband. Ann sent another Mailgram to Doris in care of her business office, demanding that she leave Ann's husband alone and threatening to fly a plane in pursuit of her if she did not desist.[7]

Then, on September 8, 1976, a man named John wrote to her at the Doris Duke Foundation, claiming a long-ago relationship with Doris through a great-great-grandfather who had married into her mother's family. John, referring to himself as "one," asked for permission to move into one of Doris's houses. One was gay and persecuted by one's parents, who were about to throw one out of the house. Requesting a ticket and security clearance in order to visit Doris and explain himself in person, one revealed that one was about to be put back into a psychiatric hospital. After an hour's conversation with someone who answered the telephone in Newport, one advised Doris that an unlisted number was essential for a celebrity. One ended with an apology and a request for a letter.[8]

John's appeal revealed that just about any psychologically unstable person could figure out where Doris lived and how to reach her. At all of her houses, she was now surrounded by security in the form of uniformed guards, but this may not have prevented the uncomfortable feeling of being "known" by strangers.

In December 1980, she received an airmail letter addressed to "Mrs. Doris Duke, (multimillionaire) AMERCA." Writing her from Andhra Pradesh, India, on letterhead from the Rural Health, Education, and Agriculture Project and Aid, its chairman, D. Konda Reddy, began by explaining the rewards of spending money on worthy projects of social betterment rather than on meaningless frivolity. He insisted that true happiness was derived not from self-indulgence but from giving to the impoverished. He wanted Doris to consider that the amount of money she presumably spent on entertainments could feed a large group of poor people who would be immensely grateful for her generosity.

Suggesting that Doris invest her entertainment money in donkey carts, water wells, hospitals, schools, nursing homes, and orphanages, Reddy assured her that he was dedicated to these issues but had no money of his own to put into them. He was turning to her because she was known around the world for her generosity. Understanding that she might want to meet with him before undertaking his mission, Reddy asked that she send him $25,000 for travel and other expenses. Once her check arrived, he would come to see her at any time and place she chose.[9]

Worthy and unworthy, certifiably insane or in support of important causes, those who wrote such letters all depended on a definition of Doris Duke, a woman most of them never met, that was entirely founded upon her wealth and a belief in her boundless generosity. These preconceived notions were, at times, not only at odds with reality but as constraining as a straitjacket from which she would never be released.

These letters and others like them may have fueled Doris's decision to bring suit against the short-lived *World Journal Tribune* in 1966, even though Jack O'Brian's mention in his November 18 gossip column seems relatively harmless. O'Brian listed celebrities sighted around New York, including a hatless Greta Garbo in Sherry's, a jacketless Bobby Kennedy wherever he went, and a barefoot Doris Duke in Delmonico's wine cellar. It seems highly likely that Garbo or Bobby Kennedy would not have given a thought to legal action. Not so Doris Duke.

The day O'Brian's column appeared, an unsigned piece of paper outlined possible legal steps for Doris's consideration. The first line of action would be an attempt to get Mr. O'Brian on the telephone and request a retraction of his statement. If that didn't work, the next step would be to write to both O'Brian and the newspaper's editor, calling the statement "untrue" and threatening legal action if there was no timely retraction. Alternatively, a columnist at the newspaper whom Doris knew, and who had been helpful in a similar situation, might intervene.

The unnamed letter writer reminded Doris that a "fuss" would bring increased attention to the column, and a retraction, if printed, might lead readers to suspect something more serious than kicking off her shoes. It might be wiser to let sleeping dogs lie. Further, a lawsuit was sure to cause reporters to dig into Doris's past, creating a swarm of revived and recirculated rumors.

On November 29, Wesley N. Fach, one of Doris's lawyers, wrote her about a telephone conversation he'd had with a reporter at the *World*

Journal Tribune. The reporter had a personal reason to be grateful to the Doris Duke Foundation: a grant from the foundation had helped to pay for the treatment of his mentally disabled son. He had been working at getting the publisher to print a retraction, but without success.[10]

This use of a charitable donation was surely not the first or the last time Doris's generosity had been brought to bear in a totally inappropriate way. Philanthropists desperate to protect themselves sometimes resort to these means, which besmirch their reputations and the reputations of the not-for-profit foundations they create. This may be one of the reasons that the tax-exempt status of foundations is scrutinized by the federal government.

In the end, Doris chose not to sue. Her decision was most likely influenced by the 1964 Supreme Court decision in *New York Times v. Sullivan*, which mandated that a finding of actual malice would have to be made before defamatory action could be instituted. Besides, it would have been virtually impossible to prove that O'Brian had shown malice in reporting that Doris had kicked off her shoes, especially since she removed her shoes whenever she could.

On June 5, 1975, *The Courier-News* in Somerville reported an attempt to force the newspaper to abandon its plan to publish Doris's photograph, taken without permission by a reporter to whom she had repeatedly refused an interview. According to the article, Doris had instructed the director of the Newport Restoration Foundation to call the newspaper and threaten that Doris would retaliate if the film wasn't returned. The retaliation would take the form of ending all restoration work in the colonial neighborhood at Newport. This would put eighty-one tradesmen out of work.

Doris seemed to have lost all sense of proportion in making this threat. The suffering that loss of their jobs would cause these men and their families, who had nothing to do with the stolen photograph, would in most people's eyes dwarf Doris's discomfort at having her sixty-three-year-old face printed in a newspaper. The terrible price celebrities sometimes pay to preserve what they feel is their essential privacy is revealed here in all its ugliness. It is one of the worst episodes in Doris's life, and shows a decay of integrity that was probably part of her great discomfort with aging.

The newspaper's executive editor then decided to forgo printing the photograph. He knew she was capable of carrying out her threat—comparing it, perhaps unfairly, to Doris's use of a donation to persuade the Somerset College trustees not to attempt to have her land condemned so that it could be appropriated. After Doris donated $419,519 to the town of Branchburg, New Jersey, near where the college was located, the condemnation proceeding was summarily dropped.

This was a sinister interpretation of what, at least on its face, seemed an act of philanthropy. The column concluded with an unsmiling shot of Doris, taken on another occasion. This photograph did not trigger Doris's threat.

**26** The 1960s provide many examples of Doris's attempts to define further the range of her personal power. In this she benefited from, without acknowledging it, the support of the burgeoning women's movement. The Miss America protest in Atlantic City on September 7, 1968, may well have caught her attention: Atlantic City is 118 miles from Duke Farms.

Widely covered and fueled by the civil rights movement (in a far less noticed ceremony, the civil rights leader J. Morris Anderson had announced the first Miss Black America on August 17), the four hundred marchers in Atlantic City crowned six sheep and disposed of false eyelashes, girdles, makeup, high-heeled shoes, and perhaps even a few bras in a "Freedom Trash Can." Doris, who reveled in physical freedom, would have felt some sense of connection.

Raised in the heart of the patriarchy and benefiting enormously, both financially and socially, from that position, Doris still found herself at odds with one of its most stalwart manifestations: the Duke Endowment, which was coming into conflict with the 1969 Tax Reform Act.

As a trustee, Doris had never attended board meetings regularly.

There were ten of them each year, and it would have been impossible for someone who traveled so often to get to them all. Her spotty attendance certainly didn't help her efforts to change the endowment's approach to child welfare in the Carolinas, questioning the running of the orphanages it supported. Having visited several of these institutions much earlier with Marian Paschal, Doris attempted in vain to persuade her fellow trustees to hire more trained social workers to help the children.[1] The other trustees, all men except for Mary Semans, probably would not have been sympathetic to her attempts to initiate change. Since she did not believe she could resign as trustee, her only recourse was, finally, to cease to attend meetings, a decision that left her mired in frustration and confused about her role as enforcer of her father's legacy.

She began to create serious difficulties when she opposed the endowment's selling its stock in Duke Power to comply with the regulations of the Tax Reform Act. This law required that a tax-exempt foundation limit its ownership of common stock in a for-profit business to 25 percent. In fact, 79 percent of the Endowment's investments were in Duke Power Company stock. A vote to change the investments had to be unanimous.[2]

In 1974, the Duke Endowment found itself in the cross hairs of the Subcommittee on Domestic Finance of the House Committee on Banking and Finance. Wright Patman, a progressive Texas Democrat whose committee would play a role during Watergate in helping to bring down President Nixon, was the subcommittee's chairman. He wrote Richard B. Henney, at that time director of the endowment, to ask whether it was in compliance with the Tax Reform Act of 1969. Henney replied that, to the best of the trustees' knowledge, yes, the Duke Endowment was in compliance.

The endowment had been audited twice in the previous two years, with the outcome still in abeyance, Henney wrote. Before the results of the audit were known, the trustees had "instituted a judicial proceeding in the Superior Court of Mecklenburg, North Carolina," to excuse the endowment from compliance with the Tax Reform Act. Due to the enormous prestige of the Duke family, the court granted the endowment the exemption. Moreover, Henney wrote, the endowment had begun to diversify its portfolio of investments to help meet the minimum payout requirements.[3]

Perhaps the makeup of the board of the endowment had raised a red flag. Of the twenty-six board members listed for 1974, seven were chairs of private foundations that might hope to receive grants from the Duke Endowment. Of the other nineteen board members, seven were executives of the endowment, which may have raised questions about self-dealing, especially in view of the "commissions" of more than $47,000 that each of the nineteen trustees received. Further, the endowment's charitable contributions in 1973 would total $19,279,470, falling just under the federal guidelines of 5 percent.

Doris's opposition reflected a failure to understand the nuances of her father's instructions for the endowment, and an overvaluing of what she believed was her father's intent. For instance, he had suggested rather than ordered retention of Duke Power stock. Doris also failed to appreciate the serious legal jeopardy the endowment faced by failing to comply with federal law—the loss of its tax-exempt status. During a 1963 conversation with the endowment chair, Tom Perkins, Doris had said that she felt certain her father would have wanted to comply with changes in the tax code, yet five years later she no longer concluded that he would have wished to do so.[4]

Doris's annoyance with the endowment increased when she saw that the May 1968 minutes did not reflect the opinions she had expressed. As a result, she refused to sign the minutes, complaining that they were incomplete. Perkins responded that the minutes of board meetings customarily include only actions taken by the board, but he went on to say that her objections and questions would nevertheless be added to the minutes. Finding herself nearly powerless to change what she described as "rule by the patriarchy," Doris seldom attended the Duke Endowment board meetings after this period.[5]

In the late sixties, Doris was beginning to recognize something feminists would call "sisterhood." In November 1968, for instance, she lent the Redwood Library and Athenaeum in Newport a marble bust of the pioneering activist Julia Ward Howe. This forbidding sculpture of a pointy-nosed, grimly smiling Howe in nun's attire had been "unearthed" in a Newport garage (Howe had long lived in the town), according to a story in *The Newport Daily News*. The bust, created by a Newport visitor, Hendrik Christian Andersen, had disappeared after its exhibition at the Metropolitan

Museum in 1900, and was rescued from untimely burial in the garage by Doris.

Although Howe is best known for having written "The Battle Hymn of the Republic," she was also a noted fighter for suffrage. With Lucy Stone, she founded the New England Woman Suffrage Association and, for twenty years, published and contributed to the widely read weekly *Woman's Journal*. Since Doris doubtless knew something about Howe's activism as well as her connection with Newport, she could have preserved the bust in acknowledgment of Howe's life and mission.

Doris's continued absence from board meetings caused one trustee, Archie Davis, to request a private meeting with her in 1979. Doris replied that she couldn't possibly meet at the moment and reminded Archie that when she had gone to a planned meeting several months earlier, no one from the endowment had shown up. Now she was packing to leave for Hawaii; everyone knew she spent her winters there. In September 1981, the trustees arranged to meet at the Mayfair Regent Hotel in New York, apparently hoping Doris would attend. She did not.

Doris's confusion about her role as trustee of the endowment was in evidence during her 1979 testimony at a civil proceeding concerning the endowment. Prior to the civil proceeding, held in a lawyer's office in Newark, New Jersey, Doris made a deposition. Asked by the opposing attorney if she was concerned about the large amount of Duke Power stock held by the endowment, she replied that she wasn't at all concerned, because she knew her father's wishes based on the indenture, which she had read.[6]

Her lawyer stopped her from replying to the next question: whether she believed in the principle of investment diversification. He may have known that for Doris that principle would have seemed little more than a tiresome obstruction of her father's will. From the early days, when she used political contributions to try to forward Jimmy Cromwell's ambitions, Doris had always privileged her autonomy over federal laws governing the use of private wealth.

Doris then admitted that she had never read the indenture that established the Doris Duke Trust, executed through her father's will. She knew it was the source of her money, most of which came in the form of dividends from Duke Power Company stock. Years earlier, her father had mandated that the bulk of her inheritance be in Duke Power Company stock, perhaps anticipating future criticism of a fortune based too largely on tobacco.

Doris reminisced that Buck had taken great satisfaction in showing her all the mechanics of the Duke Power Company plant. He'd told her that since water was a basic, unchanging necessity, the power company's stock was more reliable than any other form of investment, sure to provide the Endowment with big dividends, year after year.[7]

Her growing frustration with Tom Perkins exploded when he tried to persuade her to agree to the sale of the stock. Their estrangement had begun earlier, when Doris had asked him to fire one of her employees at Duke Farms and he refused, insisting that she fire the man herself.[8]

Her disillusionment with Tom seems to mark the beginning of her loss of trust in other men whose advice and support she had once valued. Dr. Erno Laszlo, the cosmetologist, who got to know Doris in the late 1960s, wrote suggesting a man he knew at a Swiss bank to handle her affairs after her disappointing exchanges with earlier advisers. Laszlo's suggestion was part of a flirtatious correspondence. Thanking Doris for her telephone call, Laszlo wrote that he would rather hear from her that she missed him than that she wondered if he missed her. But since she had sent him a box of chocolates, he joked, she could be sure he would never forget her. He signed the letter with love and added that his wife, Sibille, sent good wishes.[9]

Doris's father, who created the institution that frustrated her attempts to follow what she believed were his wishes, was like all the other fathers, biological or symbolic, who magnetize the loyalty of their daughters. These daughters inherit institutions so opaque and resistant to change that they must either fight lifelong battles to exercise influence or retreat, defeated, from the battle. In the case of the Duke Endowment, Doris chose to retreat.

The endowment did not sell its Duke Power Company Stock for twenty years, nor did it lose its tax-exempt status. By that time, Buck Duke's daughter had died and could no longer obstruct the process.

**27** On April 12, 1962, thirty-six years after her husband's death, Nanaline Holt Duke died in New York, at the age of ninety-two. Doris, who was in San Francisco at the time, traveled to Durham for her mother's funeral. Nanaline was buried in the crypt beneath her husband's marble sarcophagus in Memorial Chapel at Duke University. Her tomb, unvisited and unseen, is essentially invisible. Doris chose to mourn her mother's death in private, away from the intrusion of reporters.

After arranging to ship Nanaline's marble bathtub to Shangri La—it didn't work there, and was eventually returned to Doris's penthouse in New York—Doris spent much of the summer of 1962 redecorating Rough Point, which till then had been primarily Nanaline's summer domain.

Doris's whirlwind travels—Paris, Thailand, Puerto Rico, India, Egypt, Morocco, Kenya, Italy—often included a stop at the previously titled Falcons' Lair, her house in Bel Air. She had changed its name, tellingly, to Falcon's Lair, indicating that a single raptor now lived there.

Falcon's Lair provided Doris with a convenient stopping-off place when she was on her way to Honolulu. The house also gave her a foothold in

Hollywood screen society and put her closer to the West Coast jazz musician Joey Castro. In Doris's snapshots, Joey often appears on the beach at Shangri La, frolicking shirtless with her dogs. He brought a badly needed note of fun to Doris's increasingly complicated life.

Although their relationship had begun nine years earlier—at the time, Doris often introduced Joey as her piano teacher—it only became public in Geneva in 1959, when reporters chased him right into the steam bath to find out the truth. A French newspaper described Joey as a "pretty enough boy," clearly a successor to Porfirio Rubirosa.

But by the 1960s, Joey was becoming an increasingly disturbing presence in Doris's life, even though they remained so close that gossip had them married, in 1956, either in Providence or in Philadelphia. On January 1, 1966, after one of their increasingly frequent arguments, Doris ordered Joey to leave Falcon's Lair. He then filed an injunction to prevent Doris from selling the house, claiming that it was joint property since they were married by common law—which was not the case. But Joey's injunction went nowhere. Though he continued to file lawsuits claiming Doris owed him financial restitution, he finally dropped all of his suits, saying that his lawyer had made him bring them in the first place.[1] In spite of all this, Joey continued a friendship with Doris for many years.

In a long, handwritten letter, dated only "Sunday, 9:30 p.m.," Joey wrote in small, dark script the details that convey the tone of their relationship. Now living on his own, since Doris had thrown him out, he wrote that she would be gratified to hear that, as soon as he got home, he'd scrubbed the kitchen. Perhaps she had commented on its bachelor messiness. Joey added that he was delighted by the way his apartment had been changed by Doris's visit. Sharing the space with her had created a homelike atmosphere, and he thanked her for it.

Confident that Doris still loved him, he wrote that he was beginning, at last, to find out who he was. He'd benefited from the treatment for alcoholism she'd suggested, and he was so grateful for her emotional support and her constant love. He apologized for having had so much difficulty giving her what she wanted, despite his passionate love for her. But now he was going to make up for disappointing her. He'd completely stopped drinking, and proved it to her by the fact that his handwriting was not shaky.

He wanted to tell her over and over how grateful he was that she had never abandoned him, even during the rough times they'd had together. Their love, he believed, was one of the most perfect experiences any man and woman could have.

Joey went on to describe how he was taking care of himself for a change, heating up bean stew and pouring a beer—Doris must have wondered how the beer fit his pronouncement about having stopped drinking. He added that he was so encouraged by how they had managed to survive a lot of real problems in their relationship. He signed off with a host of lover's terms, including calling himself her "Boy," which he explained was a jazz term. He vowed to love Doris forever, with his whole heart.[2]

It didn't last. In another undated letter, Joey wrote that he'd found he could live without Doris but pleaded with her for help in recovering from their affair. He called himself ruined by an experience he hadn't known how to manage. He simply lacked the worldly knowledge to negotiate Doris's world. Confessing that he was praying to Thundercloud and to Arden (Doris's stillborn daughter) and to Doris's spiritual adviser and dance teacher, Eleanor Johnson Lawson, he said he was suffering from nightmares again and could no longer depend on alcohol's numbing effect. Finally, he was even praying to Doris.[3]

His letter may have moved Doris, because they tried again to make the relationship work. In a letter dated only "Monday morning, 10:30 a.m.," Joey recounted a dream—or a nightmare—of trying to get to Doris in a house in California but being unable to push his way through the crowd. This may have referred to the horde of helpers—servants, friends, security guards—with whom Doris now surrounded herself.

In the hope of healing him, Doris had begun to include Joey in some of her spiritual practices. He wrote that he had performed the rite she'd taught him, using a lighted candle, and promised that he would repeat it every night and every morning. Emotionally, he was trying to get back to the way he had felt before he had become so distressed.

Although Joey had probably never heard Clare Boothe Luce's dictum that anyone who marries a Duke becomes a Duchess, he clearly experienced the problem to which she referred: a kind of social and sexual castration. Still, Joey wrote that now he and Doris were heading into the light,[4] but the shadows soon closed in again. This time, there would be no brightening.

In an accusatory undated letter to Doris, Joey alluded to a physical confrontation that had occurred between them. He complained that when he'd wanted to move out, to lessen the strain between them, Doris had at first refused to allow it, which she could have done only if Joey had become financially as well as emotionally dependent. Something very destructive had then happened, which, Joey wrote, could have been avoided if he'd had his own place. He couldn't understand why she'd stopped him from moving out—and now she no longer loved him.[5]

On October 12, 1966, Peter R. Brooke, a Beverly Hills lawyer who was attending to Doris's problems with Joey, wrote to Peter Cooley at Duke Farms. He enclosed a newspaper article that was stirring up a lot of gossip. The article referred to an earlier suit that Joey had brought against Doris, which must have been settled out of court and apparently forgotten, but now it was being dragged up again. Since this recent article had failed to mention that the only basis for Joey's suit had been his contention that he and Doris had a common-law marriage (not recognized in California), it might be possible to bring an action against the newspaper, claiming defamation, Brooke thought. The article, Brooke believed, referred in veiled terms to Doris's violent tendencies.

Apparently, Joey had claimed to a reporter for the *Los Angeles Times* that, in the course of breaking up, he and Doris had had a fight and Doris had slashed his arm with a knife. He also claimed that they were married by common law, which led Doris to institute a lawsuit.

Brooke believed that he could push for a retraction, or at least a correction, through his contacts with reporters at the local newspapers. But he admitted to Cooley that it might be better to let the story quietly disappear, as it was sure to do in time. This is what must have happened, since no retraction was published and no libel suit was brought. Instead, Doris launched a legal action in Hawaii to obtain a court order forbidding Joey to claim he was her husband.[6]

Johnny Gomez helped Joey deal with the final separation. In his next letter, Joey—now signing himself "Joe"—wrote to let Johnny know that he had arrived safely back in L.A. from Hawaii and was feeling better. He asked Johnny to send him the clothes, music paper, pens, and records that he had left behind at Falcon's Lair, adding that he appreciated Johnny's having made sure he boarded the plane.[7]

Meanwhile, Doris was moving on. In 1969, during one of her many trips to the Middle East, she had met a thirty-year-old Moroccan decorator named Leon Amar. A dark, soulful-looking young man with a thin mustache and deep-set, brooding eyes, Leon quickly became involved in helping to decorate and run Doris's houses. He was also seen as her partner—at least by Jackie Kennedy, who, in a thank-you note for flowers Doris had sent, closed by sending love to both Doris and Leon.[8]

In choosing Leon as her beau, Doris once again flouted convention. Not only was he of a different social class and skin color, but Doris was older by twenty-seven years. She was uninterested in limiting herself, at fifty-seven, to amatory choices from the crumbling remains of New York's upper class.

The romance with Leon continued for six years, until Doris broke it off abruptly and without explanation in 1976. Her decision may have had something to do with Leon's deep incursions into her philanthropic life. In April 1973, he began meeting, as Doris's representative, with Robert J. Tashjian, veterinarian and founder of Massachusetts's Animal Medical Center. In a letter to "Miss Duke" dated April 15, 1973, Tashjian spoke of a productive meeting with Leon during which some issues relating to Tashjian's Animal Medical Center, one of Doris's projects, had been resolved. Tashjian went on to say that Mr. Amar's devotion to Doris was striking.

After Tashjian had established his second Animal Medical Center at Duke Farms in 1969, a foal stabled there had contracted equine infectious anemia and had to be moved to another farm at night. Because this move was in violation of the law, the incident resulted in a fine and the removal of the Animal Medical Center from Duke Farms.[9]

As well as representing Doris with Tashjian and others soliciting funds from her, Leon got to know her friends, including Marion Oates Charles (Oatsie), Doris's neighbor in Newport and her fellow trustee at the Newport Restoration Foundation. One day in Newport, Oatsie remembered, Leon called to say that Doris had asked him to remind Oatsie that, since Doris loved Southern cooking, perhaps Oatsie, who had been born in Alabama and had a Southern cook, would invite them both to dinner. She did, and she and Leon became friends.[10]

But if the past was any indication, the more closely entwined Leon became with Doris's life, the more likely it became that she would break those links to regain her sense of independence. Whatever the cause of the breakup, Leon Amar was devastated. On July 27, 1976, he cabled that he felt he'd been misrepresented by Robert Tashjian. Hoping that she would accept his telephone call, he explained that he felt he had a right to explain himself. He was totally shocked that Doris had believed a cruel rumor, especially since she had often told him that she was never influenced by gossip. He closed by professing his love.[11]

In October, he wrote to Doris in dark, flowing script, begging her to resume their relationship. He was desperate, nearly suicidal, and ready to admit that he'd been wrong in an undescribed incident. Now all he wanted was to be forgiven by her.[12]

In helping her to redecorate Rough Point, Leon had run afoul of Doris's staff, in a turf war detailed in an unsigned "report" dated April 12, 1976. The report described a difference of opinion between Leon and a member of Doris's staff who wanted to do things her way without interference. She complained that, after she'd finished making some nightstand covers, Mr. Amar had told her they were all wrong and ordered her to remake some pillows—without welts—even though Doris had explicitly ordered welts. And that was not the end of it. After volunteers had spent hours restoring a valance in the dining room, Doris herself had ordered it taken down, apparently because Leon didn't like it. Now he was telling the staff to do nothing without his express permission, an impossible situation.

Doris reacted to this complaint by firing Leon. Never adept at sorting out problems among the people who worked for her, she often took the quickest way out: firing even people who had worked for her and with her for years.

Leon may never have known why he was abruptly fired, but, like others who at one time were intimate with Doris, he was able to dine out on the relationship for decades. He showed up at the 2004 Christie's auction of Doris's furniture and jewelry and insinuated to a reporter that he had known Doris perhaps too intimately.

Her jewelry and Nanaline's, which she inherited at her mother's death, were sold at Christie's in New York on June 2, 2004, to benefit the Doris Duke Charitable Foundation, established through Doris's will, its mission trumping sentimental associations that might have led Doris to leave various pieces to friends or relatives. Heirloom pieces, all bought in the 1920s by Doris's father for her mother, are examples not so much of the "gaiety and optimism of the Gilded Age," as the Christie's catalogue claims, but of its sheer extravagance.[13]

A few years before the Depression, which would sweep away modest incomes while having a limited effect on enormous fortunes, Buck had supplied Cartier with a set of large diamonds for a diamond-and-pearl pendant necklace to be made for Nanaline. It was valued in 2004 at $800,000 to $1.2 million. Nanaline's rectangular-cut diamond ring from Tiffany, which featured a spectacular diamond from Golconda, India, was also appraised at $800,000 to $1.2 million, and Buck's gift of an Art Deco diamond-and-pearl bandeau was estimated at $200,000 to $250,000. Doris wore her mother's pair of diamond-and-cultured-pearl multistrand bracelets (estimated at $12,000 to $15,000 each) when she was photographed by Cecil Beaton.

The Art Deco Cartier pearl, diamond, and emerald bracelet she had bought when she was twenty-one was estimated to be worth $250,000. Cartier's interpretation of Mughal jewels, commissioned by Doris before her first visit to India, was a lotus-shaped brooch (estimated at $40,000 to $60,000). Two emerald necklaces bought on her honeymoon in India in 1935 were valued at $300,000 to $400,000. Jewelry Doris later commissioned from Flato, Verdura, and Seaman Schepps, boutique jewelers in New York City, showed the evolution of her interest in large, bold pieces, topped by David Webb's 1969 Burmese ruby-and-cultured-pearl necklace (estimated at $80,000 to $120,000), the design a collaboration between Webb and Doris.

Christie's estimated the total value of the jewelry collection at $3 to $4 million. A small dance company somewhere in the Midwest perhaps survives because of Doris's investment in a diamond-and-pearl necklace. The modest rhinestone barrettes she wore as a girl were not included in the auction. These were examples of the simpler and freer life she had enjoyed before she was seen as the richest girl, and then the richest woman, in the world.

The Christie's auction also featured the contents of Duke Farms, including furniture and decorative arts. The eighteenth-century Badminton overmantel mirror (estimated at $250,000 to $400,000) came from the Chinese bedroom at Badminton House in England, home of the Dukes of Beauford. A set of eighteenth-century silk-and-wool embroidered hangings depicting Chinese scenes, a rare Queen Anne gilt chandelier, rosewood bedside cabinets from Windsor Castle, a pair of nineteenth-century porcelain Tibetan deer, Ming-dynasty stoneware lions, and a Chelsea 1755 tureen in the shape of a crouching hare with pink-lined ears—all attest to Doris's exquisite taste and wide-ranging interests.[14] But the Christie's auction, which raised $33 million, was just one aspect of Doris's use of her fortune.

**28** In the 1980s, Doris traveled extensively in the Middle East and in Europe, as well as between Rough Point, Newport, Falcon's Lair, and Shangri La. In 1991, she settled for a while at Shangri La, where she staged an odd mock wedding ceremony.

The groom, Paul Reubens, who created the character Pee-wee Herman, was small and dapper, with smooth dark hair, his comic persona pasted over his pale face. The bride, Chandi Heffner, Doris's live-in companion at the time, was awhirl in lavender-and-orange skirts, a sprite, always dancing. She had one attendant, a bridesmaid, none other than Doris's friend Imelda Marcos, widow of the late president of the Philippines. Her neck festooned with diamonds, her stout fingers thick with rings, Imelda carried the bouquet that the bride later threw with such abandon it landed in the swimming pool. Imelda, crouching, fished it out—a briary mass of cactus with a single orchid placed at its center. The ceremony included no vows or prayers, although Chandi chanted something about universal love.

Unlike most other occasions in Doris's life, there were no reporters or photographers from whom she needed to hide.[1] The night before, fueled by the rum cocktails Joey Castro had produced in cheerful abundance, the idea of the wedding sprang up, was applauded, accepted, and planned. No one could remember who had suggested it.

No matter. For a few days, the friends were together, before Doris flew off to New York, trailing Chandi, who for once would not be dancing, because New York was not her spiritual home, as Hawaii and California were. Joey would begin another national tour with his jazz quintet, and Pee-wee, who was expected in Florida, would move swiftly to his undoing in a Sarasota movie house.

Servants peeping from the windows would have been familiar with Pee-wee from his signature movie, *Pee-wee's Big Adventure*, and from *Pee-wee's Playhouse*, which CBS had aired for five years. He would have looked much as he did on the screen, wearing his narrow suit, white shirt, and tiny red bow tie, which looked like a little boy's clip-on. Pee-wee's shy, down-turned eyes, even under his receding hairline, created an impression of devilish innocence, prompting David Letterman to include him often on his show: Pee-wee impersonating a naughty little boy.

Pee-wee's smooth, funny, eccentric persona included an element of ambiguity, as when he explained to the *Playhouse*'s adoring Miss Yvonne, "There are things about me you don't understand and that you shouldn't understand." Pee-wee made a career of his oddity, connecting with the dispossessed child in all of us. This included Doris, whom he had met a few years earlier in Hollywood.

After the scandal and trial following his apparently "masterbating"—as the Florida police spelled it—in the Sarasota porno movie theater, Pee-wee resurrected his professional life with the support of devoted fans. Doris, too, knew how to survive the rumors that had always pursued her, but she lacked a chorus of applauding strangers. The support of her intimate circle was crucial, but it was also unreliable. There were feuds, separations, and firings, especially as Chandi assumed control of Doris's household.

But by the pool at Shangri La, the five friends played like children, released momentarily from the bonds of adulthood. Even Imelda was far removed from the reversals that were coming a year later. In 1986, the People Power Revolution Movement would finally sweep Imelda and her husband, Ferdinand, from power in the Philippines, although Imelda would be elected four times to the House of Representatives after Ferdinand's death in 1969.

Doris never explained why she adopted Charlene "Chandi" Heffner, leaving others to speculate. Chandi was a pretty young woman, the daughter of an attorney and bank-president father and a surgical-nurse mother. She had graduated in 1971 from Notre Dame Academy, a private preparatory school in Towson, Maryland, before fleeing her parents' suburban Baltimore life, first to California and then to Hawaii, where she moved in 1972.

In 1973, Charlene met Gary Winslow McElroy, who had studied fine arts at the University of Texas and was establishing a Hare Krishna temple on Oahu. In 1977, the two went to India and met with A. C. Bhaktivedanta Swami Prabhupada, spiritual leader of the International Society for Krishna Consciousness. The guru gave Charlene the name Chandi, after a Hindu goddess, and baptized her as the embodiment of female spiritual energy. Chandi then began to wear the orange robes of the Hare Krishnas. Back on Oahu, she took up dance, especially hula, and met Doris for the first time in a dance class. Their love of dance would form the basis of their bond.

Chandi procured an introduction to Doris through Bobby Farrah, founder of an Eastern-inspired dance company that had once received a grant from Doris. It seems that Doris was enchanted by the pretty, lively young dancer, who shared some of her fascination with Hawaiian music, dance, and New Age spiritual practices—the chanting, prayers, crystals, candles, and incense first introduced to Doris by Eleanor Johnson Lawson. In 1986, just a few months after their first meeting, Chandi moved into Shangri La with Doris. The two had "channeling sessions" during which Doris became convinced that Chandi was the reincarnation of her lost daughter, Arden. On April 17, 1993, Doris formally adopted Chandi at the Somerville, New Jersey, courthouse.

Enormously grateful for Chandi's companionship and increasingly dependent on her, emotionally and physically—they exercised together every day and traveled extensively—Doris may have given Chandi reason to believe that she could, at least in certain household matters, take charge. Eventually, this led to disputes, as friends and employees tried to hold on to their places in the shifting hierarchy.

If Chandi had asked, Doris might have explained that things were pretty well organized in all her houses, but recently she had fired several employees, possibly at Chandi's suggestion, and the daily routine had, ever so slightly, suffered.

If Doris objected to her taking over, Chandi might have replied, with vigor, that she had every right to oversee all aspects of Doris's well-being, possessing as she did her benefactor's heart, body, and soul, an argument she would make in a slightly different form, with limited effect, to lawyers five years later.

And Chandi was expensive. Doris, who carefully tracked her expenses, may have bridled eventually at the cost of expensive jewelry, a ranch in Hawaii, and purebred horses, all of which she had given to Chandi at the start of the relationship. Chandi's materialism seemed to contradict her devotion to the selflessness of Hare Krishna. That devotion might have provided an answer to Doris's spiritual search, which she, now seventy-four, badly needed. But the two women were, at least for a time, compatible. Chandi would have seemed the perfect pretend bride for Pee-wee.

Shortly after the wedding, Chandi would find herself cut off not only emotionally but financially, as Doris tried to ensure that she (whom Doris could not, legally, unadopt) had no access to the Duke fortune. Doris had grown her wealth through economic booms and smart investing, from around $80 million to $1.2 billion. Removing Chandi from her will, Doris wrote, "I have come to believe that her primary motive was financial gain."

There had been good times earlier, when Chandi and Doris traveled together, their enthusiasm palpable in their joint telegram to Mr. Yang Zigang, deputy director of the Chinese Ministry of Foreign Affairs in Washington, D.C. Thanking him for making the arrangements, they wrote: "For us this trip opened up a far greater understanding of both your people and your country." This is an example of the way their shared travel enhanced both their lives and their relationship.

In the mornings, Doris and Chandi often read the newspapers in bed together, discussing problems they felt they might use Doris's fortune to address. They shared a faith in the moral power of wealth, as well as a commitment to correcting what they considered society's injustices.

Fighting after Doris's death for what she viewed as her rightful inheritance, Chandi lacked the legal and financial firepower to overcome the forces marshaled against her, which included the Doris Duke Charitable Foundation, which would be endowed through Doris's will. Chandi would not be granted what she petitioned for: Doris Duke's entire estate.

Before long, Imelda Marcos, too, would experience problems. In exile from the Philippines in 1988, she had flown from Hawaii to New York to face federal charges for racketeering. Doris had loaned her her plane for the trip. She also put up a $5 million bond, as well as $10 million for her legal fees. Doris was nothing if not a loyal friend.

Their friendship had begun in 1979, when Doris had stayed in the Marcoses' ornate, Spanish-style guesthouse on the grounds of Malacanang Palace. She and Imelda had grown close during the three years that Imelda and Ferdinand had lived in exile in Hawaii. In *The New York Times* on November 4, 1988, Celestine Bohlen reported that Doris believed that the case against the Marcoses contradicted basic American values, quoting Doris as saying, "I have always believed that an accused person is innocent until proved guilty. I wish the rest of America agreed with me."

Her responses to Bohlen's questions were relayed by her lawyer, Donald A. Robinson. "We have agonized with our families for a solution. I hope justice prevails," Robinson quoted Doris as saying: "But as events continue, I worry that another 'Bonfire of the Vanities' is exploding at the expense of my friend's honor and freedom." Doris was referring to Tom Wolfe's 1987 bestselling novel, which, among other things, satirized ambition, politics, class, and the excessive display of wealth in 1980s New York City.

Imelda and Doris shared a passion for music. Imelda was an exuberant cabaret performer who often burst into impromptu song. More important, Doris believed that the Marcoses provided a buffer against communism in the Philippines. For Doris, this may have had more significance than the charge that the Marcoses had plundered $103 million from the Philippine treasury, using the money to buy Manhattan real estate, art, and shoes.

In the same *New York Times* article, Imelda spoke of her great respect for Doris. The syndicated gossip columnist for the New York *Daily News*, Liz Smith, reported that Imelda's portrait was the only one on Doris's piano in her penthouse at 475 Park Avenue.

Doris may well have identified with Imelda because of the way she was portrayed in the press. Most commentators focused on Imelda's lavish lifestyle, caricaturing her vast collection of Manolo Blahniks and other possessions. Her role in the despoiling of the Philippine treasury evoked less censure than her commitment to enjoying herself. The fact that those she called "the little people" in her country idolized her and drew vicarious pleasure from her lifestyle paled, as did her building of a hospital and a cultural center, in the glare cast by her remorseless hedonism and materialism.

Imelda and Doris were further united in their hatred of governmental authority, particularly when it intruded on areas of their personal lives that they considered inviolable: their right to spend freely and to enjoy themselves. In Imelda's case, she believed she had an inborn right to pile up millions pillaged from the people of the Philippines. Doris, meanwhile, felt she could exercise her right as a landowner over the land she coveted in Hawaii, but was thwarted when denied permission to build a swimming pool extending over the beachfront. She also tried to siphon water she needed from the Raritan River for the man-made lakes and fountains at Duke Farms, ignoring the fact that the water was needed for the people of New Jersey.

Imelda Marcos's story has been somewhat revised in recent years, especially after she was ultimately cleared of all charges in the U.S. courts. She returned to the Philippines in 1991 and was elected four times in subsequent years to their congress. Then, in 2013, David Byrne wrote *Here Lies Love*, a widely praised musical about Imelda that opened at the Public Theater in New York in 2017. Byrne said she was a star for whom the songs in the show seemed to write themselves. Although the show stresses, almost equally, Imelda's triumph and her downfall, the lyrics allow the audience to appreciate the ingenuity of the poor girl who rose to power and represented the dreams of her people.

Imelda, who was called "The Fabulous One," became the incarnation of beauty, power, and success after she married Ferdinand Marcos. He forcefully remade her into the perfect political wife. Claiming that she was too fat, he even weighed her food—something Doris would have related to, given her efforts to influence Marian Paschal's weight.

In 1965, Imelda's popularity was crucial to her husband's election as president. He promised roads, schools, and hospitals—promises that were at least partially fulfilled. Doris may have remembered her attempts to promote the political career of her first husband, Jimmy Cromwell. And, like Imelda, Doris was both admired and vilified for her glamour, money, and power.

As for Pee-wee, Doris would give him refuge after he was indicted and condemned for the incident in the Sarasota cinema. Many of his friends in Hollywood spoke up in his defense, among them the now disgraced Bill Cosby. But Pee-wee, whose strange gamin charm seldom failed to please, would bounce back. Ten years later, he resumed his TV career. He never needed to become dependent on Doris. Nor did Imelda, who has outlived Doris by many years.

It may have been Doris's longtime servants, peering from the windows at the wedding party, whose future was most secure. Though Doris frequently shifted responsibility among the various men in her life, most of the staff these men were supposed to supervise stayed in their jobs longer than their overseers.

Perhaps, in the end, their work of cooking, cleaning, gardening, and driving had a legitimacy, for Doris, that outweighed whatever loyalty she felt to her consorts. Since she had been raised by servants, their work— the basic hard work of housekeeping—may have provided her only sure connection to ordinary reality and affection.

 In 1987, Chandi met Bernard Lafferty at a party at
the Beverly Hills home of Elizabeth Taylor, and, know-
ing that Doris was in search of a butler to replace Phil
Strider, who was retiring, Taylor recommended him.
Encouraged by Chandi, Doris met Bernard, liked him, and hired him
on the spot.

The routine Phil had inherited would continue under his successor.

According to a later interview with Phil, he had been working for
a bachelor on Park Avenue when he sometimes noticed a tall, elegant
woman leaning against a building when she was fatigued during her
walks. One day they struck up a conversation, and before long Phil was
hired to oversee a domestic routine established in the 1930s by Doris's
then butler, Henry Spragg, who served her for thirty years, until his
death. Meals were served in a style that Phil called "European Service,"
which involved passing each dish to each guest at the table. He remembered that the most formal meal at Doris's house was lunch, which was
always served in the dining room. Phil communicated with the waiters
through hand signals, since they were not allowed to speak. Guests were

offered one drink before lunch, and ushered to the table at exactly twelve-forty-five. Doris never waited for latecomers.

No matter where she was in residence, Doris never ate lunch alone. In addition to Chandi, her two secretaries would join her, or Johnny Gomez—with much talk and laughter—or friends like Carolyn Lynch, co-founder with her husband of the Lynch Foundation, or Malcolm Forbes, or Betty Hutton. When Betty came for Sunday lunch, she and Doris would sometimes read *Arsenic and Old Lace* afterward, each taking a part; this play about two genteel but wicked old ladies must have delighted Doris. Or she would sing after lunch, sometimes with a black gospel singer from Newark, doing jazz improvisations on the hymns they would sing in choir.

According to Phil, during his tenure in the late 1980s, the staff started to quarrel, sometimes at Chandi's instigation, and the atmosphere became toxic. One time, Johnny Gomez added to the tension by throwing a tantrum over a ninety-dollar bottle of wine used to poach mussels, even though Doris pronounced the mussels delicious.[1]

Around this time, the staff began leaving, one by one. Doris did not understand what was happening, and Phil remembered her being very hurt and mystified by these departures. Apparently, she was unwilling to look into the reasons for their dissatisfaction. Phil was a huge admirer of Doris. He considered her a very classy, even regal woman, one of the best, and later said he regretted leaving. He did concede, however, that even though Bernard Lafferty came into a household of fixed routines, it was one beset with dissension.[2]

By the time Bernard arrived, Chandi was involved in all of Doris's personal philanthropic giving. She also encouraged Doris to spend money on herself, above all on projects that delighted her, such as setting up a state-of-the-art music studio at Duke Farms to record performances of the gospel singer Constance Pitts-Speed. At Chandi's urging, Doris had a Kurzweil orchestral keyboard installed there, with a Macintosh computer attached to it.

In Somerville on November 10, 1988, two years after their first meeting, Doris and Chandi drove to the courthouse to sign adoption papers following a brief hearing in family court. For three more years, the two women lived and traveled together, until their disputes began to draw the attention of Doris's staff, including Bernard, who appeared to keep what he saw to himself, a quality that made him precious to Doris.

In February 1991, at Falcon's Lair, the tensions between Doris and Chandi erupted, and the young woman was terminated. As was her wont, Doris did not explain her actions, nor did she tell Chandi herself that she was out. Doris simply left the premises and had her staff throw Chandi out.

In May 1991, Doris was informed by Howarth & Smith, Chandi's attorneys in Los Angeles, that their client was seeking payment for medical bills and transportation to San Diego, where she saw a doctor for an unspecified ailment. She hoped at the same time to meet with Ronald T. Oldenburg, a Hawaiian attorney Doris had hired to help acquire green cards for her staff. Chandi wanted to work out a reconciliation with Doris, but Oldenburg was advised by Doris's attorneys that he was under no obligation to comply. He sent a letter to Doris to inform her that he would not meet with Chandi.

On May 27, Irwin Bloom, one of Doris's many lawyers, advised her that Oldenburg was conveying Chandi's questions about the state of Doris's health, even though Bloom had insisted that Doris was fine. Apparently, Chandi was trying to prove that the people now taking care of Doris—primarily Bernard Lafferty—were not competent to do so. Bloom also surmised that Chandi might be preparing to seek guardianship of Doris's affairs on the grounds that Doris was unable to take care of them herself. He suggested that Doris write a letter to one of her other lawyers, specifically mentioning Samuel N. Greenspoon, who had drawn up her will in 1970, stating that she was in good health and felt about Chandi as she had when she dismissed her in February. Indeed, Doris had dictated a letter to Walker Jr. and to her trusts and estates lawyer Sam Greenspoon in New York City, in April 1992, to head off this very situation. "Dear Walker and Sam," she wrote: "In the event any attempt is made to have me declared incompetent, you have agreed that you will oppose any such attempt, including taking necessary appeals." The letter was signed, in typescript, "Sincerely, Doris Duke." On the back of this letter, both men are named as conservators of Doris's property should she become incapacitated. Neither side is signed in her handwriting.[3] If Doris had in fact dictated the letter, it shows a clear mind and a determination to protect herself from fortune seekers. The lack of a handwritten signature, however, raises doubt about the legitimacy of the letter.

On February 10, 1993, in the midst of a storm of publicity provoked by Chandi's claims, Doris asked Bloom whether she should try to annul the adoption. Bloom felt that Chandi's adoption gave her no legal basis for her demands, especially in view of the terms of James B. Duke's 1917 will, which limited inheritors to biological heirs. He advised Doris to forget about an annulment, which would have been difficult if not impossible to achieve. Still, Chandi's chances were somewhat enhanced by the language in Doris's will, which named lineal descendants rather than biological issue as heirs. This opened the way for an adopted daughter's claim, and raised the possibility that Doris had intended at one point for Chandi to be an inheritor.

Throughout this turbulent time, Doris found herself turning to Bernard Lafferty more and more. Bernard's sexual ambiguity may have reassured Doris. They seemed immediately to understand each other as two beings who were not neatly categorizable. Although Bernard was her butler, his relationship with Doris was not constrained or defined by that position. Who was he, really, bringing in her evening cocktail on the small silver tray, hesitating in the doorway, almost bowing? Who was she, really, now that she sometimes needed a cane to walk—although she would never agree to use one?

Despite her increasing frailty, between 1990 and 1993 Doris traveled extensively. She visited Austria and Morocco, as well as Switzerland, Poland, Romania, Vietnam, Thailand, and Laos, and, only a few months before her death, Australia and Holland. In 1993, she had an operation for a broken hip as well as two knee replacements, which she undertook in the hope that she could once again dance. Eleanor Johnson Lawson, Doris's former yoga and dance teacher as well as close personal confidante, advised against the knee surgeries, but Doris took no notice. The surgeries were not a success, and Doris would never dance again.

Bernard was always waiting to welcome Doris back from her travels and to let her know that he had missed her. Except for his wages, he asked for, and received, few expensive gifts, loans, bonuses, or handouts, which again marked him as exceptional in Doris's life. Increasingly, she relied upon him to help her navigate the stairs, to hoist her in and out of cars, and even to support her when walking.

Doris's friends came to know and like Bernard, partly because of his devotion to Doris but also because he never seemed to take advantage of his relationship with her to improve his own status. At parties, he hovered in the background even after Doris had urged him to take off his white butler's coat. He was always solicitous of her comfort and that of her guests, hurrying to serve food and drink or to recover coats at the end of the evening. Even those inclined to doubt the sincerity of the men who attended Doris were eventually persuaded that Bernard's affection was sincere. Of course, there were always those among Doris's acquaintances who would never be able to see Bernard as anything other than a butler.

Her friends were becoming aware of Doris's increasing vulnerability, given her loneliness and partial disability. Like all women who have prized their bodies and lived through them, she felt the loss of her physical strength and beauty as severe blows. And by now, Nana Veary was no longer at Doris's side; even Eleanor Lawson faded into the background. Close friends who might have offered comfort were held at arm's length, finding it more and more difficult to reach Doris on the telephone. Her increasing isolation was blamed on Bernard, but it is just as likely that Doris, aware of her physical deterioration, no longer wanted to be seen by her friends. Yet her end was not as pitiable as that of other rich women of her generation, despite certain sad similarities.

Huguette Clark, a copper heiress, spent the last twenty years of her life at the Beth Israel Medical Center in New York, her only friends her doctors and nurses. After she died in 2011, at the age of 104, distant relatives charged the hospital with coercing Huguette into leaving it a large chunk of her $300 million estate. Before she died, she had given the hospital $4 million as well as paying millions more for living there, even when she was not actually in need of medical care. The relatives suing for a larger share of her estate had never visited her, giving as their excuse that she was such a private person.

Although the case seemed to turn on whether or not Huguette liked, or even saw, her relatives, or whether they liked, or even saw, her, there is another factor that operates powerfully when, through her will, a woman makes decisions about passing on great wealth to an institution rather than to her family. It is sometimes not clear to the public that inherited money belongs to the inheritor, rather than the extended family. Huguette, disposing of her fortune as she wished, may not have guessed that her relatives doubted her right to make the decision.

Attitudes had changed to some degree by 2014, when Huguette's second will was vindicated by the courts. Proof rested on the fact that she had not only authorized the sale of her fine Stradivarius violin and Renoir painting but also kept her checkbook on her bedside table at the hospital, and wrote out large sums for gifts in a steady hand. She chose to enrich the people who had been kindest to her in her last years.[4] Like Doris, Huguette had no relatives to whom she felt especially close.

Although friendly in a formal way, Doris had never been intimate with her Duke relatives. The only exceptions were her half brother, Walker Jr., and her cousin Mary Semans, who was a devoted friend. In 1989, Mary wrote a four-and-a-half-page letter to Doris from Durham, North Carolina, emphasizing that everyone had missed Doris at a recent family reunion. She also gave her news of the endowment—Doris had not attended board meetings in years. Mary wrote of changes in the field of child care, special conferences on subjects like medical ethics and infant mortality, and the challenges for those caring for AIDS patients. Doris gave generously to the latter cause, including a $2 million contribution for AIDS research at Duke University and $1 million to the Elizabeth Taylor AIDS Foundation in 1993 alone. Unfortunately, Mary did not see Doris during her last years.

Rumors and suspicions cloud the picture of those final years. Doris may have suffered a fall in 1990, but a joyous snapshot from her February 1992 trip to Southeast Asia, taken eighteen months before her death, shows her in an open boat, arms outspread and face aglow, with Bernard and her maid, Nuku Makasiale, beaming behind her.[5]

This photograph seems to trump rumors that she was isolated by her staff during her final months. But her lifelong friend Oatsie remembered that she couldn't reach Doris during this time. Her phone calls were answered by someone who always said that Doris was unavailable. However, Oatsie, who knew Bernard, did not think it was him.[6]

Bernard was at Falcon's Lair when Doris died, at the age of eighty, on October 28, 1993. He immediately arranged to have her body cremated and scattered her ashes, with flowers, in the Pacific, though Doris had requested that her body be buried at sea. There was no autopsy; the death certificate was signed by Dr. Joshua Trabulus, stating pulmonary edema as the cause. This information was given to the press by the noted public-relations man Howard J. Rubenstein, who was identified as "an advisor to Bernard Lafferty." This merely added fuel to the fire of escalating suspicions of Bernard's wrongdoing.

On December 5, 1993, Mary wrote to Bernard, whom Doris had named as her executor, to offer her support and to ask for a portrait of Doris to hang in the library at Duke University. But there was no portrait, except the one of the bored blond girl in the entrance hall at Rough Point. There is still no portrait of Doris Duke to be found at Duke University.

Nannerl O. Keohane, president of Duke at the time of Doris's death, also called Bernard to offer support. Bernard responded that he was touched by her phone call.

After attending a ceremonial occasion at Duke University in June 1994, Bernard thanked John J. Piva, Jr., head of the university's development office, adding that he was considering Piva's suggestion that the Levine Science Research Center be renamed for Doris, in gratitude for her $10 million bequest. This did not happen.

On October 15, Peggy Lee wrote to Bernard that she missed seeing him at her dinner party. She wondered if he remembered the pink cabbage rose she had fastened to the top of her oxygen tank.

Kelly Morgan, a major donor to AIDS research who had known Doris through this shared concern, wrote to Bernard in July to express pain at the gossip swirling around Doris's death. She praised him for not adding to the furor, and also for caring for Doris during her last days.[7]

Rumors of foul play and a storm of legal debate tied up Doris's estate for three years. An army of lawyers—forty, in ten law firms—worked on the suits, charging more than $10 million in legal fees. The suits were aimed first at Bernard, to whom Doris had left $5 million as well as an annual income of $500,000 for life and a seat on the board of the Doris Duke Charitable Foundation. She also named Bernard as coexecutor of her estate, along with the United States Trust Company.

Irwin Bloom, whom Doris had removed in 1992 as coexecutor of her will, filed objections, claiming that Doris told him she was frightened of the medicines she was being given. He also objected, as did Chandi, to Doris's cremation, saying that Doris had explicitly told him she wanted to be buried at sea.

After Doris's death, in the spring of 1994, Chandi had filed a breach-of-promise suit, claiming that Doris, in her will, had reneged on a promise to make Chandi sole beneficiary of her estate. Chandi sought compensatory and punitive damages, and an order preventing Doris's estate from going to anyone else. But Doris had made it clear before her death that she regretted having adopted Chandi. She had also stated that her father would not have wished Chandi to inherit any of the proceeds of the trusts he had established for Doris, for other relatives, and, finally, for charity. She did not wish Chandi to be deemed her lineal descendant, adding that she was worried that Chandi would find a way to draw income from the trusts.

On November 2, 1993, Chandi's lawyer, Benjamin Michel, asked the Supreme Court of New Jersey on behalf of his client to rule that Doris's will be filed in that state, which he called the site of her primary residence. Lloyd Kaplan, representing Doris's estate, said it was properly filed in New York City, because the United States Trust Company, the corporate fiduciary, was located there. Most of Doris's assets were in New York.

In *The New York Times* on November 2, Kaplan, who had acted as Doris's public-relations consultant, described Bernard in glowing terms as Doris's best friend. He believed that they shared in all the decisions that mattered, adding that they had many common interests and that she had respected him. Attempts to reduce him to her "traveling butler," as Chandi's lawyer had done, were meant to discredit the depth and importance of the relationship between Doris and Bernard.

According to an article in the February 23, 1994, *New York Times*, Chandi alleged in court that Bernard had used illegal means to persuade Doris to disinherit her. She also testified that Doris was no longer competent when she signed her will on April 5, 1993.

Doris's bequests to Bernard, small in the context of her $1.2 billion estate, might not have raised these concerns, but when she named him coexecutor and a trustee of her foundation, with the power to appoint the other three members of the board, she ensured that he would face intense scrutiny and eventually censure.

To back up her claim, Chandi stated in court that she had always seen that Doris received proper medical care, and that she had worked tirelessly to reorganize each of Doris's three estates, which she claimed were run-down and neglected. In a strange assumption of authority, Chandi also said that she had bought Doris a $25 million private jet (which of course could only have been financed with Doris's own money) and had saved her bene-factor's life twice: once when she collapsed in the bathroom, and a second time when she was almost swept out to sea while swimming in Hawaii. It was difficult for Chandi's lawyer to substantiate these claims.

Chandi was partially successful in getting the money she was after, apparently pledging to the executives of the Doris Duke Charitable Foun-dation lifelong silence about her relationship with Doris in return for a settlement of $65 million. Given this outcome, it is unlikely that any-one will ever know the truth of Chandi's relationship with Doris. But, as is the case with many secrets, the concealed reasons for this accommo-dation with Chandi will forever spawn gossip about the nature of the relationship.

Bernard's claim took longer to settle. In May 1995, Judge Eve Preminger of the Manhattan Surrogate Court ruled that Bernard had used Doris's fortune to finance his luxurious way of life and that he was unfit to be executor of her estate. She noted that he had traveled in her chauffeured limousine and her private jet, had run up huge credit-card bills for antiques, clothes, and jewelry, and had renovated her bedroom at Falcon's Lair so that he could enjoy bigger windows and a spa. The fact that he had been hospitalized for alcoholism was also cited.

Further, Judge Preminger condemned the United States Trust Com-pany as coexecutor of Doris's estate, for failing to control Bernard's spending and for lending him $825,000. She ruled that the United States Trust Company should be removed and replaced by the Morgan Guar-anty Trust Company, under the guidance of Alexander D. Forger, a trust and estates lawyer who had represented the Kennedys.[8] The judge also presided over the formation of a new board of seven trustees for the Doris Duke Charitable Foundation. Among the new trustees was Doris's former doctor Harry Demopoulis, who had vigorously attacked her will, claiming that she had been unduly influenced by Bernard.

Judge Preminger cut the trustees' compensation in half and engineered Bernard's final payment of $4.5 million plus $500,000 a year for life, contingent on his resigning as coexecutor and member of the foundation board, which he agreed to do. Bernard told the press that, since litigation was holding up the charitable work Doris's will had mandated, he would step down rather than contest the verdict and cause more delays.

Chen Sam, one of Doris's public-relations spokespersons, said she felt the ruling, relying as it did on Bernard's drinking and lack of education, was unfair. Many uneducated people do well in life, she asserted, and practically everybody is addicted to something.[9]

Had she been able to foresee the outcome of three years of lawsuits, Doris would have been irritated that one of her last wishes was flouted and her affection for Bernard questioned. She had spent much of her long life fighting to protect and control her fortune, only to have one of her final decisions overturned.

Doris's will—signed in April 1993, the signature shaky—left the bulk of her net worth, valued at $1.2 billion, to the Doris Duke Charitable Foundation. In line with the causes she had supported throughout her life, the foundation's ongoing mission is to support the arts, the environment, child welfare, and the prevention of cruelty to animals.

Ten-million-dollar bequests went to the Metropolitan Museum of Art and to Duke University. Although the Met was probably grateful for the bequest, the university may well have been disappointed, since the bequest represented less than 1 percent of Doris's total estate. Regardless, the chapel bells on the Duke University campus tolled eighty times, and flags were flown at half-mast during the week of her death.

Duke's president Nannerl O. Keohane placed Doris's philanthropy in the context of the generous giving of her family to the university. The family's support began with Buck Duke's founding endowment of $40 million in 1924, and continued with Doris's 1992 gift of $2 million to the Duke Medical Center for AIDS research.

The New York Zoological Society received $1 million, and $500,000 went to the Self-Realization Fellowship in Los Angeles, which Doris had contributed to for many years. Gifts of various sizes went to friends and to each of the 150 employees on Doris's three estates. Three and a half million would be dispensed to her longtime friend Eleanor Johnson Lawson; $1 million to the Reverend Lawrence Robert of the First Baptist Church of Nutley, New Jersey, where Doris had sung in the choir; $350,000 to Walker Jr.; and $200,000 to Johnny Gomez. Her will also established lifetime trusts for long-term employees and directed $100,000 for the care of her dogs.

Nothing was left to Doris's six Duke cousins. There were no ill feelings; her family was already wealthy. Doris's cousin Angier Biddle Duke, former ambassador to Spain, Denmark, and Morocco, had tried to persuade Doris to attend Founder's Day at Duke University in 1992, where the ceremonies would include a tribute to Doris's father. He understood from her absence that she had an aversion to the place but hoped the arrival of younger people might persuade her to share his hope for the future. But Doris had not gone. During the controversy over her will, Angier reported that he had never met Bernard, but found him very polite when he telephoned to announce Doris's death.

Although Doris's will forgave a loan of $158,000 to the estate of the late Italian film producer Franco Rossellini, it stipulated that Imelda Marcos must repay the money Doris had loaned her for her legal defense against criminal charges brought by the U.S. government, but not until Imelda had settled her financial disputes.

Doris's will established two other independent foundations in addition to the Doris Duke Charitable Foundation, one to administer open, natural spaces at Duke Farms for the benefit of threatened wildlife, and the other to ensure the welfare of New Jersey farmland and farm animals. Doris's two beloved camels and her two horses were left to the Duke Farms Foundation, probably a not entirely welcome gift.

Rough Point would go to the Newport Restoration Foundation, to be preserved as a historical property open to the public, but there was no financial bequest. The continuing work of restoration and maintenance would be paid for by rentals of the number of houses Doris had restored, and by other donors and grants. Her apartment at 475 Park Avenue in Manhattan and Falcon's Lair in Los Angeles would be sold, for $1.4 million and $2,294,000, respectively, with the proceeds going to the Doris Duke Charitable Foundation.

A fourth foundation, the Doris Duke Foundation for Islamic Art, would support Shangri La and provide programming and fellowships to promote understanding of Middle Eastern art and culture, an area of study that has become increasingly important over the years.[10]

After his legal claims were settled, Bernard disappeared into the shadows. In 1996, just three years after Doris's death, he died in Los Angeles, at fifty-one. He was alone in his bed, and there was no evidence of foul play. In its obituary, *The New York Times* reported that it was commonly known that Bernard struggled with alcoholism and took various medications. He had been so vilified during the court battle that it might have been difficult for him to imagine a future, especially without Doris.

Few of us can say that, at the end of our lives, we have preserved the spark of originality we had at the beginning, the originality of the little girl carving an American flag and an eagle in the sand at Bailey's Beach.

For Doris Duke, that original spark faded, nearly went out, but flared again when she finally succeeded in becoming a reporter during World War II. Its small light guided her through the preservation of Rough Point and the creation of Shangri La and its Islamic Study Center in Hawaii. It lighted her imagining of conservation projects at Duke Farms.

By its light, she established the Newport Restoration Foundation and the Doris Duke Charitable Foundation. Its glow was warmest in her grants to artists like Louise Duncan and activists like Margaret Sanger. Their work, and that of many others, could not have been accomplished without Doris Duke's support.

And the spark was still with her near the end, when she spread her arms wide in joyous celebration in an open boat. Doris said once that beauty—its creation, restoration, and preservation—was the goal of her life.

Joy was its enduring spark.

EPILOGUE

For two decades after her death, Doris Duke was defined by tales of the disastrous personal consequences, at least for women, of possessing great wealth. Ignoring her achievements and focusing on her personal difficulties, the stories explained not only our cynicism about inherited money but also our willingness to see the punishment as fitting the crime—even when there is no crime.

If wealthy women are, in many people's minds, cursed from childhood with their ill-gotten gains, there is no need to examine the sources of the great inequality that bedevils contemporary life in the United States, no need to address problems of tax evasion, generation-skipping trusts, protection of corporate earnings, and all the other engines of capitalism that allow the gross accumulation of wealth by a few individuals, nearly all of them men.

"Poor Little Rich Girl," so inappropriate it was never used during her life, is after her death the definition from which Doris Duke will never entirely escape. And it has claws. Since Doris chose to protect herself by leaving no diaries or journals and few letters, nothing that has been written or said about her can be proved—or disproved.

The vast cache of papers she gave to her archive at Duke University correct some misinterpretations, but since they include so little of her own voice, there will always be gaps for innuendo to fill. In this, she was like the women of earlier generations who did not feel they deserved to be remembered, women who accepted society's dictum that a lady should appear in the newspapers only at her birth, her marriage, and her death.

Much influenced by her father's example, Doris began, very early and somewhat successfully, to hide. There would be no later letters as revealing as the few she wrote in the early 1940s; in fact, there would be almost no letters from her at all, because she didn't write any—as many of her friends and lovers complained. Allowing herself to be defined by glamorous photographs and increasingly malevolent gossip, she never realized that she was, unwittingly, lending credence to rumors: that she was a closeted lesbian and/or sexually voracious with men. These assumptions would come in the end to obscure her originality, her generosity, the great delight she took in the energetic and courageous use of her body, and the joy in living she expressed to lovers and friends.

Secrecy became her métier. Lacking a political understanding of the liabilities of her status and class, convinced of the evil intentions of many who did not actually know her, she became more exposed to misunderstanding the more she hid.

Because of her access to a battalion of lawyers and the means with which to pay them, she sometimes embroiled herself in hopeless lawsuits. She did not see herself as entitled, and therefore failed to understand that others did—and they resented her for it. She did not ally herself with the progressive social movements of her period, and never developed a relationship with a female mentor after her first mentor, Marian, died. Her lovers to some extent became her muses, without the will or the experience to offer guidance, and she sometimes separated from employees and friends who perhaps knew her best.

Many women face a version of these issues. The size of the fortune is not what exposes us to misunderstanding; it is our innate power. It may be a power we never choose to wield, but if, as in Doris's case, we decide to live conspicuously and to spend money on the people and things and causes that fascinate us, it is our power that terrifies, amplified by, but not based on, our financial means.

What if she had succeeded in her dream to transport a threatened Egyptian temple to each of the U.S. state capitals? The extravagance of that gesture would have exposed her to scorn, not because her idea lacked value but because her plan would have been so large in her imagination, so dependent on her international connections, and so illustrative of her vivid and outrageous use of her fortune. The fifty temples would have affected the reality of many ordinary citizens in those fifty cities. And that, at least if a woman is executing it, is not acceptable.

Doris, like most inheritors, found that criticism made it even harder to consider the source of her fortune or to question her father's role in the spread of smoking. This Doris could never do, hampered by her unquestioned reverence for Buck Duke and all he stood for. If he made a large part of his fortune out of a product that has sickened and killed millions—and that continues to do so—that she could never admit into her imagination. It may have helped to assuage her conscience that most of her fortune was in the form of Duke Power Company stock.

Nicotine addiction continues to kill. A report from an Australian study published in *BMC Medicine* in February 2015 states, "Two-thirds of smokers will die early, from cigarette-triggered illness, higher than doctors had estimated." There are 480,000 smoking-related deaths in the United States every year, making it the leading cause of preventable death. However, thanks to decades of information about health and to aggressive anti-smoking campaigns, the number of smokers in the United States continues to decline. This is not true of the rest of the world, especially Asia.

The cigarette manufacturers, several of them offshoots of Buck Duke's British-American Tobacco Company, finally succumbed to a 2006 order forcing them to admit that they have lied for decades about the effects of smoking. In 2018, they took out full-page ads in *The New York Times* admitting their culpability.

But they continue to blanket the world with their advertisements. In China, which Buck Duke considered his prime target, 60 percent of the men now smoke. In Indonesia, two-thirds of the population smokes, and Philip Morris sponsors kiosks outside of schools, selling cigarettes and offering—supposedly for safety's sake—a lighter attached to a string. Even the tiny country of Togo is not exempt: 40 percent of the largely illiterate population smokes, and one two-year-old cigarette-addicted boy became an international sensation.

Would any of this have mattered to Doris Duke? Probably not.

To the degree that she was able to think about it at all, she might have relied on her father's dictum that people have always smoked and will always smoke, and that an entrepreneur who fails to take advantage of this fact is a fool.

But when the root is denied, its fruits shrivel. No matter how large her charitable contributions, they cannot make up for the deaths of millions. No matter how personally generous Doris Duke was, the root evil remains.

Doris Duke created worthy memorials: the foundations she endowed through her will; the three outstanding houses that began as personal refuges but are now refuges and places of learning for the public; the continuing work of the Newport Restoration Foundation; and the lives and legacies of the multitudinous throng she benefited during her lifetime and that the terms of her will continue to benefit.

Doris was able to recognize talent and to give across the barriers of race and class. Her understanding and liking of dark-skinned men and women is certainly one of the reasons she has been traduced; it also produced her most original acts of generosity.

In the end, her good works remain.

"The evil that men do lives after them; / The good is oft interred with their bones." This line, spoken by Shakespeare's Antony at Caesar's burial, cannot be Doris Duke's epitaph. The evil assigned to her is largely imaginary. She was attacked in the press, pilloried because of her wealth and the size of her intentions. But the good—the enormous, the magnificent good, the fruit of her imagination, her gift for empathy, and her astonishing generosity—lives on.

NOTES

ABBREVIATIONS USED IN THE NOTES

DDP: Doris Duke Papers, Doris Duke Charitable Foundation Historical Archives, David M. Rubenstein Rare Book & Manuscript Library, Duke University.

DDPPC: Personal Correspondence Series, Doris Duke Papers, Doris Duke Charitable Foundation Historical Archives, David M. Rubenstein Rare Book & Manuscript Library, Duke University.

DDPSF: Subject Files Series, Doris Duke Papers, Doris Duke Charitable Foundation Historical Archives, David M. Rubenstein Rare Book & Manuscript Library, Duke University.

DDCFRL: Doris Duke Charitable Foundation Historical Archives, David M. Rubenstein Rare Book & Manuscript Library, Duke University.

DDPC: Doris Duke Photograph Collection, David M. Rubenstein Rare Book & Manuscript Library, Duke University.

JBDP: James Buchanan Duke Papers, David M. Rubenstein Rare Book & Manuscript Library, Duke University.

CCOHC: Columbia Center for Oral History Collection, Columbia University.

Bold Entrepreneur: Robert F. Durden, *Bold Entrepreneur: A Life of James B. Duke* (Durham, N.C.: Carolina Academic Press, 2003).

Dukes of Durham: Robert F. Durden, *The Dukes of Durham*, 1865–1929 (Durham, N.C.: Duke University Press, 1975).

Lasting Legacy: Robert F. Durden, *Lasting Legacy to the Carolinas: The Duke Endowment, 1924–1994* (Durham and London: Duke University Press, 1998).
DD: Doris Duke
JBD: James Buchanan Duke
ACR: Alec Cunningham-Reid

PREFACE

1. Virginia Woolf, *Mr. Bennett and Mrs. Brown* (London, England: Hogarth Press, 1924), p. 4.
2. Ibid., p. 24.

PROLOGUE

1. Alletta Morris later married Peter McBean and founded the Alletta Morris McBean Charitable Trust.

CHAPTER 1

1. Passport, Doris Duke Business Office Safe Series, box 350, folder 15, DDP.
2. Divorce proceedings, *Cromwell v. Cromwell*, Dec. 21, 1943, box 350, folder 12, Doris Duke Business Office Safe Series, DDP.
3. United States Seaman's Service Correspondence, box 302, folder 6, Miss Duke's Office Series, DDP.
4. J. Edgar Hoover to DD, Sept. 1942, box 15, folder 25, DDPPC.

CHAPTER 2

1. "Foreign News: Old Boys," *Time Magazine*, Aug. 9, 1943. http://content.time .com/time/magazine/article/0,9171,766957,00.html.
2. ACR, *Blame the Old Gang!* (London, England: W. H. Allen & Co., 1942).
3. "Two Members of Commons Apologize for Fist Fighting," *Evening Independent*, July 28, 1943, pp. 1, 6.
4. Letters, ACR to DD, boxes 14 and 15, DDPPC.
5. Ibid.
6. Ibid.
7. Ibid.
8. Photographs with correspondence regarding Cunningham-Reid children, box 299, Miss Duke's Office Subseries, DDPSF.
9. Correspondence, ACR to DD, boxes 14 and 15, DDPPC.
10. Ibid.
11. Ibid.
12. Ibid.
13. Ibid.
14. Ibid.

15. ACR to DD, n.d., box 299, folder 1, DDPSF.

16. Correspondence concerning the Cunningham-Reid children, box 298, folder 10; and box 299, folders 2–5, both in DDPSF.

17. Ibid.

18. Ibid.

19. Correspondence, ACR, box 14, folders 2–5; and box 15, folders 1–3, both in DDPPC.

20. Ibid.

21. Michael Cunningham-Reid to DD, box 299, folders 2–4, DDPSF; and box 15, folder 3, DDPPC.

22. Letters, Marian Paschal correspondence, box 16, folder 22, DDPPC.

23. Ibid.

24. B. F. Giles to DD, box 15, folder 22, DDPPC.

25. Letters, Marian Paschal correspondence, box 16, folder 22, DDPPC.

26. Ibid.

27. News articles, box 254, folders 1–4, DDPSF.

28. Ibid.

29. Documents regarding travel orders, International News Service, box 254, DDPSF.

30. Stanley P. Hirshson, *General Patton: A Soldier's Life* (New York: HarperCollins, 2002).

31. Tom Perkins to DD, Duke Business Office Safe Series, box 350, folder 15, DDP.

32. Nancy Caldwell Sorel, *The Women Who Wrote the War: The Compelling Story of the Path-Breaking Women War Correspondents of World War II* (New York: Skyhorse Publishing, Inc., 2011), p. 173.

CHAPTER 3

1. The aims and uses of the OSS came into question when the Freedom of Information Act opened the OSS/CIA archives, revealing that seventy-five thousand American men and women had undertaken some form of secret activity during the Second World War, including Julia Child, Noël Coward, and my father.

2. Douglas C. Waller, *Wild Bill Donovan: The Spymaster Who Created the OSS and Modern American Espionage* (New York: Free Press, 2011).

3. B. F. Giles to DD, Aug. 25, 1945, Giles correspondence, box 15, folder 22, DDPPC.

4. Ibid.

5. Tex McCrary to DD, Feb. 1945, McCrary correspondence, box 16, folder 14, DDPPC.

6. Ibid.

7. Ibid.

8. Ibid.

9. Charles J. Kelly, *Tex McCrary: Wars, Women, Politics: An Adventurous Life Across the Twentieth Century* (Falls Village, Conn.: Hamilton Books, 2009).
10. Ibid.
11. Tex McCrary to DD, n.d., McCrary correspondence, box 16, folder 14, DDPPC.
12. Ibid.
13. Tex McCrary to DD, 1969, McCrary correspondence, box 16, folder 14, DDPPC.
14. Ibid.
15. Passport and visa applications and related material, box 350, folder 15, Doris Duke Business Office Safe Series, DDP.
16. Travel orders, Jan. 5, 1945, International News Service files, DDPSF.
17. Tex McCrary to DD, n.d., McCrary correspondence, box 16, folder 14, DDPPC.
18. Print #PH.DD072h, box 8, folder PHDD072, DDPC.
19. Dispatches in International News Service Subseries, box 254, folders 1–4, DDPSF.
20. Ibid.
21. Ibid.
22. Ibid.
23. Letters, Nanaline Duke to DD, box 15, folder 13, DDPPC.
24. Dispatches by DD, 1945 and 1946, International News Service Subseries, box 254, folder 3, DDPSF.
25. Ibid.
26. Ibid.
27. Ibid.
28. Ibid.
29. DD to Marian Paschal, n.d., Paschal correspondence, box 16, folder 22, DDPPC.

CHAPTER 4
1. Nanaline Duke to DD, 1945, box 15, folder 13, DDPPC.
2. Documents in International News Service Subseries, box 254, DDPSF.
3. Carl Bernstein, "The CIA and the Media," *Rolling Stone*, Oct. 20, 1977.
4. Penelope Rowlands, *A Dash of Daring: Carmel Snow and Her Life in Fashion, Art, and Letters* (New York: Atria Books, 2008).
5. Ibid.
6. "Heiress Doris Duke Sues Confidential Magazine," *Lewiston Evening Journal*, July 19, 1955, p. 6.
7. Russell McKinnon to DD, 1957, box 16, folder 15, DDPPC.
8. Ibid.
9. Ibid.
10. "People in the Collections: Doris Duke, 1912–1993," David M. Rubenstein Rare Book & Manuscript Library, Duke University, http://library.duke.edu/rubenstein/collections/people/dorisduke/#item-39.

11. Marty Wall et al., *Chasing Rubi: The Truth About Porfirio Rubirosa, the Last Playboy* (Newport Beach, Calif.: Literary Press Publishing, 2005), p. 59.

12. Gary Cohen, "The Legend of Rubirosa," *Vanity Fair*, Dec. 2002, https://www.vanityfair.com/news/2002/11/porfirio-rubirosa-200211.

13. Ibid.

14. Walker Inman to DD, Nov. 14, 1947, box 7, folder 1, Administrative Records Series, DDP.

15. Ibid.

16. Richard Kent to James Cromwell, Oct. 17, 1968, box 340, folder 6, Duke Business Office Safe Series, DDP.

17. Marriage contract, Sept. 1, 1947, box 350, folder 10, Duke Business Office Safe Series, DDP.

18. DD to Nanaline Duke, Oct. 10, 1947, box 15, folder 13, DDPPC.

19. Ibid.

20. Cable, DD to Walker Inman, n.d., box 7, folder 1, Administrative Records, DDP.

21. DD to Walker Inman, Oct. 9, 1947, ibid.

22. Documents, box 350, folder 12, Duke Business Office Safe Series, DDP.

23. Wall et al., *Chasing Rubi*, p. 173.

CHAPTER 5

1. Porfirio Rubirosa to DD, n.d., box 16, folder 29, DDPPC.

2. Gary Cohen, "The Legend of Rubirosa," *Vanity Fair*, Dec. 2002, https://www.vanityfair.com/news/2002/11/porfirio-rubirosa-200211.

3. *Rubirosa v. Rubirosa*, Certified Findings of Fact, Conclusions, and Decree, Oct. 27, 1948, box 350, folder 7, Duke Business Office Safe Series, DDP.

4. Letters, Porfirio Rubirosa to DD, box 16, DDDPC.

5. Ibid.

6. Ibid.

7. "Fusses over Ladies and a Ladies' Man," *Life*, Jan. 11, 1954, pp. 24–25.

8. Shawn Levy, *The Last Playboy: The High Life of Porfirio Rubirosa* (New York: Harper Perennial, 2016).

CHAPTER 6

1. Draft of letter, DD to Michael Chinigo, box 12, DDPPC.

2. Correspondence and documents, box 254, folders 9 and 10, DDPSF.

3. Michael Chinigo to DD, March 10, 1955, box 12, folder 5, DDPPC.

4. Bayard Stockton, *Flawed Patriot: The Rise and Fall of CIA Legend Bill Harvey* (Washington, D.C.: Potomac Books, 2006), pp. 278–87.

5. DD to Stuart Hawkins, May 15, 1947, box 254, folder 9, DDPSF.

6. "People in the News," *Kentucky New Era*, Dec. 7, 1974, p. 2.

7. DD to William deMeza, Aug. 15, 1951, box 254, folder 9, DDPSF.

8. Ibid.

CHAPTER 7

1. *Bold Entrepreneur*, p. 139.
2. JBD to Benjamin and Sarah Duke, Aug. 18, 1880, box 1, Correspondence Series, JBDP.
3. Advertisement, *Hillsborough Recorder*, Oct. 7 and 14, 1863.
4. *Dukes of Durham*, pp. 8–9.
5. Ibid., p. 13.
6. JBD to Benjamin and Sarah Duke, Aug. 18, 1880, box 1, Correspondence Series, JBDP.
7. *Dukes of Durham*, pp. 11–19 and 125.
8. Wendell Berry, "It All Turns on Affection," 2012 Jefferson Lecture, National Endowment for the Humanities, https://www.neh.gov/about/awards/jefferson -lecture/wendell-e-berry-biography.
9. Reminiscences of Bernard Baruch, James B. Duke Oral History Interviews, CCOHC.
10. Reeves Wiedeman, "Honest Honus," *New Yorker*, May 16, 2013.
11. Iain Gately, *Tobacco: A Cultural History of How an Exotic Plant Seduced Civilization* (New York: Grove Press, 2003), pp. 206–13.
12. *Bold Entrepreneur*, pp. 14–37.
13. Jennifer Dawn Farley, *Duke Homestead and the American Tobacco Company* (Mount Pleasant, S.C.: Arcadia Publishing, 2013), pp. 63–71.
14. *Dukes of Durham*, pp. 204–205.
15. Farley, *Duke Homestead*, pp. 80–81.
16. *Bold Entrepreneur*, pp. 81–84.
17. Martha McCulloch-Williams, "The Tobacco War in Kentucky," *The American Review* 37 (Feb. 1908), pp. 168–70.
18. My grandfather Robert Worth Bingham tried to help the Kentucky tobacco growers, building warehouses where they could store their crop until prices rose, but his attempt failed, partly because he tried to create another monopoly tobacco business, which could not compete with Buck Duke's.
19. *Dukes of Durham*, pp. 70–71.
20. A. K. Leake, "Anti-Monopoly," *Southern Planter* 53, no. 5 (May 1892), p. 292.
21. Gately, *Tobacco: A Cultural History*, pp. 284–85.
22. *Bold Entrepreneur*, pp. 167–69.
23. JBD to Benjamin Duke, Feb. 1919, box 1, Correspondence Series, JBDP.
24. *Lasting Legacy*, pp. 1–28.
25. *Dukes of Durham*, pp. 92–191.
26. Ibid., pp. 82–97.
27. Reminiscences of Edward Hansen, James B. Duke Oral History Interviews, CCOHC.

CHAPTER 8

1. *Bold Entrepreneur*, pp. 35–36.
2. New York Mansion Series (1 E. 78th St), Duke Family New York Apartments Collection, DDCFRL.
3. Clarice Stasz, *The Vanderbilt Women: Dynasty of Wealth, Glamour and Tragedy* (Lincoln, Neb.: iUniverse.com, Inc., 1999), p. 273.
4. Telegram, JBD to Lady Paget, Nov. 22, 1912, "People in the Collections: Doris Duke," Rubenstein Library, http://library.duke.edu/rubenstein/collections/people/dorisduke/.
5. James B. Duke correspondence, box 15, folder 12, DDPPC.
6. Ibid.
7. Interview, Edward Hansen, CCOHC.
8. Ibid.
9. Joseph Duveen, the eldest of eight sons in a family of British Jews, developed his eye for art while working in his father's prosperous antiques business in London. Later, he transferred his interest and expertise to paintings, which he sold to the new "squillionaires," as he called them, in America. According to Susan Stamberg's story on National Public Radio's "Morning Edition" on March 9, 2015, he once observed, "Europe has a great deal of art, and America has a great deal of money."
10. Reminiscences of Norman Atwater Cocke, James B. Duke Oral History Interviews, CCOHC.
11. James B. Duke correspondence, box 15, folder 12, DDPPC.
12. Ibid.
13. L. Emmett Holt, *The Care and Feeding of Children* (New York and London: D. Appleton and Company, 1894).
14. Daniel Beekman, *The Mechanical Baby: A Popular History of the Theory and Practice of Child Raising* (New York: Lawrence Hill & Company, 1977).
15. Mary Lillian Read, *The Mothercraft Manual* (Boston: Little, Brown, and Company, 1916).
16. Correspondence and related materials, box 258, folders 1–3, Jenny Renaud Series, DDPSF.
17. Notebook, box 287, folder 1, Miscellaneous Series, DDPSF.
18. Jenny Renaud to DD, 1955, box 258, folder 2, Jenny Renaud Series, DDPSF.

CHAPTER 9

1. Reminiscences of Wilburt Davison, James B. Duke Oral History Interviews, CCOHC.
2. Reminiscences of Mrs. John Williams, James B. Duke Oral History Interviews, CCOHC.
3. Unidentified clipping, box 7, Miscellaneous Papers Series, Washington Duke Papers, David M. Rubenstein Rare Book & Manuscript Library, Duke University.

4. B. N. Duke to J. B. Duke, Dec. 29, 1893, B. N. Duke Letterbook, Benjamin Newton Duke Papers, David M. Rubenstein Rare Book & Manuscript Library, Duke University.
5. *Bold Entrepreneur*, p. 94.
6. Documents and clippings in the James B. Duke and Lillian McCredy Duke Divorce Records, 1904–1906, Duke University Archives, David M. Rubenstein Rare Book & Manuscript Library, Duke University.
7. Richard Kluger, *Ashes to Ashes: America's Hundred-Year Cigarette War, the Public Health, and the Unabashed Triumph of Philip Morris* (New York: Vintage Books, 1997), p. 94.
8. "Notorious Big," *New Yorker*, March 28, 2016, p. 72.
9. Reminiscences of Mrs. E. C. Marshall, James B. Duke Oral History Interviews, CCOHC.
10. "What Happens When You Smoke," *Harper's Weekly* 50 (May 26, 1906), p. 751.
11. "Harmless Smoking," *Harper's Weekly* 56 (Aug. 3, 1912), p. 24.
12. Interview, Edward Hansen, CCOHC.
13. Clippings and photographs, box 66, Miscellaneous Series, JBDP.
14. "James Buchanan Duke, Tobacco King, 68, Dies of Pneumonia," *New York Times*, Oct. 11, 1925, p. 1.
15. *Bold Entrepreneur*, pp. 170–91.
16. Rough Point deed, March 18, 1927, and Duke Farm indenture, Sept. 20, 1926, box 341, Duke Business Office Safe Series, DDP.
17. "Former Wife of James B. Duke Dying in Poverty," *Bridgeport Telegram*, Oct. 24, 1925, p. 19.
18. Legal Papers, 1878–1926 and n.d., JBDP.
19. Photograph, box 1, DDPC.

CHAPTER 10

1. Reminiscences of Mary Few, James B. Duke Oral History Interviews, CCOHC.
2. Ibid.
3. Reminiscences of John Fox, James B. Duke Oral History Interviews, CCOHC.
4. Interview, Mary Few, CCOHC.
5. Ibid.
6. Reminiscences of E. R Bucher, James B. Duke Oral History Interviews, CCOHC.
7. Reminiscences of Bennette Eugene Geer, James B. Duke Oral History Interviews, CCOHC.
8. Ibid.

CHAPTER 11

1. Notebooks, box 8, folders 26, 28, and 30; box 10, folder 1; box 16, folders 5–16, Miscellaneous Series, Doris Duke Memorabilia Collection, DDCFRL.

2. Interview, Edward Hansen, CCOHC.

3. Memorabilia from DD's childhood, box 10, folders 6–9, Miscellaneous Series, Doris Duke Memorabilia Collection, DDCFRL.

4. Interview, Edward Hansen, CCOHC.

5. Ibid.

6. "Doris Duke Feted at Newport Dance," *New York Times*, Aug. 24, 1930, p. N8.

7. George Wein et al., *Myself Among Others: A Life in Music* (Boston: Da Capo Press, 2004), p. 134.

8. *Brooklyn Life and Activities of Long Island Society*, Aug. 9, 1930, p. 10.

9. Harry Crocker Correspondence, 1932–1934, 1946, box 13, folders 1–6, DDPPC.

CHAPTER 12

1. "Oliver E. Cromwell, Dead," *Forest and Stream* 74 (Jan. 1, 1910), p. 25.

2. Wayne C. Willcox, "A Biography in Progress: Stotesbury," http://www.stotes bury.com.

3. Ibid.

4. Mara Bovsun, "Broadway Butterfly, Dorothy King, Dead in Bed with Her Jewels Gone," *Daily News*, April 17, 2011, http://www.nydailynews.com/news/crime/ broadway-butterfly-dorothy-king-dead-bed-jewels-article-1.116132.

5. Rachel Hildebrandt, *The Philadelphia Area Architecture of Horace Trumbauer* (Mount Pleasant, S.C.: Arcadia Publishing, 2009), p. 79.

6. "Road Show," *MTI Music Theatre International*, http://www.mtishows.com/ show_detail.asp?showid=000363.

7. Charles K. Hyde, *The Dodge Brothers: The Men, the Motor Cars, and the Legacy* (Detroit, Mich.: Wayne State University Press, 2005), pp. 137–40.

8. Brett Anderson, "From the Editors: Wheels and Deals," *Robb Report*, http:// robbreport.com/paid-issue/editors-wheels-and-deals.

9. Newsreel, "Dodge-Cromwell Wedding," 1920, https://www.youtube.com/watch ?v=FxO4wIEF7Fk.

10. James H. R. Cromwell, *The Voice of Young America* (New York and London: Scribner, 1933).

11. Letters, James Cromwell to DD, box 14, folder 1, DDPPC.

12. Ibid.

13. Douglas MacArthur to American Embassy in Paris, Sept. 5, 1939, box 294, folder 4, Miscellaneous Correspondence Series, DDPSF.

14. Letters, James Cromwell to DD, box 14, folder 1, DDPPC.

15. Ibid.

16. Ibid.

17. Ibid.

18. Ibid.

19. Ibid.

20. Ibid.
21. Ibid.
22. Cromwell, *Voice of Young America*.
23. James H. R. Cromwell and Hugo E. Czerwonky, *In Defense of Capitalism* (New York: Scribner, 1937).

CHAPTER 13

1. "1914 Agreement," Student Record Collection, box 30, folder 3895 (Cromwell, James Henry Roberts, Class of 1915), Lawrenceville School Stephan Archives, Lawrenceville, N.J.
2. Eva Stotesbury to Headmaster McPherson, Nov. 8, [1913], ibid.
3. Headmaster McPherson to Eva Stotesbury, Spring [1914], ibid.
4. Eva Stotesbury to Headmaster McPherson, Sept. 19, 1914, ibid.
5. Headmaster McPherson to Eva Stotesbury, Nov. 2, 1914, ibid.
6. Ibid.
7. Eva Stotesbury to Headmaster McPherson, Nov. 3, 1914, Student Record Collection, box 30, folder 3895 (Cromwell, James Henry Roberts, Class of 1915), Lawrenceville School Stephan Archives, Lawrenceville, N.J.
8. Miscellaneous notes, ibid.
9. Duke Cromwell Honeymoon Scrapbooks, Shangri La Historical Archives, Doris Duke Foundation for Islamic Art, Honolulu, Hawaii.
10. Ibid.
11. C. David Heymann, *Poor Little Rich Girl: The Life and Legend of Barbara Hutton* (New York: Pocket Books, 1987).
12. "Gandhi Receives World's Richest Bride and Groom," *Chicago Tribune*, March 17, 1935, p. 19A.
13. James Cromwell to Miss Knox, May 28, 1935, box 1, folder 2, Correspondence Series, Doris Duke Papers on the Shangri La Residence, DDCFRL.
14. Documents, Administrative Records Series, ibid.
15. Michael Beschloss, "Duke of Hawaii: A Swimmer and Surfer Who Straddled Two Cultures," *New York Times*, Aug. 23, 2014, http://www.nytimes.com/2014/08/23/upshot/duke-of-hawaii-a-swimmer-and-surfer-who-straddled-two-cultures.html?abt=0002&abg=1.
16. Photograph, box 8, DDPC.
17. Audio Series, Doris Duke Audiovisual Collection, 1919–2012 and n.d., box 16, DDCFRL.

CHAPTER 14

1. Independent Aid, Inc., Records, DDCFRL.
2. Glenda Riley, *Divorce: An American Tradition* (Lincoln, Neb.: University of Nebraska Press, 1997), p. 115.
3. "The Equal Rights Amendment: Unfinished Business for the Constitution, a

project of the Alice Paul Institute, http://www.equalrightsamendment.org/about.

4. Independent Aid, Inc., Records, DDCFRL.
5. Reminiscences of Mary Duke Biddle Trent Semans, James B. Duke Oral History Interviews, CCOHC.
6. Independent Aid, Inc., Records, DDCFRL.
7. Ibid.
8. Ibid.
9. Correspondence between Marian Paschal and W. L. Baldwin, box 298, Miss Duke's Office Subseries, DDPSF.
10. Documents, box 301, folder 12, DDPSF.
11. Ibid.
12. DD to Marian Paschal, 1945, box 17, folder 11, DDPPC.
13. Staudinger to DD, Sept. 12, 1946, box 333, folder 9, Duke Business Office Safe Series, DDP.
14. DD to Marian Paschal, May 7, 1945, box 17, folder 11, DDPPC.
15. Marian Paschal to DD, 1945, box 16, folder 22, DDPPC.

CHAPTER 15

1. Board of Trustees of the Society of the New York Hospital to Nanaline Duke, box 3, folder 6, Correspondence Series, Duke Family Papers, DDCFRL.
2. *Lasting Legacy*, pp. 184–85.
3. Walker Inman to DD, 1945, box 7, folder 1, Administrative Records Series, DDP.
4. Walker Inman to DD, June 7, 1945, ibid.
5. Reminiscences of Watson S. Rankin, James B. Duke Oral History Interviews, CCOHC.
6. "Free to Dance: Katherine Dunham," PBS Great Performances, http://www.pbs.org/wnet/freetodance/biographies/dunham.html.
7. Katherine Dunham, "The Rabbit Hunt," in Dunham, *A Touch of Innocence* (Chicago: University of Chicago Press, 1994), pp. 3–12.
8. Katherine Dunham et al., *Kaiso!: Writings by and About Katherine Dunham* (Madison: University of Wisconsin Press, 2006), p. 264.
9. Ibid., p. 64.
10. Ibid., p. 179.
11. "How Katherine Dunham Revealed Black Dance to the World," *New York Times*, May 23, 2006, http://www.nytimes.com/2006/05/23/arts/dance/23appr.html?_r=0.
12. Independent Aid, Inc., Records, DDCFRL.
13. Margaret Sanger to Georgea Furst, Jan. 21, 1951, S33:0801 (microfilm), Margaret Sanger Papers Project, Department of History, New York University.
14. Ellen Chesler, *Woman of Valor: Margaret Sanger and the Birth Control Movement in America* (New York: Simon & Schuster, 1992), p. 352.

15. Ibid.
16. "W.E.B. Du Bois on Black Eugenics," *Western Voices World News* website, http://www.wvwnews.net/story.php?id=4391.
17. Margaret Sanger to Georgea Furst, box 55, folder 9, Doris Duke Foundation Records, DDCFRL.
18. Georgea Furst to Margaret Sanger, April 11, 1952, box 44, folder 10, ibid.
19. Margaret Sanger to DD, April 18, 1952, S37:0454 (microfilm), Margaret Sanger Papers Project, Department of History, New York University.
20. Margaret Sanger to DD, Feb. 20, 1956, S49:0421 (microfilm), ibid.
21. W-Miscellaneous file, box 82, folder 1, Subject Files, Doris Duke Foundation Records, DDCFRL.

CHAPTER 16

1. Documents, box 1, Correspondence Series, Doris Duke Papers on the Shangri La Residence, DDCFRL.
2. Arthur Upham Pope (1881–1969) was best known as an American expert on Iranian art. He edited the authoritative six-volume *A Survey of Persian Art* (Oxford University Press, 1938–39).
3. Documents, boxes 1 and 2, Correspondence Series, Doris Duke Papers on the Shangri La Residence, DDCFRL.
4. Documents, box 168, folder 4, Legal Records Series, DDP.
5. Documents, box 1, Correspondence Series, Doris Duke Papers on the Shangri La Residence, DDCFRL; and documents, box 301, folders 3–5, DDPSF.
6. Documents in box 2, folder 7, Correspondence Series, Doris Duke Papers on the Shangri La Residence, DDCFRL.
7. Letters, box 16, folder 11, DDPPC.
8. Photograph, folder PHSL001, box 64, Shangri La Series, DDPC.

CHAPTER 17

1. Sandra Kimberley Hall, *Duke: A Great Hawaiian* (Honolulu: Bess Press, 2004), p. 81.
2. Documents, box 1, folder 9, Correspondence Series, Doris Duke Papers on the Shangri La Residence, DDCFRL.
3. Ibid.
4. Interview OH.036, Johnny Gomez, Jan. 20, 1998, and Feb. 21, 1998, box 14, Doris Duke Oral History Collection, DDCFRL.
5. Mario Braggiotti to DD, box 11, folder 7, DDPPC.
6. Aly Khan to DD, Dec. 1949, box 16, folder 5, DDPPC.
7. Jacqueline Kennedy to DD, June 17, 1968, box 16, folder 3, DDPPC.
8. Jacqueline Kennedy to DD, n.d., box 16, folder 3, DDPPC.
9. Interview OH.030, Grace Cohen and Eleanor Freedman, Jan. 24, 2009, Doris Duke Oral History Collection, DDCFRL.

10. Louis J. Camuti, *All My Patients Are Under the Bed* (New York: Simon & Schuster, 1980).
11. Interview, Cohen and Friedman, Doris Duke Oral History Collection, DDCFRL.

CHAPTER 18
1. Newport Restoration Foundation, "Rough Point: History and Architecture," http://www.newportrestoration.org/visit/rough_point/history_architecture.
2. Alletta Morris McBean's diary, 1924–1925, photocopy, box 8, folder 27, Miscellaneous Series, Doris Duke Memorabilia Collection, DDCFRL.
3. Leta to DD, n.d. letter, box 16, folder 13, DDPPC.
4. Interview OH.001, Marion Oates Charles, April 25, 2005, box 1, Doris Duke Oral History Collection, DDCFRL.
5. "Auto Driven by Doris Duke Kills Friend," *Chicago Tribune*, Oct. 8, 1966, p. 1.
6. Interview OH.017, Fred Sopko, Aug. 24, 2004, box 8, Doris Duke Oral History Collection, DDCFRL.
7. Kaffe Fassett to DD, 1966, box 18, folder 22, DDPPC.
8. Interview OH.012, David Rimmer, Nov. 20, 2003, and Dec. 18, 2004, box 5, Doris Duke Oral History Collection, DDCFRL.
9. Documents, box 166, folder 4, Legal Records Series, DDP.

CHAPTER 19
1. "Newport Restoration Foundation: Mission and History," http://www.newportrestoration.org/about/mission_history.

CHAPTER 20
1. Deeds for Duke Farms, box 15, folder 4, Administrative Records Series, Duke Family Papers on the Duke Farms residence, DDCFRL.
2. Letters, George LaFever to DD, box 294, folder 7, Miscellaneous Correspondence Series, DDPSF.
3. Documents, box 241, folder 2, Administrative Records Series, Duke Family Papers on the Duke Farms Residence, DDCFRL.
4. Documents, box 59, folder 15, ibid.
5. Doris Duke's Last Will and Testament and Codicil, box 170, folder 1, Legal Records Series, DDP.
6. William Russell, "Doris Duke: East Meets West in the Many Spectacular Homes of the Glamorous Heiress," Christie's website for the Doris Duke Collection, https://www.christies.com/special_sites/duke_jun04/saleinfo.asp.

CHAPTER 21
1. Daniel Bratton and Carol Williams, *Yrs, Ever Affly: The Correspondence of Edith Wharton and Louis Bromfield* (East Lansing: Michigan State University Press, 2000).

2. "Event Timeline," Malabar Farm Historic Landmark website, http://www .malabarfarm.org/history/historical-timeline.

3. Interview, David Rimmer, Doris Duke Oral History Collection, DDCFRL.

4. Bromfield correspondence, box 11, folder 9, DDPPC.

5. David A. Anderson, "Louis Bromfield's 'Cubic Foot of Soil,'" http://www .ohioana.org/features/legacy/lbromfield.asp.

6. Correspondence, box 11, folders 8 and 9, DDPPC.

7. Correspondence and documents, box 294, folder 17, Miscellaneous Correspondence Series, DDP.

8. Ibid.

9. Ellen Bromfield Geld to DD, Nov. 10, 1957, box 11, folder 9, DDPPC.

10. A. W. Short to DD, 1968, box 11, folder 9, ibid.

11. Interview, David Rimmer, Doris Duke Oral History Collection, DDCFRL.

12. Personal interview, Hutton Wilkinson, May 30, 2016.

13. Documents, Administrative Records Series, Doris Duke Papers on the Falcon Lair Residence, DDCFRL.

CHAPTER 22

1. Letters, Charles Asfar to DD, box 11, folders 2–4, DDPPC.

2. Ibid.

3. Ibid.

4. Ibid.

5. Obituary, Charles Trenet, *The Telegraph*, Feb. 20, 2001, https://www.telegraph .co.uk/news/obituaries/1323305/Charles-Trenet.html.

6. Charles Asfar to DD, Aug. 9, 1954, box 11, folder 4, DDPPC.

7. Ibid.

8. Ibid.

9. Ibid.

CHAPTER 23

1. Arnold Miller to DD, Jan. 22, 1974, box CF8, Duke Endowment Archives, David M. Rubenstein Rare Book & Manuscript Library, Duke University.

2. Ibid.

3. DD to Arnold Miller, Feb. 7, 1974, box CF8, ibid.

4. Antoine Robideaux to DD, Dec. 2, 1958, box 333, folder 8, Duke Business Office Safe Series, DDP.

5. Postcard, Walker Inman to DD, n.d., box 7, folder 1, Administrative Records, DDP.

6. Bob Burnette to DD, Oct. 31, 1968, box 11, folder 10, DDPPC.

7. Letters, Bob Burnette to DD, ibid.

8. Ibid.

9. Ibid.

10. Ibid.

CHAPTER 24

1. Letters, Anne Morrow Lindbergh to DD, box 16, folder 9, DDPPC.

2. Ibid.

3. Ibid.

4. Ibid.

5. Letters, Ruth B. Elwell to DD, 1960, box 15, folder 17, DDPPC.

6. Letters, Ananda Kumar to DD, 1963, box 16, folder 6, DDPPC.

7. Letters, Ruth Montgomery to DD, 1983, box 16, folder 17, DDPPC.

8. Nana Veary, *Change We Must: My Spiritual Journey* (Blue Hill, Maine: Medicine Bear Publishing, 1990).

9. Paramahansa Yogananda, *The Law of Abundance: Principles of Spiritual, Mental, and Material Abundance* (Los Angeles, Calif.: Self-Realization Fellowship, 1959).

CHAPTER 25

1. DD to Angier Biddle Duke, April 17, 1966, box 166, folder 2, Legal Records Series, DDP.

2. Walker Inman, Jr., to DD, 1965, box 16, folder 1, DDPPC.

3. Sabrina Rubin Erdely, "The Poorest Rich Kids in the World," *Rolling Stone*, Aug. 12, 2013, http://www.rollingstone.com/culture/news/the-poorest-rich-kids-in-the-world-20130812.

4. Aaron Kirschenfeld, "They Laughed 'Til It Hurt: A History of Humor Magazines at Duke," *Duke Magazine*, July–Aug., 2011, http://dukemagazine.duke.edu/article/they-laughed-til-it-hurt.

5. Jay to DD, Oct. 17, 1966, box 296, Miscellaneous Correspondence Subseries, DDPSF.

6. Joe Cahill to DD, Apr. 12, 1968, box 11, folder 12, DDPPC.

7. Ann to DD, Mar. 10, 1975, box 296, Miscellaneous Correspondence Subseries, DDPSF.

8. John to DD, Sept. 8, 1976, ibid.

9. D. Konda Reddy to DD, Dec. 1980, ibid.

10. Wesley N. Fach to DD, Nov. 29, 1966, box 67, folder 2, Doris Duke Foundation Records, DDCFRL.

CHAPTER 26

1. *Lasting Legacy*, pp. 96–101, 288–89.

2. Ibid., pp. 216–17.

3. Ibid., pp. 188–213, 320–21.

4. Ibid., p. 321.
5. Ibid., pp. 311–13.
6. Ibid., p. 321.
7. Ibid., p. 322.
8. Ibid., p. 313.
9. Letters, Erno Laszlo to DD, box 16, folder 7, DDPPC.

CHAPTER 27

1. Stephanie Mansfield, *The Richest Girl in the World: The Extravagant Life and Fast Times of Doris Duke* (New York: Kensington Publishing, 1992), pp. 287–88.
2. Letters, Joey Castro to DD, box 12, folder 1, DDPPC.
3. Ibid.
4. Ibid.
5. Ibid.
6. Documents, box 166, folders 5–7, Legal Records Series, DDP.
7. Letters, Joey Castro to DD, box 12, folder 1, DDPPC.
8. Jacqueline Kennedy to DD, box 16, folder 3, DDP.
9. Documents, box 6, folder 9, Administrative Records Series, DDP.
10. Interview, Marion Oates Charles, Doris Duke Oral History Collection, DDC-FRL.
11. Letters, Leon Amar to DD, box 11, folder 1, DDPPC.
12. Ibid.
13. Christie's, "Doris Duke: An American Original," https://www.christies.com /special_sites/duke_jun04/article.asp?article=1.
14. Ibid.

CHAPTER 28

1. Bruce Handy, "Return from Planet Pee-Wee," *Vanity Fair* 62 (Sept. 1999), p. 344.

CHAPTER 29

1. Interview OH.012, Phil Strider, June 1, 2005, box 8, Doris Duke Oral History Collection, DDCFRL.
2. Ibid.
3. DD to Walker Inman, Jr., and Samuel N. Greenspoon, Apr. 1992, box 376, folder 2, Administrative Records Series, DDP.
4. Bill Dedman and Paul Clark Newell, Jr., *Empty Mansions: The Mysterious Life of Huguette Clark and the Spending of a Great American Fortune* (New York: Ballantine Books, 2013).
5. Photograph, box 7, DDPC.
6. Interview, Marion Oates Charles, Doris Duke Oral History Collection, DDCFRL.

7. Kelly Morgan to Bernard Lafferty, box 1, Bernard Lafferty Papers, DDCFRL.

8. James C. McKinley, Jr., "Judge Removes the Executors of Duke Estate," *The New York Times*, May 23, 1995, http://www.nytimes.com/1995/05/23/nyregion/judge-removes-the-executors-of-duke-estate.html.

9. Ibid.

10. Doris Duke's Last Will and Testament and Codicil, Legal Records, DDP.

ACKNOWLEDGMENTS

I would like to thank the following for their invaluable assistance: Ileene Smith, Melissa Delbridge, Melissa Chinchillo, Donald Lamm, Betty Waynick, the Lawrenceville School Stephan Archives, the Sophia Smith Collection at Smith College, the Center for Oral History Archives at Columbia University, and the staff at the David M. Rubenstein Rare Book and Manuscript Library at Duke University, especially Elizabeth Dunn, Mary Samouelian, Laura Micham, and Robert L. Byrd. Without their guidance and help, this project would not have been possible. I am grateful.

INDEX